DIGITAL PUBLIC EMPLOYMENT SERVICES IN ACTION

Edited by
Didier Demazière, Ray Griffin,
Janine Leschke and Magnus Paulsen Hansen

P

First published in Great Britain in 2025 by

Policy Press, an imprint of
Bristol University Press
University of Bristol
1–9 Old Park Hill
Bristol
BS2 8BB
UK
t: +44 (0)117 374 6645
e: bup-info@bristol.ac.uk

Details of international sales and distribution partners are available at policy.bristoluniversitypress.co.uk

British Library Cataloguing in Publication Data
A catalogue record for this book is available from the British Library

ISBN 978-1-4473-7188-5 paperback
ISBN 978-1-4473-7190-8 ePub
ISBN 978-1-4473-7189-2 OA PDF

Cover design: Chris Wilson
Front cover image: Alamy/Heritage Image Partnership Ltd
Bristol University Press and Policy Press use environmentally responsible print partners.
Printed and bound in Great Britain by CPI Group (UK) Ltd, Croydon, CR0 4YY

To all whose paths cross in public employment services

Contents

List of figures and tables

Figures

Tables

Notes on contributors

Clément Brébion is a researcher in labour economics at Rockwool Foundation Research, Denmark. His research is mostly empirical. In his work, he strives to explain how institutions affect decision-making on the labour market. His main focus is on the demand side: he investigates how firms strategically design their employment and training practices according to the rules governing unemployment insurance, collective bargaining and apprenticeship training systems. Past publications include articles in the *European Economic Review* and *Industrial Relations*.

Alizée Delpierre is a sociologist, researcher at the Centre national de la recherche scientifique (CNRS) and member of the lab Printemps (University of Paris Saclay, France). She specialises in domestic work, exploitation at work and the wealthy, and has published several papers and books on these areas of research. She has also been part of a collective and international research focused on public employment services policies for digitalisation, in a comparative perspective. She has recently started a new research fieldwork on 'modern slavery', which questions the borders of exploitation, through the interweaving of work, vulnerability, immigration, from an intersectional perspective.

Didier Demazière is a sociologist, senior researcher at the CNRS and member of the Centre for the Sociology of Organisations at Sciences Po, France. As a sociologist of work and professions, he has carried out a great deal of research in the field of unemployment and employment, analysing different facets of work such as support for the unemployed in public employment services in Europe, or the job-seeking activities of unemployed people. He also conducts surveys on elected politicians, their activities, remuneration and working conditions. He has recently published several articles on the public employment service and the unemployed (in *Regulation & Governance* in 2023, *Sociologie du travail* in 2022, *Social Policy and Society* and *Critical Policy Studies* in 2021). He is currently preparing an issue of the *Journal of European Social Policy* on 'Active social policy and labour market integration in the digital era'.

Zeta Dooly is Lecturer, Researcher and Supervisor in the School of Education and Lifelong Learning at South East Technological University, Ireland. Zeta holds a doctorate in Structural Embeddedness of Research Networks and Collaborations, and has lectured, researched and led research projects on digital transformation, education, cybersecurity, privacy and the recognition of prior learning.

Aurélie Gonnet is a sociologist, Associate Professor at the University of Paris Cité and Associate at the Employment and Work Study Centre, France. As a specialist in issues relating to work, employment and career paths, she has conducted and participated in several research projects on career change services (guidance, career development, job search), the experiences of unemployment and transformations in the public employment service. These studies have resulted in several articles and a recently published collective book. She is currently taking part in a research project on (in)dignity from the margins of (un)employment, using a comparative approach (France, United States, Denmark) and a local approach (ethnography of small working-class towns).

Patrick Gallagher is a postdoctoral researcher in the Department of Management and Organisation, South East Technological University, Ireland, working on the Horizon 2020 HECAT project. Prior to that he worked as an scholar at Maynooth University working with the New Deals in the New Economy team. His work focuses on the political economy of finance, financialisation and labour markets.

Ray Griffin is Senior Lecturer in Management and Organisation at the South East Technological University, Ireland. He is the principal investigator for the EU Horizon 2020-funded HECAT and - Taighde Éireann – Research Ireland funded PEStech projects that explore the sociotechnical organising around unemployment.

Magnus Paulsen Hansen is Associate Professor at the Department of Social Sciences and Business, Roskilde University, Denmark. He has a long-standing interest in the politics and sociology of unemployment and the turn towards active labour market policies and workfare across the Organisation for Economic Co-operation and Development countries. His book, *The Moral Economy of Activation*, maps the moral ideas legitimising activation reforms in France and Denmark since the 1990s.

Órla Hayes is Lecturer in Marketing Communications at Technological University Dublin, Ireland. She was a postdoctoral researcher on the H2020 HECAT project at South East Technological University, Ireland. Dr Hayes's expertise ranges from marketing, online media, omni-channel to small- and medium-sized enterprise and community engagement. In 2022 Dr Hayes completed her PhD thesis titled 'Exploring Data Utilisation Strategies for Marketing Campaign Development Across the Omni-Channel for Small-to- Medium Sized Business-to Business Enterprises', at South East Technological University.

Antoinette Jordan is Lecturer in Business Information Systems at the South East Technological University, Ireland. As an interdisciplinary researcher, her expertise combines sociology, political science and computer science in science and technology studies and organisation studies. Her research interests combine social policy with digital transformation, most recently in the areas of public services, European affairs and digital education. She has significant experience in managing large, interdisciplinary research projects across academic, research and public sector environments as a project manager in EU-funded projects, including the Horizon 2020 HECAT project on disruptive technologies in public services and FP7 TRANSFORM project on eHealth and patient safety. As a member of Waterford Un/Employment Research Collaborative she researches the lived experience of the digital transformation of unemployment and was a researcher on the Horizon 2020 HECAT project and SFI-funded Future Digital Challenge PESTech project.

Antoinette Kelly is a case officer working in the Local Employment Services in Ireland. Antoinette recently completed her MA degree in Social Policy at the South East Technological University and is knowledgeable about the policies and practice of welfare in Ireland.

Janine Leschke is Professor of Political Economy of Labour Markets at the Department of Management, Society and Communication at Copenhagen Business School, Denmark. Her main research interests comprise non-standard employment, unemployment benefits, job quality, EU labour migration, gender and labour markets and digitalisation. She is editor of the *Journal of European Social Policy*. From 2020 to 2023, she was the Danish lead partner of the EU Horizon 2020 project HECAT – Disruptive Technologies Supporting Labour Market Decision Making. She has published extensively including in *Work, Employment and Society*, *Journal of Ethnic and Migration Studies*, *Social Politics* and *European Journal of Industrial Relations*. She is co-editor of several edited volumes including on youth labour in transition and EU labour mobility.

Maggie Müller is PhD Fellow in the Department of Social Sciences and Business Roskilde University, Denmark. She is currently working on experiences of (in)dignity from the margins.

Ayo Næsborg-Andersen is Associate Professor of Law, University of Southern Denmark, researching at the intersection of human rights and new technologies.

Sabina Pultz is Associate Professor in the Department of People and Technology at Roskilde University, Denmark. As a social psychologist

Pultz explores unemployment experiences and other experiences of being marginalised in the labour market in Europe and the United States. In particular Pultz explores the role of emotions and how they are linked to underlying value system and thus address the intersection between psychology and politics. Currently Pultz is co-leading a research project (Indigma) comparing experiences of marginalisation in Denmark, France and the United States, theorising the concept of (in)dignity. Her book, *Emotionally Indebted* (Palgrave Macmillan) investigates the many ways unemployed people are governed in the Danish welfare state and how they govern and relate to themselves.

Martina Rameša is an analyst at Zavod Republike Slovenije za zaposlovanje/ Employment Service of Slovenia.

Zach Roche is Assistant Lecturer in Management Studies at the South East Technological University, Ireland. His recent book, *Thriving Beyond Debt* (2024), investigates how the Irish insolvency and bankruptcy system operate as a form of welfare protection.

Aisling Tuite is Lecturer in Management at the School of Business, South East Technological University, Ireland. An interdisciplinary sociologist, organisation studies and science and technology studies researcher, she explores the lived experiences of work and unemployment. Her current research runs along three tracks: transformation and change in organisations and work, including being Principal Investigator on two research projects on banking (the effects of the Irish marriage bar and the digital transformation); exploring changing practices of care in places of work through tracing flows between policy/rules and relational practices; finally, as a member of Waterford Un/Employment Research Collaborative she researches the lived experiences of unemployment and has been a senior researcher the Irish Research Council-funded Understanding Unemployment in the Era of Big Data (PEX project), Horizon 2020 HECAT, Disruptive Technologies Supporting Labour Market Decision Making and the SFI-funded PEStech project.

Introduction

*Didier Demazière, Ray Griffin,
Magnus Paulsen Hansen and Janine Leschke*

This book explores the rise of digital public employment services (PES). While digital services have been in progress for at least 40 years, some PES are now envisioning them becoming the default means of delivering public services (Schou and Pors, 2019). We are now at an inflection point where new ideas and approaches are needed to animate the, almost inevitable, transformation of this vital social service.

The title of this book – *Digital Public Employment Services in Action* – captures our unique take on this digital transformation. Almost all of the contributors' research, often over decades, is immersed in contemporary PES practice, and so we follow the action from there. This approach contrasts and complements the mainstream of digital development in which technologists and policy makers have tended to explore new and imagined tools and devices, with little heed to established PES practice, constraints and wisdom. In this way, this book reconnects the ongoing digital transformation of PES to older and deeper discussions over the purpose, value and limits of PES.

As digitalisation recomposes and reanimates the service provision of PES, everything is at stake once more. Technological development in public policy, animated by visions of innovation and disruption, is often disconnected from the corresponding research on unemployment and the long tradition of front-line PES practice. As a result, digitalisation is a new theatre of global policy reform – where rationalisation, New Public Management, privatisation, competition and ambitions for cheaper, more efficient services are contested once again. As digitalisation often disintermediates front-line professionals, digitalisation is also a space for 'double activation', accelerating work-first conditionalised welfare and workfare (Peck, 2001) by activating both the unemployed and PES. And yet, the missing part of debates on digitalisation is practice – particularly how digitalisation alters the professional front-line work of PES and changes the service for unemployed people. As a result, the book will more forcefully analyse the various ways digital PES is imagined, and how it actually unfolds in practice and in action.

A third age of public employment services

We are now at the dawn of the third age of unemployment, as European PES face the significant upheaval of becoming ever more digital. The welfare state and its master concept of unemployment emerged as part of a grand settlement after the great wars of the 20th century. With it emerged PES, as a technology of the state to administer worklessness, alleviate absolute poverty and acts as an automatic stabiliser for internal tensions within market economies. Any significant transformation of PES raises fresh questions over our brittle, often frayed, yet enduring, social harmony. As such, the digital transformation of PES, just like the activation transformation before it, is a significant matter of concern.

The first age of unemployment saw the problem of worklessness become a public concern, eventually coming to colonise almost all of the political and policy problems of poverty and inclusion. Somewhere between German Chancellor Bismarck's introduction of social insurance laws in the 1880s and the 1960s, almost every nation has, to a greater or lesser extent, accepted responsibility for supporting unemployed people through PES. Underpinning PES is the master concept of unemployment, the definition generated by the International Labour Organization (ILO) that calls it into being, and allows it to be consistently measured and evidenced across the world. The ILO, now an agency of the United Nations was conceived of, largely from J.M. Keynes' interventions, in the Treaty of Versailles, and soon after advanced unemployment as being people 'without and available for work', a category of people to be measured and managed in every society. Despite the social and political monopoly the concept generates, it emerges contingently rather than inevitably, displacing older social policy perspectives and colonising national and eventually global approaches to the problem of worklessness. When rendered as a service, administering this form of unemployment entails the dispensing transfer payments to the entitled in relatively simple administration offices for doling out money.

Definitionally the unemployment we understand today crystallised in 1954 as the ILO revisited the definition for the last time to add a third element – seeking work. It is this definition that leads to the second age of unemployment, where unemployment gives way to job seeking and universal supports are disparaged as passive, and the unemployed are stigmatised and in need of activation (Van Berkel et al, 2017). The instinct was present at the formation of universal services for the unemployed but has now come to rebalance PES provision with incentives and sanctions designed to promote access to jobs (Clasen and Clegg, 2006; Bonoli, 2010), where social benefits now come with responsibilities (Brodkin and Marston, 2013; Watts and Fitzpatrick, 2018; Dwyer, 2019) such as active job search and more generally the assessment of effort and merit (Dean,

2003; Knotz, 2018). This movement was supported by reforms inspired by the New Public Management and oriented towards the rationalisation of organisations, cost-cutting and the search for efficiency. Here, the task of PES becomes a far more complex human service, counselling, mentoring, motivating, training and evidencing job search, and at times punishing the recalcitrant (van Gerven et al, 2024).

Digital firsts

This book explores the emergence of digital public employment services. To a certain extent, like all revolutions, the antecedents can be detected after the fact. In one way of thinking, both *welfare* and *PES* have always been digital, a conversion of analogue systems of poverty alleviation often grounded in moral judgement, community and workfare, into a bureaucratic, rights-based, rule-based computational system. Thinking more narrowly of digitalisation, as the increasing involvement of computers, data and the withdrawal of human-to-human services, PES digitalisation has been in progress for at least 40 years, and is now becoming the totality of some public services. The movement towards digitalisation of PES has been growing, with some governments on the cusp of launching digital-first or digital-by-default PES (Ball et al, 2023).

This vision of digital PES extends from procedural automation, sorting and judging systems to engagement services. When we imagine digital services we often think of the more mechanical procedural automation of PES operations where data input is pushed back onto claimants, and data cleaning, wrangling and processing is done at scale by specialists who work remotely from the unemployed. Perhaps the most sustained area for digital PES is the range of back-office technologies used to streamline administering and judgement processes, with statistical and artificial intelligence (AI) algorithmic profiling used to classify and sort unemployed people into the frictionally unemployed and those at risk of becoming long-term unemployed and thus targeted for intensive supports and conditionality. Here, the firmness of faceless digital rules and the standardisation of service marginalises discretion and the ambiguity of human-to-human service provision. The rationality of Weberian bureaucracy, the iron cage of control based on knowledge, intellectually analysable rules and calculability of operations, for good and ill, takes hold of PES. Claims of efficiency are also made, that digital services will, ultimately after considerable investment, reduce spending on PES, particularly replacing expensive human services. Increasingly, digital technologies are being explored for the more complex engagement services, such as identifying training, mentoring and skills gaps, developing CVs and applications, and matching as well as counselling and mentoring all being piloted and rolled out as digital services.

Digitalisation is frequently identified as a revolutionary and disruptive transformation. Digital, or what counts as digital today, emphasises electronic and computing technology that generates and stores and processes data in terms of two states – one or zero, something or nothing. The origin of our enumerative and calculative abilities emerges in embodied digitality, the presumed ancient technique of using our body as an abacus, the 12 thick phalanges of each of our four fingers as the original counting tool – thought to have been first used to count livestock. So digital transformations are not simply utilitarian machines and instruments under human control, rather they are extensions of hominisation, of human beliefs, values and modes of being. Here, digital means breaking things up to classify them, first our bodies, but now we break the complex bonds of society and community into individuals or clumps of problem people to be managed. Like every extension of mankind, every technique that affords more range and capability, there is an often poorly perceived amputation (McLuhan, 1951) – with cars we walk less, with phones we write less – we often embrace the extension but fail to notice what is lost. This begs the question when we transform our PES into digital services what are the extensions and amputations, and what do we break apart and put back weaker?

While there are legitimate rationalities for universal service provision, and for activation and active labour market policies, it is not altogether clear what the digital revolution of PES attempts to accomplish. Digital PES is a container for both utopian and dystopian dreamers with few alighting on a shared programme. Some envision digital PES as more flexible and user-friendly – rather than attending an office for a specific appointment or time slot, individuals, particularly those with caring obligations, are free to access services at times that suit them. Australia, with its low population density, has advocated for PES at a distance, and here digital services are just an extension of call centre PES. Equally, PES staff have more flexibility in managing their work, are less tied to meetings and appointments, and so can work more reactively and time-shifted from service users. There are also a range of opportunities that come from aggregate data for the unemployed, front-line workers and PES management, where they can track productivity and anomalies and make useful comparisons. Digital PES also offers the promise of mass customisation with greater standardisation and centrally controlled compliance, while at the same time more personalisation and targeting of services. Beyond this, in vague ways, there is the sense that digital PES will also be more efficient, frictionless and cost-effective, perhaps ultimately with fewer offices and staff delivering higher service levels. Overall, many understand digital PES as inevitable, simply a political and public expectation.

However, many commonly identified amputations emerge with digital PES. First is the significant risk of double social exclusion as a result of digital access and literacy challenges (Schou and Pors, 2019). Many unemployed people do not have the technology or optimal technology to access digital services – such as internet quality and devices. Beyond this many do not have the basic literacy or digital skills to access appropriate PES support. Such exclusion is not evenly experienced, and often impacts more vulnerable or marginalised service users, indeed such users experience multiple forms of bias, particularly in profiling (Körtner and Bonoli, 2023). Indeed, much of the technology is not visible and readable by the public, not only does welfare need to be provided, it needs to be seen to be provided along the lines of natural justice – fair, independent, impartial, free of bias and open to scrutiny, appeal and accountability. Digital PES is rarely people-less welfare, rather it is that the people providing the welfare are largely unseen and so their mode of work is not visible. For these reasons, many welfare professionals, both in policy and front-line services, as well as academics, have an unfathomable unease about the ongoing digital transformation of PES. The fear is that the brittle and complex machinery of welfare falls under the control of technologists and policy makers with little accountability to the front line (Allhutter et al, 2020; Sztandar-Sztanderska and Zielenska, 2020). Some have argued that, subject to the principles of New Public Management, street-level bureaucracy (Lipsky, 1980) is tending to disappear in favour of a system-level bureaucracy guided by digital technology, in which the processing of individual cases has given way to the optimisation of processes for storing, processing and circulating information (Bovens and Zouridis, 2002). Undoubtedly, the progress of digital administration has direct consequences for the place of front-line professionals (Jansson and Erlingsson, 2014), and current technological development is somewhat disconnected from practice and research on unemployment.

Everything at stake

Digitalisation also affects the work of these professionals. However, there has been little study of what this digitalisation entails. Does it involve developing algorithmic decision-making for social benefit allocation? Is it about shifting information system input tasks to the unemployed? Or is it about providing counsellors with tools for more intensive support and creating automated systems to monitor both counsellors and the unemployed? Similarly, there is a lack of solid results of the consequences on the work of professionals, that is, on the uses they make of digital tools, on how these tools interfere with their expertise and working relations, particularly with regard to hierarchies.

Time and time again, PES has done a remarkable job in stabilising society through macroeconomic crises such as the global financial crisis and the COVID-19 pandemic; and preventing the worst effects of the poverty and hardship that comes with labour market failure. In many ways, PES is a perpetual political and policy calibration of what is needed to deliver social protection, preserve liberal market capitalism and personal freedom against demands, at times violent demands, for redistribution. The fabric of European welfare goes beyond addressing material wants to offer recognition, dignity, security, justice and democratic participation. Beyond those who actually draw on PES, welfare policy, in providing a reservation wage and a floor in the labour market, ensures a high-quality labour market for all workers and a real promise of ontological security and basic wellbeing (Sage, 2018) to every citizen of the European Union (EU). As such, PES is a core technology, perhaps the only durable technology for maintaining internal state cohesion and stability. As such, PES is an essential to ensuring post-war European peace and preserve the shared European economic, political, social and cultural way of life. As digital innovation leads the reanimation of service provision, often without a deep understanding of service provision, all of the accomplishments of PES are at stake.

We are now at an inflexion point where new ideas and approaches are needed to reanimate this vital social service. The backdrop to this book is an action learning EU project that seeks to develop a new disruptive technology for PES, giving the contributors unique access to the digital transformations underway in PES. The book is sociological and anthropologically led, focusing on the lived experience of practice in deploying technology in the field. As such, it does not draw from the techno-utopian register of exploring possible PES futures, rather we are resolutely committed to the existing capacity and accomplishments of PES. Here we extend our deep understanding of the operation of PES, from multiple perspectives – primarily social policy and practice, but also sociology, labour market data, political science as well as information data science. In part, the diffuse disciplinary conversations around digital welfare have siloed various understandings of this emerging policy problematic, so a central aspiration of the volume is to bring the field together across disciplines and country-specific perspectives to find common ground. There is a pressing need for a collection of expert voices to gather the field of digital welfare together, with a shared aspiration of generating an authoritative, provocative and optimistic engagement between traditional social policy and theory, now that the digital-first genie is out of the bottle. As an approach, our volume integrates the digital with traditional concerns of social policy, with and against the grain. Our volume follows the action (Dourish, 2001) of contemporary, state-of-the-art digital services as PES practises them. In this, we call the field together.

This volume, across 15 chapters, explores the complexities of digital PES. The first part of the book explores the ongoing datafication and governance of unemployment, offering a critical perspective on current state-of-the-art practices in PES. This sets the scene for the following two parts which explore specific aspects and opportunities of the digitisation agenda, and reflect on how they might be enacted at the front lines of welfare delivery.

The book then considers the movement from software-enabled welfare to software-defined welfare – exploring how unemployed people are constructed through processes of datafication, inherent in policy, policy techniques such as profiling tools and statistical counting of the unemployed. This section begins by examining the overarching digital aspirations of the EU and the practical challenges of translating these policies into action.

Jordan and Griffin, in Chapter 2, highlight the curious demand for fully digital-first, software-defined public services across the EU. By focusing on the Irish PES and the evolution of the Probability of Exit AI algorithm, the authors explore the tension between top-down political aspirations translated into public services, or from politics to code, as the authors put it.

Chapter 3, by Gallagher and Griffin, considers one of the oldest and most problematic big data and algorithmic control technologies used by PES – profiling algorithms. The chapter illustrates the gap between the stated ambition of these algorithms and how they operate in practice at the front line of PES. It also shows how digitalisation can go wrong, accelerating and weaponising the bias of the labour market in the very system that is supposed to counterbalance such biases.

The first part of the book concludes with Chapter 4, by Jordan, Dooly and Griffin, who, informed by philosophers of science and technology, consider the emergence of unemployment in practice, as an active practice of turning people into data. They approach this by exploring the production of statistical knowledge about unemployment, drawing on ethnographic fieldwork with a national statistical agency during formal public data collection. Following the action, ethnographically, they highlight the moments in which complex messy and unique people are somehow flatted into their data – where the analogue becomes digital, how digital data becomes the basis for the governance of unemployment, and how people are then perceived and managed within digital systems.

The book then explores considerable challenges in digital service innovation and development, highlighting the challenge of co-designing disruptive digital systems, the legal considerations for algorithm development, and the limitations and affordances of our existing labour market data ontologies. Tuite, in Chapter 5, provides an autoethnographic account of the development of a disruptive digital system for deployment in public service, in the EU-funded HECAT project, one that aspired to place service users' experience at its centre. The project was co-developed with stakeholders from social sciences, data and technical sciences and users in a collaborative setting, and so the chapter offers a rich account of the micro-practices of innovation across disciplines and locations.

At a very different register, highlighting the organisational complexity of digital PES, Næsborg-Andersen's Chapter 6 examines rules governing the development of public algorithms, against the backdrop of the new EU AI

Act, and more established General Data Protection Regulation (GDPR), human rights law (particularly the EU Charter of Fundamental Rights) and general Administrative Law. The chapter highlights pivotal principles, such as proportionality, discrimination, fairness and protection of sensitive data, all of which will be an essential part of the principles of legally compliant digital PES.

Brébion and Leschke, in Chapter 7, demonstrate how vital data infrastructure and availability is when generating digital tools for PES – showcasing the multidimensional concept of job quality with a view on whether and how job quality items can be integrated into matching and profiling tools. This hopeful chapter highlights how digital-first tools do not need to be activation or job-first orientated, but how, with some thought, they can be used to support unemployed people towards high-quality work, where quality is determined by their particular needs and context.

Following on from this, in Chapter 8, Demazière approaches the issue of digital services from the bottom up, by drawing on a large number of interviews with jobseekers to develop an informational approach to job search. The chapter explores how different forms of information shape the job search potential of an unemployed person, acting in different ways to inform, offer hope, realism and support. This chapter offers a richer understanding of job search, a necessary prelude to developing supportive, rather than undermining or authoritative, digital tools.

Kelly and Roche tackle the issue of digital exclusion in Chapter 9. Starting by noting the policy rush to digital-first services, they introduce their primary data from experienced case officers on how digital systems are engaged with at the front lines and by service users. The case highlights the complex nature of digital exclusion and how we are moving towards an era of 'double exclusion' – first from the labour market and then from welfare.

The third part of the book, across five chapters, focuses on the translation of digital welfare to the front line of public service delivery – at the street and screen level. Chapter 10 relays the experience of using co-design methods to bring unemployed people, caseworkers, senior policy makers and actors into the development of a disruptive PES technology. Using a vignette scenario methodology, across four countries, with three different stakeholder types, the exercise surfaces the complex views and trade-offs that emerge when key stakeholders and users engage with concrete dilemmas around trust in data, job quality and discrimination in the use of digital technologies in PES. This chapter concludes with a reflection on the affordance and limitations of expert panels in co-designing.

Delpierre, Demazière and Gonnet in Chapter 11 offer an in-depth exploration of the emergence of statistical profiling by French PES. Drawing on interviews and textual analysis, Delpierre et al examine the adoption of profiling against the backdrop of the restructuring of the PES institutional landscape and the change in PES adviser profiles, orientation and training. The chapter demonstrates the complexity of introducing new technologies, and while a new welfare state is emerging – at different paces in different contexts, but with a common international dynamic.

More speculatively, Tuite's Chapter 12 considers the potential of AI technologies to deliver care in welfare services. Theories of care define care as a human-to-human activity, so the very possibility of technology-delivered care is an open question. Here, Tuite considers the integration of digital PES technologies into an assemblage of caring. The chapter draws on investigations into previous and existing PES technology, along with focus groups made up of caseworkers and unemployed people to consider the potential for adoption of such digital technologies as part of a cyborg merging of human and non-human for delivering care. The data indicates support for the potential of digital PES technologies as part of a hybrid service but is limited by the discretionary powers of PES advisers.

In Chapter 13, Hayes, Tuite and Griffin explore the communication confusion that emerges as welfare moves from a single point of service – the welfare office – to multiple, technology-enabled and hybrid channels and touchpoints. They draw on empirical insights from a dialogical study of both caseworkers and their long-term unemployed clients to explore the various implications of human and technologically delivered service provision. Echoing Kelly and Roche, they also find evidence of an intense digital divide, raising questions of digital inclusion in this new era of hybridic welfare. As PES mismanage the coherence of omni-channel welfare, issues of mistrust, inconsistency of experience and reliability weaken the quality of welfare. The worth of this chapter lies in highlighting the institutional changes needed to make omni-channel welfare work for all, across this digital divide and beyond.

Finally, Pultz's Chapter 14 uses a governmentality framework to explore how unemployed people are governed through digital services and especially profiling tools, and, as a consequence, how they govern themselves. Drawing on interviews with 45 unemployed people in Slovenia, Pultz explores the effects of technologies of power and technologies of the self that emerge from entangling unemployed people with profiling tools.

Together, these chapters show the complexity, wide contextual and situational inconsistencies in digital PES, the gap between policy imaginaries, the front line of service delivery and service users. As a whole, they announce the incoherence of the field, which should be a concern to all, as we consider a radical transformation that is more likely to weaken the fabric of welfare. This sentiment is gathered together in a concluding reflection, Chapter 15, a manifesto on what can be done to positively shape digital PES in action. This chapter is a plea to turn back towards the citizen experience, the deep and broadly positive history of the welfare state, renewing rather than just automating services and exploiting technology to develop personalised welfare services by embracing interdisciplinary and inclusive research on PES.

As editors, we have been driven by the pressing questions surrounding the digital transformation of PES and the need to critically engage with its implications across Europe and beyond. This volume brings together key insights from a diverse and interdisciplinary academic community, reflecting the richness of our collective research. We hope it will serve as a valuable resource for scholars, policymakers, and practitioners alike.

We extend our gratitude to all contributors and collaborators who made this work possible. In particular, we acknowledge the generous support of European Union funding, which has been instrumental in facilitating this research and fostering academic exchange across borders.

This book is attached to the HECAT project Disruptive Technologies Supporting Labour Market Decision Making, supported by funding from the European Union's Horizon 2020 Research and Innovation Programme under Grant Agreement No 870702.

References

Allhutter, D., Cech, F., Fischer, F., Grill, G. and Mager, A. (2020) Algorithmic profiling of job seekers in Austria: How austerity politics are made effective. *Frontiers in Big Data*, 3: 502780.

Ball, S., McGann, M., Nguyen, P. and Considine, M. (2023) Emerging modes of digitalisation in the delivery of welfare-to-work: Implications for street-level discretion. *Social Policy & Administration*, 57(7): 1166–1180.

Bonoli, G. (2010) The political economy of active labor-market policy. *Politics & Society*, 38(4): 435–457.

Bovens, M. and Zouridis, S. (2002) From street-level to system-level bureaucracies: How information and communication technology is transforming administrative discretion and constitutional control. *Public Administration Review*, 62(2): 174–184.

Brodkin, E.Z. and Marston, G. (eds) (2013) *Work and the Welfare State: Street-level Organizations and Workfare Politics*. Washington, DC: Georgetown University Press.

Clasen, J. and Clegg, D. (2006) Beyond activation reforming European unemployment protection systems in post-industrial labour markets. *European Societies*, 8(4): 527–553.

Dean, M. (2003) Culture governance and individualisation. In H.P. Bang (ed) *Governance as Social and Political Communication* (pp 117–139). Manchester: Manchester University Press.

Dourish, P. (2001) *Where the Action Is: The Foundations of Embodied Interaction*. London: MIT Press.

Dwyer, P. (ed) (2019) *Dealing with Welfare Conditionality: Implementation and Effects*. Bristol: Policy Press.

Jansson, G. and Erlingsson, G.Ó. (2014) More e-government, less street-level bureaucracy? On legitimacy and the human side of public administration. *Journal of Information Technology & Politics*, 11(3): 291–308.

Knotz, C.M. (2018) A rising workfare state? Unemployment benefit conditionality in 21 OECD countries, 1980–2012. *Journal of International and Comparative Social Policy*, 34(2): 91–108.

Körtner, J. and Bonoli, G. (2023) Predictive algorithms in the delivery of public employment services. In D. Clegg and N. Durazzi (eds) *Handbook of Labour Market Policy in Advanced Democracies* (pp 387–398). Cheltenham: Edward Elgar.

Lipsky, M. (1980) *Street-Level Bureaucracy: Dilemmas of the Individual in Public Services*. New York: Russell Sage Foundation.

McLuhan, H.M. (1951) *The Mechanical Bride*. London: Routledge & Kegan Paul.

Peck, J. (2001) *Workfare States*. New York: Guilford Press.

Sage, D. (2018) Well-being and the welfare state. In B. Greve (ed) *Routledge Handbook of the Welfare State* (pp 101–112). New York: Routledge.

Schou, J. and Pors, A.S. (2019) Digital by default? A qualitative study of exclusion in digitalised welfare. *Social Policy & Administration*, 53(3): 464–477.

Sztandar-Sztanderska, K. and Zielenska, M. (2020) What makes an ideal unemployed person? Values and norms encapsulated in a computerized profiling tool. *Social Work & Society*, 18(1).

Van Berkel, R., Caswell, D., Kupka, P. and Larsen, F. (eds) (2017) *Frontline Delivery of Welfare-to-Work Policies in Europe: Activating the Unemployed*. Taylor & Francis.

van Gerven, M., Malava, T., Saikku, P. and Mesiäislehto, M. (2024) Towards a new era in the governance of integrated activation: A systematic review of the literature on the governance of welfare benefits and employment-related services in Europe (2010–21). *Social Policy & Administration*, 58(3): 329–343.

Watts, B. and Fitzpatrick, S. (2018) *Welfare Conditionality*. London: Routledge.

2

From politics to code: the unfolding of EU digital aspirations into practice

Antoinette Jordan and Ray Griffin

Introduction

Governments are increasingly using technology to deliver public services. Strategies for this implementation are categorised as digital transformation, digitalisation or eGovernment. The European Union (EU)'s digital strategy was launched in 2021, setting targets for 100 per cent of services available online by 2030 in each Member State. Digitalisation of public services is seen as a positive intervention that benefits citizens (European Commission, 2021; Negreiro, 2021). This approach raises the question of whether existing street-level bureaucratic processes are being digitised into code-level bureaucracies with little input from caseworkers, or whether more radical reforms are taking place, reforms that change the politics and policy underpinning public services.

Despite technological advancements and digital transformations, globally the welfare state remains intact and maintains its mission to protect citizens against social risks, providing social security and insurance (Ewald, 2020; van Gerven, 2022). Social protection policies address poverty, social exclusion, unemployment, inequalities, and remain a key element of public administration. In the EU, general government expenditure on social protection in 2022 was 22 per cent of gross domestic product, which makes the activities of public employment services (PES) a significant investment in citizen welfare, one which Member States are committed to maintaining despite constraints on public financing (European Commission, 2023).

While new digital labour platforms and the impact of artificial intelligence (AI) on the digitalisation of work is being tackled by the EU (European Commission, 2023) and others, the digitalisation of welfare state systems themselves deserves further study. PES is a useful and important place to explore the impact of digital transformation on social policy, particularly in Ireland given the rapid transformation of welfare services since 2011. Ireland's PES changed from a system of voluntary engagement with active labour market policies (ALMPs) to the introduction of profiling, conditionality and sanctions, and mandatory engagement with ALMPs. This change in policy was facilitated by the global financial crisis, where a solution was required to tackle the urgent organisational problem of welfare resource allocation, in response to the bailout agreement between the Irish government and the Troika. A solution was found through new digital technologies featuring the Probability of Exit (PEX) statistical profiling model based on algorithmic technology. It was designed to help manage government spending and resource allocation, during the critical bailout period when government budgets were tightly monitored for excess spending.

However, PEX had a real impact on the experience of unemployment, as it profiled all unemployed jobseekers who entered the PES system, predicting the likelihood that a claimant would still be employed 12 months after they made their initial claim (McGuinness et al, 2022). The resulting PEX score determined the pattern of interaction with PES case officers, creating categories of low, medium and high-risk citizens involuntarily entered into a welfare system of conditionality and possibly sanctions for non-compliance. This transformation of welfare policy remains in operation today, rebranded as a personalised service, with PES building on digital welfare advances introduced during the COVID-19 pandemic response and working towards the EU digital innovation goals.

Foucault's concept of governmentality (Foucault, 1978) dominates much of the literature on social policy, however policy making in the datafied state has moved away from governmentality. It is no longer defined as a network (Law and Callon, 1988; Latour, 2005) but instead is comprised more of an assemblage of things (Deleuze and Guattari, 1987). In the analysis of a public sector algorithm or technology, the design can be studied and documented, however only through looking at the whole assemblage can the complex social life of an algorithm, once deployed, be explored. Exploring this assemblage provides a better understanding of the sociology of policy and code in assembling public employment services and code-level bureaucracies.

The study explores the first ten years of the PEX algorithm implementation (2011 to 2021), from the impact of the global financial crisis to the COVID-19 pandemic response. An assemblage ethnography was used (Wahlberg, 2022), with an approach inspired by science and technology studies (STS) and actor-network theory (ANT) (Law and Callon, 1988; Latour, 2005; Ingold, 2016). Ireland's digital welfare policy-making ecosystem is largely inaccessible to researchers, which created the challenge of researching the black-box of AI and algorithms, combined with difficulties in gaining access to stakeholders (Pasquale, 2015; Danaher et al, 2017; Geiger, 2017; Hynes, 2017; Lee and Björklund Larsen, 2019; Raymond and Connelly, 2020). Working with the concept of what is accessible, rather than focusing on gatekeepers and barriers to access, proved to be a motivating factor (Seaver,

2017). Morton's (2013) theory of visualising the ecosystem as a hyper-object was also helpful, along with the Glaser et al (2021) framework which offers a pathway to see algorithms as entangled nested assemblages. The dataset comprised 96 documents (government policies, press releases, legislation, reports) plus interviews with academics, civil servants, technology experts and public sector consultants who led the rollout of the PEX and AI in PES.

This chapter contributes to a better understanding of the sociology of policy and code, focusing on how policy, code and human services interact and are assembled into public employment services. This ongoing digital transformation of PES reassembles the welfare state, and so needs to be considered sociologically to reveal the deeper transformation underway. This includes implications for citizen interaction with PES, economic considerations of PES resource allocation, the digital divide and educational implications, plus implications for service delivery going forward to the 2030 digital future in Europe.

In the next section, the main concepts underlying the rise of digital public services are explored, with a focus on social protection and statistical profiling and particular reference to Ireland. In the third section, the methodology of the study is outlined. In the fourth section, the main findings are presented, which explore the social life of the PEX algorithmic model in Ireland through the concepts of the apparatus and assemblage. Finally, the last section presents the conclusion and value of the study.

Digital transformation of public services

The digital transformation of public services has been underpinned by initiatives such as the European Commission's digital compass. The availability of 100 per cent of public services online by 2030 is a key goal, supported by initiatives to upskill millions of citizens in digital skills and support the rollout of 5G networks to boost online connectivity. 'A Europe fit for the digital age' was one of six priorities of the von der Leyen European Commission (2019–2024), highlighting its key policy position amid a time of energy crisis, increased military spending and other competing priorities (European Commission, 2021; 2023; European Parliament Directorate-General for Parliamentary Research Services and Bassot, 2022). Indeed many Member States celebrated their accelerated digital activities, as exemplified here by the Irish example: 'these gains, along with an accelerated response via digital solutions to the continued provision of services and information during the pandemic, bodes well for our ambitions … leveraging the substantial progress made during the pandemic' (Government of Ireland, 2022c).

The literature on the digital transformation of public services uses many terms – digitalisation, digitisation, datafication, automation, AI, digitisation, automated decision-making, technology adoption, digital transformation, digital by default and the datafied state (Mejias and Couldry, 2019; Schou and Pors, 2019; Karsten, 2021; Considine et al, 2022; Dencik, 2022; Henman, 2022; OECD, 2022; Gallagher and Griffin, 2023; Ingold et al, 2024; Kopper and Knox, 2024). At an organisational level, there are differences between digital transformation and IT-enabled organisational transformation (Wessel et al, 2021). Digital transformation uses technology to redefine an organisations value proposition and a new organisational identity emerges, while IT-enabled organisational transformation uses technology to support the existing value proposition and enhance the existing organisational identity. Using this framework, multi-country initiatives such as the EU digital decade are aspiring towards the implementation of full digital transformation by 2030, and therefore a full redefinition of their value proposition and service delivery to citizens. The national digital implementation strategy of Ireland outlines what is required at Member State level – digital transformation of government, redesigning and rebuilding government processes and services, if necessary across organisations, and using digitalisation and data to provide an integrated experience for our people, businesses and policy makers (Government of Ireland, 2022b).

At a process level, digitalisation of services can be defined as implementing ready-made technologies into organisational settings, thus bringing about changes in practices and processes (Karsten, 2021) and organisational renewal through new information and communication technologies. At a data level, digitisation occurs where practices are transformed from analogue into digital form (Plesner and Husted, 2020; Karsten, 2021; Trittin-Ulbrich et al, 2021), including the management of mass payments and processing of large amounts of data. Datafication also occurs, where data is recorded and analysed in digital and quantifiable forms (Mejias and Couldry, 2019; Trittin-Ulbrich et al, 2021). This leads to the concept of the datafied state, with its three key elements of algorithms, automation and surveillance (Burrell et al, 2022).

Digital transformation of public employment services

PES are the authorities that connect jobseekers with employers, help match supply and demand on the labour market and provide information, placement, financial supports and active supports to jobseekers and citizens (Department of Social Protection, 2023). The digital transformation of public employment services has been underway for almost 40 years, with some service delivery models now embracing digital-first and digital-by-default assistance to citizens. However the period of 2011–2021 is particularly relevant as efficiencies in PES became critical during this time due to the global financial crisis, and rapid digital transformation became a key element of the COVID-19 pandemic response from 2020.

Statistical profiling is a technological solution in use since the 1990s, promoted to PES management as an invaluable tool in the provision of employment services, for early identification of jobseekers who need extra support and for cost efficiencies in PES. Profiling is endorsed by the Organisation for Economic Co-operation and Development (OECD), the World Bank and the EU (Blázquez, 2014; Loxha and Morgandi, 2014; OECD, 2018). Profiling assesses the prospects of clients finding work, places them in different groups as a function of their needs, then targets and tailors PES inputs to meet these demands (OECD, 2018). There is no common standard for the use of statistical profiling technology and accuracy rates remain inconsistent, with reported rates of 50–80 per cent and risks of misclassification of jobseekers (Griffin et al, 2020).

An analysis of the development of the PEX profiling model in Ireland clearly shows a reaction to crisis. When the Irish government agreed to austerity measures in social protection beyond what was required by the Troika bailout package in 2010, profiling was seen as international best practice for rationalising limited resources and allowing those scarce resources to be directed to those most in need (Dukelow, 2015; Hick, 2018; OECD, 2018; Murphy and Hogan, 2020; McGann and Murphy, 2021). This introduction of statistical profiling in welfare service delivery marked the cornerstone of PES reforms in Ireland (O'Connell et al, 2009; Kelly et al, 2019). In other contexts, profiling was promoted as helping to deliver employment services more efficiently, tailor services to jobseekers' individual needs and assess the prospects of finding work (OECD, 2018).

The implementation of these policy changes had an immediate impact on jobseekers in Ireland. Besides introducing profiling, the new reforms introduced conditionality and sanctions at the same time. This policy reimagined the experience of unemployment in a non-strategic way, foraging ahead with operationalisation of non-inclusive policy-to-code implementation, in reaction to a crisis. Conditionality meant that payment of benefits was now dependent on the jobseeker meeting certain conditions set out by the PES (such as attending meetings or participating in courses), while sanctions in the form of benefit reductions were negative interventions for non-compliance.

The use of statistical profiling by PES is widespread, identified in Ireland, Australia, Italy, the Netherlands, the United States, Austria, Belgium (Flanders), Denmark, New Zealand, Latvia and Sweden. Countries implementing non-statistical profiling tools, such as caseworker-based profiling and rule-based profiling include Estonia, Germany, Greece, Luxembourg, Norway, Poland, Slovenia, Switzerland and the UK. Only three countries are considered to be using AI in PES, with Flanders clearly using AI, and Denmark and New Zealand using machine learning techniques (McGuinness et al, 2022).

Research design

This chapter draws on a three-year assemblage ethnographic study of the first ten years of statistical profiling in the Irish PES (2011–2021). Given the complex, unboundedness of social phenomena such as a policy, a method that allowed multiple data sources to be brought together was required. This method is a methodological response to new forms of technologically underpinned social organisation, empirically focusing on the technologies of government identifiable within various forms of technocratic organisation such as governments, ministries, commissions and institutions (Wahlberg, 2022). Assemblage ethnography draws on the work of Foucault (1980), Deleuze and Guattari (1987) and Latour (2005), and has proved useful in the study of China's one-child policy (Greenhalgh, 2008), EU migration apparatus (Feldman, 2011), biotechnology (Rabinow, 1996), the war on drugs (Zigon, 2015) and youth services in the UK (Youdell and McGimpsey, 2015). This method also includes an STS and ANT-inspired approach (Law and Callon, 1988; Latour, 2005; Ingold, 2016), with the theoretical framework informed by assemblage thinking (Foucault, 1978; Deleuze and Guattari, 1987).

Data collection and analysis

The use of an assemblage ethnography approach combined genealogy, archival work, policy analysis, ethnography and qualitative interviews. Use of this approach aimed to counteract the challenge of researching potential 'black box' aspects of AI and algorithms (Pasquale, 2015; Danaher et al, 2017; Geiger, 2017; Hynes, 2017; Lee and Björklund Larsen, 2019; Raymond and Connelly, 2020). Working with an ethnographic triangulation approach, the focus remained on accessible pathways and ecosystems, rather than on gatekeepers or barriers to access (Morton, 2013; Seaver, 2017; Glaser et al, 2021).

The dataset comprised 96 artefacts (government policies, press releases, legislation, reports, presentations, spreadsheets, research papers, procurement documents, booklets, leaflets, flyers, policy briefs, handbooks, webinar recordings, web pages, YouTube videos, newsletters, action plans) dating from 2005 to 2021, encompassing the background to statistical profiling and the first ten years of its implementation in the Irish PES (2011–2021). The data also included ten semi-structured interviews with academics, civil servants, technology experts and public sector consultants undertaken in 2021 and 2022. Fieldwork took place during the COVID-19 pandemic response and the interviews were conducted and recorded online. The interviews explored topics such as public service policy, digital transformation policy, Irish and EU policy, implementation and COVID-19 related digital transformations in service delivery.

Ethnographic data analysis methods were used, using a triangulation of genealogy, document analysis and interviews. In exploring sociology and the ethnography of emerging digital data, ethnography is not stable and does not have a universal set of methodological principles that unify ethnographic practice (Brooker, 2022). Assemblage ethnographic fieldwork took place in multiple sites, where those involved in social practices of legislating, administering and governing (and the documents they produce) are to be found (Wahlberg, 2022). This study offers a pathway for the study of PES profiling, algorithms and AI in digital welfare, through the use of assemblage ethnography.

Findings

This section demonstrates assemblage thinking and assemblage ethnography as a method of enquiry into AI and algorithmic public sector service delivery. First, the PEX algorithm as a state apparatus is explored. Second, the PEX algorithm and its social life is discussed.

Statistical profiling: the Probability of Exit algorithm in Ireland as a state apparatus

Ireland's PEX statistical profiling model is an example of AI implemented since 2012, as a solution to the urgent organisational problem of welfare resource allocation. At the time of the bailout agreement between the Irish government and the EU Troika, government spending was monitored and huge economic changes were required at a service level, amid a political discourse of austerity. The unemployment rate rose to almost 20 per cent and additional PES capacity could not be resourced by a financially troubled state. With international pressure to generate cost efficiencies in public services combined with limited national resources, profiling of jobseekers was introduced as the solution, along with an amalgamation of welfare agencies into a one-stop-shop model. The policy foundations of PEX began in 2009–2010, with a legal basis in 2012 (S.I. No. 373, 2012) and an organisational structure in 2015. The PEX model predicts the likelihood that a claimant will still be unemployed 12 months after the day that they make their initial unemployment benefit claim and the algorithm remains in use under the 2021–2025 employment policy (Government of Ireland, 2021b; McGuinness et al, 2022) despite Ireland exiting the bailout in 2013.

Despite a lack of transparency in its calculations, low accuracy rates and its unquantifiable role as the solution to the resource allocation issue, PEX remains in place as a consistent tool used by the Irish PES, throughout the changing nature of unemployment rates in Ireland since 2012. The algorithm continues to foster traditional power relationships and discriminate against those needing protection and support (Eubanks, 2018; D'Ignazio and Klein, 2020). It continues to be an 'object of concern' and an 'object of ignorance' (O'Doherty and Neyland, 2019), despite a recent rebranding as 'a personalised service' in the latest employment policy, Pathways to Work 2021–2025 (Government of Ireland, 2021b).

The techno-utopianism of welfare policy which incorporates AI and statistical profiling algorithms is evident. Irish policies on employment, digital literacy, AI, digital futures and government innovation are aligned to EU policy goals and promote organisational change and reform, with a digital personalised service for citizens (Department of Public Expenditure and Reform, 2017; European Commission, 2021; Government of Ireland, 2021a; 2021b; 2022a; 2022c). Indeed the Irish government created a Department of Public Expenditure and Reform to drive much of these endeavours, offer direction to government departments on digital best practice and liaise with EU institutions and agencies on these matters. These policies feed into the apparatus of the welfare state (Foucault, 1980), creating the PEX algorithm, encouraging apparatus-builders to continue with its recalibration, a rebranding as personalised service and an alignment to EU policy goals of digital-by-default public services. Since then, the promotion of profiling has continued through policies of the OECD, World Bank and EU, all encouraging the use of profiling as part of the digital future of government services and 'Digital PES' (Blázquez, 2014; Loxha and Morgandi, 2014; Barnes et al, 2015; OECD, 2018).

Public employment services statistical profiling: a problematic approach

This approach is problematic in several ways. First, using Ireland as an example, the PEX statistical profiling algorithm is not subject to the General Data Protection Regulation and a separate legal basis exists in specific legislation, allowing state access to the personal data required to run the algorithm. Second, profiling facilitates discrimination. In Ireland, this looks like categorising jobseekers into three groups, where PEX facilitates a first-level segmentation into low, medium or high probability of finding work, which in turn determines the engagement frequency with PES. A caseworker tailors the service based on their training and experience but they can also be informed by profiling methodologies and statistical assessment tools (Government of Ireland, 2021b). PEX profiling facilitates segmentation and is promoted as a tool to deal with the challenge of delivering a personalised service, yet misclassification can require higher frequency of interactions with PES and unnecessary redirections to irrelevant training, for example.

Third, international examples show that PES profiling tools have been rejected and abandoned, for reasons of acceptance and discrimination, with only 13 countries continuing with implementation. In Finland, the profiling tool was rejected by caseworkers, with 84 per cent surveyed noting the tool did not help to solve the client-case and the majority 'do not believe the model can predict long-term unemployment, do not use it in their day-to-day work nor discuss the results with the clients' (Riipinen, 2011). In Austria, the profiling tool raised public concerns about gender discrimination, with the documentation listing the 'female' variable as detrimental to the chances of labour market integration and the 'obligations of care' variable only applying to women (Allhutter et al, 2020). This was justified by the Austrian PES as capturing the 'harsh reality' of the labour market but ultimately resulted in the abandonment of the profiling system amid questions of accountability, transparency, bias, discrimination, objectivity and encoding past inequalities into classification models.

Probability of Exit statistical profiling algorithm and its social life

Governments promoting the model AI deployments of personalised welfare services tend to articulate a logical model, where 'customers', a term problematic in the field, follow a scheduled service model. In the circular model of policy development, the assessment of policy and implementation of AI and digital tools is part of the policy design, and seeks to validate the model delivery. In ethnography, the model is never the terrain, and certainly the rollout of logical models of service provision is distinctively different in practice.

A key finding of this chapter is to demonstrate the use of assemblage thinking as a method of inquiry into the use of AI and algorithms in public sector organisations. Assemblage thinking traces the complex social life of the PEX algorithm and shows a more in-depth picture of the whole ecosystem, the assemblage bringing the policy to life. Triggered by the global financial crisis and its impact on Ireland, the policy foundations of PEX emerged in 2009–2010, the regulations to give it a legal basis in 2012 and the organisational structures in 2015. By this time, Ireland had exited the bailout, employment rates had increased, yet government policy remained focused on PEX implementation and delivery. Focusing only on the technology and policy would highlight the big dreams and imaginaries of AI, missing key elements of the wider assemblage, therefore this method allows greater analysis of AI-driven public service delivery.

The state can show that its technology works and its policy goals have been achieved. When some systems only have a review after ten years of implementation, such as PEX (McGuinness et al, 2022), there is limited information to investigate. With the state having a monopoly on policy and on technology specifications, researchers can only study certain areas. Therefore the assemblage thinking approach offers new insights.

Much of the discussion around the use of AI in public services refers to the deployment of machine learning technologies, using statistical methods to help predict certain outcomes. This leads to the concept of 'black boxes', which is different from traditional statistical analysis, as it does not involve detailed checks of how these predictions were produced (European Union Agency for Fundamental Rights, 2020). The Irish government strategy on AI, influenced by EU policy goals, highlights potential risks for AI in the areas of discrimination, risk, transparency and accountability. It notes that public administrations are experimenting with algorithmic decision-making in high-stakes areas such as eligibility for social benefits. It highlights the importance of making information on how AI systems make consequential decisions public and understandable, using all available tools in the AI assurance ecosystem (Government of Ireland, 2021a). As a leading digital nation which promoted the regulation of data protection, the Irish government sees an opportunity to leverage its reputation to serve as a leader in ethical and trustworthy data governance for AI, drawing on a human rights-based approach to underpin AI ethics guidance (Government of Ireland, 2021a). Exploring emerging code-level bureaucracies and their social life opens up issues such as the debate on why PEX is never officially referred to as an algorithm or AI, and therefore whether the AI strategy with its goals of transparency applies to it.

With the arrival of profiling and AI-based systems, system transparency and documentation of provenance is an evolving field. It is not yet a feature of PES statistical profiling systems, but the adoption of provenance mechanisms would demonstrate the steps of data processing and help determine the trustworthiness and accuracy of the results produced (Werder et al, 2022; Kale et al, 2023). Using provenance processes has been shown to build trust and facilitate the adoption of clinical learning healthcare systems (Curcin et al, 2014; Delaney et al, 2015; Ford et al, 2021). With trust, values and accuracy emerging as potential reporting standards for algorithmic profiling in PES (Gallagher and Griffin, 2023; Hayes and Griffin, 2023), harnessing digital transformation in PES must include monitoring and evaluation of automated decisions (European Union Agency for Fundamental Rights, 2020; Lauringson, 2022).

Conclusion

The value of this study reconsiders the big dreams of AI in the organisation life of the PES, capturing the digital organisational understanding of statistical profiling algorithms in welfare systems, through the example of the PEX algorithm in Ireland. PES is particularly important and relevant as it deals with vulnerable populations. The value of such an ethnographic study exposes the social life of the algorithm from emergence, to embedding, to its role in the digital organisational future of 'digital PES'. Using Foucault's concept of the *dispositif*, the study identifies the PEX algorithm as the state

AI apparatus which shapes work practices, decision-making process and client encounters in PES (Foucault, 1980; Agamben, 2009). In exploring the PEX ecosystem evolution from 2011 to 2021 through ethnographic methods, the study further reveals the assemblage which encompasses statistical profiling systems – the assemblage plus its social life (Deleuze and Guattari, 1987). This approach provides a pathway for capturing an understanding of EU digital aspirations in practice, from politics to code in the digital welfare state.

References

Agamben, G. (2009) *'What Is an Apparatus?' and Other Essays*. Stanford: Stanford University Press.

Allhutter, D., Cech, F., Fischer, F., Grill, G. and Mager, A. (2020) Algorithmic profiling of job seekers in Austria: How austerity politics are made effective. *Frontiers in Big Data*, 3(5).

Barnes, S.-A., Wright, S., Irving, P. and Deganis, I. (2015) *Identification of Latest Trends and Current Developments in Methods to Profile Jobseekers in European Public Employment Services: Final Report*. Brussels: European Commission.

Blázquez, M. (2014) *Skills-based Profiling and Matching in PES*. Analytical Paper. Brussels: European Commission.

Brooker, P. (2022) Computational ethnography: A view from sociology. *Big Data & Society*, 9(1).

Burrell, J., Washington, A. and Mulligan, D. (2022) *Conversations on the Datafied State – Part One: What is the Public Interest?* [Podcast], 4 May.

Considine, M., McGann, M., Ball, S. and Nguyen, P. (2022) Can robots understand welfare? Exploring machine bureaucracies in welfare-to-work. *Journal of Social Policy*, 51(3): 519–534.

Curcin, V., Miles, S., Danger, R., Chen, Y., Bache, R. and Taweel, A. (2014) Implementing interoperable provenance in biomedical research. *Future Generation Computer Systems*, 34: 1–16.

Danaher, J., Hogan, M.J., Noone, C., Kennedy, R., Behan, A., De Paor, A., et al (2017) Algorithmic governance: Developing a research agenda through the power of collective intelligence. *Big Data & Society*, 4(2).

Delaney, B.C., Curcin, V., Andreasson, A., Arvanitis, T.N., Bastiaens, H., Corrigan, D., et al (2015) Translational medicine and patient safety in Europe: TRANSFoRm – architecture for the learning health system in Europe. *BioMed Research International*: 961526.

Deleuze, G. and Guattari, F. (1987) *A Thousand Plateaus: Capitalism and Schizophrenia*. Minneapolis: University of Minnesota Press.

Dencik, L. (2022) The datafied welfare state: A perspective from the UK. In A. Hepp, J. Jarke and L. Kramp (eds) *New Perspectives in Critical Data Studies: The Ambivalences of Data Power* (pp 145–165). Cham: Palgrave Macmillan.

Department of Public Expenditure and Reform (2017) *Our Public Service 2020: Development and Innovation*. Dublin. https://www.ops.gov.ie/what-is-ops2020/downloads/

Department of Social Protection (2023) *Intreo: The Public Employment Services*. https://www.gov.ie/en/organisation-information/3c095-intreo-the-public-employment-services/

D'Ignazio, C. and Klein, L.F. (2020) *Data Feminism*. London: MIT Press.

Dukelow, F. (2015) 'Pushing against an open door': Reinforcing the neo-liberal policy paradigm in Ireland and the impact of EU intrusion. *Comparative European Politics*, 13(1): 93–111.

Eubanks, V. (2018) *Automating Inequality: How High-Tech Tools Profile, Police, and Punish the Poor*. New York: St. Martin's Press.

European Commission (2021) *2030 Digital Compass: The European Way for the Digital Decade (COM/2021/118 final)*. Brussels: European Commission. https://eur-lex.europa.eu/legal-content/en/TXT/?uri=CELEX%3A52021DC0118

European Commission (2023) *The Future of Social Protection and of the Welfare State in the EU*. Brussels: Publications Office of the European Union.

European Parliament Directorate-General for Parliamentary Research Services and Bassot, E. (2022) *The Six Policy Priorities of the von der Leyen Commission: State of Play in Autumn 2022: In-Depth Analysis*. Brussels: European Parliament.

European Union Agency for Fundamental Rights (2020) *Getting the Future Right: Artificial Intelligence and Fundamental Rights*. https://fra.europa.eu/sites/default/files/fra_uploads/fra-2020-artificial-intelligence_en.pdf

Ewald, F. (2020) *The Birth of Solidarity: The History of the French Welfare State*. Durham, NC: Duke University Press.

Feldman, G. (2011) *The Migration Apparatus: Security, Labor, and Policymaking in the European Union*. Stanford: Stanford University Press.

Ford, E., Edelman, N., Somers, L., Shrewsbury, D., Lopez Levy, M., van Marwijk, H., et al (2021) Barriers and facilitators to the adoption of electronic clinical decision support systems: A qualitative interview study with UK general practitioners. *BMC Medical Informatics and Decision Making*, 21(1): 193.

Foucault, M. (1978) *The History of Sexuality, Volume I: An Introduction*. New York: Pantheon Books.

Foucault, M. (1980) *Power/Knowledge: Selected Interviews & Other Writings 1972–1977*. New York: Pantheon Books.

Gallagher, P. and Griffin, R. (2023) (In) accuracy in algorithmic profiling of the unemployed: An exploratory review of reporting standards. *Social Policy and Society*. doi: 10.1017/S1474746423000428

Geiger, R.S. (2017) Beyond opening up the black box: Investigating the role of algorithmic systems in Wikipedian organizational culture. *Big Data & Society*, 4(2).

Glaser, V.L., Pollock, N. and D'Adderio, L. (2021) The biography of an algorithm: Performing algorithmic technologies in organizations. *Organization Theory*, 2(2).

Government of Ireland (2021a) *AI – Here For Good: A National Artificial Intelligence Strategy for Ireland*. Dublin: Government of Ireland. https://enterprise.gov.ie/en/Publications/National-AI-Strategy.html

Government of Ireland (2021b) *Pathways to Work 2021–2025*. Dublin: Government of Ireland. https://www.gov.ie/en/publication/1feaf-pathways-to-work-2021/

Government of Ireland (2022a) *Adult Literacy for Life: A 10-Year Adult Literacy, Numeracy and Digital Literacy Strategy*. Dublin: Government of Ireland.

Government of Ireland (2022b) *Connecting Government 2030: A Digital and ICT Strategy for Ireland's Public Service*. Dublin: Government of Ireland. https://www.gov.ie/en/publication/136b9-connecting-government-2030-a-digital-and-ict-strategy-for-irelands-public-service/

Government of Ireland (2022c) *Harnessing Digital: The Digital Ireland Framework*. Dublin: Government of Ireland. https://www.gov.ie/en/publication/adf42-harnessing-digital-the-digital-ireland-framework/

Greenhalgh, S. (2008) *Just One Child: Science and Policy in Deng's China*. Berkeley: University of California Press.

Griffin, R., Tuite, A., Roche, Z. and Gallagher, P. (2020) *[HECAT] D1.3 Report: Ethical, Social, Theological and Technical Review of 1st Generation PES Algorithms and Data Use*. Waterford: HECAT Project. https://doi.org/10.5281/zenodo.7913459

Hayes, O. and Griffin, R. (2023) *[HECAT] D7.2 Policy Briefing Report. Algorithm Profiling in Public Employment Services (PES): Reporting Standards Policy Brief*. https://doi.org/10.5281/zenodo.7921614

Henman, P.W.F. (2022) Digital social policy: Past, present, future. *Journal of Social Policy*, 51(3): 535–550.

Hick, R. (2018) Enter the Troika: The politics of social security during Ireland's bailout. *Journal of Social Policy*, 47: 1–20.

Hynes, M. (2017) Shining a brighter light into the digital 'black box': A call for stronger sociological (re)engagement with digital technology design, development and adoption debates. *Irish Journal of Sociology*, 26(1): 94–126.

Ingold, J., Forde, C. and Robertshaw, D. (2024) Varieties of digitalisation? A comparison of employment services digitalisation in the UK and Australia. *Australian Journal of Social Issues*.

Ingold, T. (2016) *Lines: A Brief History*. London: Routledge.

Kale, A., Nguyen, T., Harris, F.C., Jr., Li, C., Zhang, J. and Ma, X. (2023) Provenance documentation to enable explainable and trustworthy AI: A literature review. *Data Intelligence*. doi: 10.1162/dint_a_00119

Karsten, M.M.V. (2021) Dislocated dialogue: An anthropological investigation of digitisation among professionals in fire safety. *Organization*, 28(1): 92–114.

Kelly, E., McGuinness, S., Redmond, P., Savage, M. and Walsh, J.R. (2019) *An Initial Evaluation of the Effectiveness of Intreo Activation Reforms*. Dublin: ESRI. https://doi.org/10.26504/rs81

Kopper, M. and Knox, H. (2024) Introduction: Number politics after datafication. *The Cambridge Journal of Anthropology*, 42(1): 1–22.

Latour, B. (2005) *Reassembling the Social: An Introduction to Actor-Network-Theory*. Oxford: Oxford University Press.

Lauringson, A. (2022) *Harnessing Digitalisation in Public Employment Services to Connect People with Jobs*. Paris: OECD. https://www.oecd.org/els/emp/Harnessing_digitalisation_in_Public_Employment_Services_to_connect_people_with_jobs.pdf

Law, J. and Callon, M. (1988) Engineering and sociology in a military aircraft project: A network analysis of technological change. *Social Problems*, 35(3): 284–297.

Lee, F. and Björklund Larsen, L. (2019) How should we theorize algorithms? Five ideal types in analyzing algorithmic normativities. *Big Data & Society*, 6(2).

Loxha, A. and Morgandi, M. (2014) *Profiling the Unemployed: A Review of OECD Experiences and Implications for Emerging Economies*. Washington, DC: World Bank. http://hdl.handle.net/10986/20382

McGann, M. and Murphy, M.P. (2021) Introduction: The dual tracks of welfare and activation reform – governance and conditionality. *Administration*, 69(2): 1–16.

McGuinness, S., Redmond, P., Kelly, E. and Maragkou, K. (2022) *Predicting the Probability of Long-Term Unemployment and Recalibrating Ireland's Statistical Profiling Model*. Dublin: ESRI. https://www.esri.ie/publications/predicting-the-probability-of-long-term-unemployment-and-recalibrating-irelands

Mejias, U.A. and Couldry, N. (2019) Datafication. *Internet Policy Review*, 8(4).

Morton, T. (2013) *Hyperobjects: Philosophy and Ecology after the End of the World*. Minneapolis: University of Minnesota Press.

Murphy, M. and Hogan, J. (2020) Reflections on post-bailout policy analysis in Ireland. *Administration*, 68(4): 145–160.

Negreiro, M. (2021) *The EU Digital Decade: A New Set of Digital Targets for 2030*. Brussels: European Parliament. https://www.europarl.europa.eu/RegData/etudes/BRIE/2021/696189/EPRS_BRI(2021)696189_EN.pdf

Northern Ireland Statistics and Research Agency (NISRA) (2022) *Census 2021: Statement about Data Quality*. Belfast: NISRA. https://www.nisra.gov.uk/system/files/statistics/census-2021-statement-about-data-quality.pdf

O'Brien, J. and Griffin, R. (2015) Statistics: On the statistical composition of unemployment. In T. Boland and R. Griffin (eds) *The Sociology of Unemployment*. Manchester: Manchester University Press.

O'Connell, P.J., McGuiness, S., Kelly, E. and Walsh, J. (2009) *National Profiling of the Unemployed in Ireland*. Dublin: ESRI. https://www.esri.ie/publications/national-profiling-of-the-unemployed-in-ireland

O'Doherty, D. and Neyland, D. (2019) The developments in ethnographic studies of organising: Towards objects of ignorance and objects of concern. *Organization*, 26(4): 449–469.

OECD (2018) *Profiling Tools for Early Identification of Jobseekers Who Need Extra Support: Policy Brief on Activation Policies*. Paris: OECD Publishing.

OECD (2022) *Harnessing Digitalisation in Public Employment Services to Connect People with Jobs*. Paris: OECD. https://www.oecd.org/els/emp/ Harnessing_digitalisation_in_Public_Employment_Services_to_connect_ people_with_jobs.pdf

Pasquale, F. (2015) *The Black Box Society*. Cambridge, MA: Harvard University Press.

Plesner, U. and Husted, E. (2020) *Digital Organizing: Revisiting Themes in Organization Studies*. London: Red Globe Press.

Rabinow, P. (1996) *Making PCR: A Story of Biotechnology*. Chicago: University of Chicago Press.

Raymond, A.H. and Connelly, C. (2020) Governance of algorithms: Rethinking public sector use of algorithms for predictive purposes. In W. Barfield (ed) *The Cambridge Handbook of the Law of Algorithms* (pp 233–250). Cambridge: Cambridge University Press.

Riipinen, T. (2011) Risk profiling of long-term unemployment in Finland. *European Commission's 'PES to PES Dialogue Dissemination Conference'*. Brussels, 8–9 September, pp 8–9.

Schou, J. and Pors, A.S. (2019) Digital by default? A qualitative study of exclusion in digitalised welfare. *Social Policy & Administration*, 53(3): 464–477.

Seaver, N. (2017) Algorithms as culture: Some tactics for the ethnography of algorithmic systems. *Big Data & Society*, 4(2).

S.I. No. 373 (2012) Social Welfare (Consolidated claims, payments and control) (Amendment) (No. 9) (Information) Regulations 2012.

Trittin-Ulbrich, H., Scherer, A.G., Munro, I. and Whelan, G. (2021) Exploring the dark and unexpected sides of digitalization: Toward a critical agenda. *Organization*, 28(1): 8–25.

van Gerven, M. (2022) Studying social policy in the digital age. In K. Nelson, R. Nieuwenhuis and M. Yerkes (eds) *Social Policy in Changing European Societies: Research Agendas for the 21st Century* (pp 251–264). Cheltenham: Edward Elgar.

Wahlberg, A. (2022) Assemblage ethnography: Configurations across scales, sites, and practices. In M.H. Bruun, A. Wahlberg, R. Douglas-Jones, C. Hasse, K. Hoeyer, D.B. Kristensen, et al (eds) *The Palgrave Handbook of the Anthropology of Technology* (pp 125–144). Singapore: Springer Singapore.

Werder, K., Ramesh, B. and Zhang, R. (2022) Establishing data provenance for responsible artificial intelligence systems. *ACM Transactions on Management Information Systems*, 13(2): Article 22.

Wessel, L., Baiyere, A., Ologeanu-Taddei, R., Cha, J. and Blegind Jensen, T. (2021) Unpacking the difference between digital transformation and IT-enabled organizational transformation. *Journal of the Association for Information Systems*, 22(1): 102–129.

Youdell, D. and McGimpsey, I. (2015) Assembling, disassembling and reassembling 'youth services' in austerity Britain. *Critical Studies in Education*, 56(1): 116–130.

Zigon, J. (2015) What is a situation? An assemblic ethnography of the drug war. *Cultural Anthropology*, 30(3): 501–524.

3

Algorithmic profiling of the unemployed

Patrick Gallagher and Ray Griffin

Introduction

Public employment services (PES) increasingly use automated statistical profiling algorithms (ASPAs) to stream unemployed jobseekers at risk of becoming long-term unemployed (LTU) into active labour market policy (ALMP) interventions.

While almost all PES policy operates as an algorithmic rule-based system, the past 20 years has seen the development of statistical profiling using the big datasets captured in PES interrogated by algorithmic techniques. Prior to ASPAs, some PES engaged in casework-led profiling or rule-based profiling and so the transformation to ASPAs is to black-box these visible processes. The international trend for ASPAs has led to the introduction of profiling into more universalistic systems. With some variations, algorithmic profiling has renewed and greatly increased the use of profiling in PES, in general bluntly identifying recipients of a passive or an active PES, based on the algorithm identifying those with a statistically high probability of becoming LTU.

Strikingly, despite over 25 years experience of ASPAs, none of the 13 countries that deploy them use a similar system – each has different statistical, processing and administrative features. As a vital first step in improving the functioning of these important pieces of social infrastructure, we introduce our comparative international study of the 14 live ASPAs in use – surfacing the mathematical and statistical infrastructure of these algorithms and addressing their operational accuracy. We demonstrate that the current, ad hoc and minimalist approaches that report a single measure for accuracy (usually a percentage) inflates the capabilities of the technology to predict LTU accurately and thus prevents a more considered use of ASPAs. We conclude the chapter with a call for a higher reporting standard, and identify the key elements of what such an accuracy reporting standard might look like.

Datafication

In this datafication process, individuals, with their complex messy lives, flatten their experience, identity and predicament into a simple category that allows the state to administer them. The term datafication captures the transformation of social action into online quantified data, thus allowing for real-time tracking and predictive analysis (Mayer-Schoenberger and Cukier, 2013), and involves processes that have become gradually ever more naturalised. The term data derives from the Latin term *datum* which literally means *a thing given*. The term's transmission into science comes in the early Enlightenment, when natural scientists explored naturally occurring things given by God. Central to this idea is that these things are natural gifts, part of a generous cycle of reciprocity (Malinowski, 1922; Mauss, 1925). In contemporary datafication practices, data does not arise from fundamental gift relations with nature; to collect data is not to receive what is given but to extract what is not (Ingold, 2018).

Although the welfare state is a bureaucratically administered system of gift relations, or mutual commitment, the process of extruding data from people requires that they break off important markers of selfhood to establish themselves in the world of welfare. For example, identifying into normative binary gender is important, complex elaborations of gender are not. In this way, data snaps apart markers from the currents and entanglements of social life. Datafication enthusiasts tend to assume a self-evident relationship between data and people, which is rooted in the prevailing social norm of statistical science. This relies on a belief in the objectivity of quantification, a seamless transmission from the corporal, biological human into a digital avatar.

In our popular imagination statistics are collected around unemployment. Neutral, passive researchers go out into the world and unproblematically collect and collate descriptions of the natural world. Such assumptions commonly fail to take account of the social and organisational processes involved in the production and dissemination of these important numbers, as well as the performative and reflexive aspects of the statistics. Statistics are political, they render vivid images of society that call for action. Performative in the sense that unemployment is not a natural or objective category; it is an organisational category of government and the act of categorising someone as unemployed, more than anything else, makes people unemployed. Reflexive in the sense that the statistics of unemployment are consumed crudely by government and individuals belying the complex issues around how they are produced, and how government and individuals make decisions based on the statistics, which in turn impact unemployment statistics. The ubiquity of statistics around unemployment gives a false sense of seeing the actual experience of being unemployed – the model is not the terrain.

Curiously, the welfare algorithms orientate towards geographic, demographic, behavioural and psychographic markers of the individual. This echoes an earlier and settled debate in marketing theory on marketing segmentation. Segmentation (along with targeting and positioning) was one of the core planks of marketing theory encapsulating the idea that customers gather, clump and cluster into tribes that have homogeneous needs and respond to homogeneous stimulation (Kotler, 2009). Before segmentation gave way to mass customisation, and segments of one, marketing produced taxonomies of customers based initially on their demographic and geographic markers until people no longer fell into the groove of their place and age, and latterly on psychographic and behavioural markets.

The extent to which a homogeneous population exists is essential for statistical modelling to work (Flyvbjerg, 2020), particularly the form of statistics that rely on regression such as algorithmic welfare. At stake is whether the labour market is complex, and so can be modelled with ever more data and processing power; or whether it is chaotic, random and without order. Complex systems can be conquered with perfect information that when fully understood can allow perfectly accurate predictions of a system, whereas chaotic systems may behave in complex ways, until they do not. We know from previous research that the labour market is chaotic and unemployment is heterogeneous, comprised of both frictionally unemployed and LTU and that the term LTU masks a host of social problems such as addiction, ill health and social exclusion.

From the raw material of individuals who are numbered and compounded into datafied clusters emerges narratives that shape meaning – data does not stand alone (Dourish, 2016), rather it is invited into models. Beyond the issues of producing data, there is considerable symbolic and imaginative effort to make data work, including the discursive, operation and material construction that surrounds data to make it self-legitimating and self-fulfilling. So it is common to discuss the issue of long-term unemployment as having a scarring effect, scarring is an allusion to physical trauma that is variously used in economics, social policy and sociology (Knabe and Rätzel, 2011). Inert data is brought to life as socially significant by narrative (Dourish, 2016; Seaver, 2017) that translates (Bolin and Anderson Schwarz, 2015) and frames (Pentzold and Fischer, 2017) social issues, such as scarring, quantifying them so they can subsequently be addressed through policy. Thus, the process of datafication legitimises itself by building a narrative of the negative impacts of LTU on the individual, all of this occurs without accounting for the actual experience of LTU (Lindsay, 2010).

Method

The central object of our investigation is algorithmic statistical profiling (Desiere et al, 2019). Statistical profiling uses a statistical model to predict the likelihood of return to work. It has proved a particularly rich terrain for social policy, with specialists in labour market economics (Loxha and Morgandi, 2014; Desiere et al, 2019), sociology (Griffin et al, 2020), science and technology studies (Allhutter et al, 2020) and critical data studies (Sztandar-Sztanderska and Zielenska, 2020) all interrogating welfare algorithms.

Generally, researchers have developed a corpus of documents around singular algorithms – from workshop presentation slides, studies, technical reports and policy documents developed by government departments, parliamentary and public body oversight and scrutiny, newspapers, blog posts and academic commentary. Documentary analysis falls into the tradition of constructionist research (Jupp and Norris, 1993), which plays down the politics and authorship of profiling algorithms, while drawing attention to their complex social consequences. This work typically has an investigative approach – seeking out information on an intricate and largely hidden system (Delpierre et al, 2024). Most profiling algorithms rely on publicly published studies and datasets, so the data used to model the labour market, the statistical strategy and the variables are usually visible when looked for. What is less visible is how the algorithm is embedded into administrative systems; whether it is compulsory, if there is a human override, what is the nature of that override and what are the implications for an individual of algorithmic judgement.

In this chapter, we develop our comparative study based on a structured technical paper and literature review (n=146), briefings with system experts supported by EU TAIEX events, a trawl of GitHub for the actual algorithms and technical support from research colleagues. From this, we find, somewhat surprisingly, that despite very different statistical, mathematical and data approaches, each algorithm performs a remarkably similar job of managing workloads in public employment services, rationing resources and targeting ALMP interventions.

As both our primary and secondary data collection surfaced data that was technical in nature, we were supported by an expert in mathematical modelling who kindly assisted us in understanding how algorithmic statistical profiling works, particularly offering plain language explanations of their complex mathematics and computer coding.

Our analysis explores six elements of each of the algorithmic statistical profiling deployments. First, we sought to secure a technical description of the project background and how the algorithm came into being. Second, we examined the process by which variables were selected to be used to compute the algorithm, understanding the testing and training data that supported the development. Third, we ascertained the statistical approach used in computation. Fourth, we examined how the algorithm was embedded within the PES processes and workflow. Fifth, we assessed the accuracy of the algorithm in use. Sixth, we sought to understand the nature of the algorithm/test and its implications for those subjected to it. Table 3.1 sets out these elements in concise form for 13 different deployments our review surfaced.

Table 3.1: Descriptive information on data infrastructure, variables and statistical approach for all unemployment profiling algorithms

Country and system name	Project background	Core variables	Statistical method	Self-reported accuracy	Function in PES process and workflow
Australia, JSCI Job Seeker Classification Instrument	1998+ 2 revisions	12	Logistic regression	70–88%	LTU
Austria, AMS Employment Prospects Model	2019–2020 aborted	8	Multivariate logistic regression models	80–85%	LTU
Belgium, VDAB Predictive Modelling	Ongoing development	9	Random forest, neutral networks and decision trees	67%	LTU
Croatia, StAP Statistically Assisted Profiling	2016 revised	8	Logistic regression	69%	LTU
Denmark, Job Barometer (2004); STAR (2015)	2004; 2015	6	Logistic regression and decision tree	66–80%	LTU
Estonia, prognosis tool	2007; 2019	6	OTT random forest model	95%	LTU
Finland, Risk Profiling Tool	2007+	7	Logistic regression	89%	LTU
France, Intelligence Emploi	2020+	n/a	Neural network	70–80%	LTU
Ireland, PEX Probability of Exit	2011; 2022	13, 8	Probit regression	50–69%	LTU
Italy, ANPAL Qualitative Profiling Service	2016+	4	Logistic regression	70–90%	LTU
Latvia, SEA State Employment Agency	2013; 2017	12	Decision tree	60–70%	LTU
Netherlands, WorkProfiler	2015+	11	Logistic regression	70%	LTU
New Zealand, CSM Client Service Matching	2017	9	Random forest and gradient boosting	63–83%	LTU
Sweden, AST Assessment Support Tool	2012+	11	Probit model- binary logistic regression	85–90%	LTU

Source: Inspired by Desiere et al (2019) and Georges (2008), based on a structured literature review (n=146) + TAIEX exchange interviews (n=6).

While we worked carefully to build a deep understanding of ASPAs, it is more arresting that these powerful technologies that sit at the heart of many contemporary welfare states are somewhat of a black box. Strikingly, we know very little about how ASPAs are used administratively in operational environments, and to what kind of accuracy and oversight they are subject. This has significant practical implications for the overall effectiveness of state expenditure on ALMPs. These policies now, on average, cost Organisation for Economic Co-operation and Development (OECD) countries 0.6 per cent of gross domestic product (Pignatti and Van Belle, 2018), and their effectiveness is in question, with the most authoritative study, a meta-analysis of the effectiveness of 200 ALMPs (Card et al, 2018), suggesting that average short-run impacts were negligible. Indeed, a recent Australian study found that jobseekers who were not 'activated' were more effective in finding work swiftly and sustainably. It may well be the case that the general opaqueness of ASPAs, particularly how they are embedded into administrative practices in PES and their accuracy, reflects a general lack of understanding on how ASPAs function.

Reviewing the archetypical profiling algorithms

Each of the 13 ASPAs use different mathematical approaches, variously using probit, logit, random forest, decision tree and neural networks (see Table 3.1). In a similar vein, there are a variety of approaches to training the algorithms, some use sample data, others use registry data, some algorithms are set and updated at intervals, others are continuously updated. All the algorithms use broadly similar variables – history of unemployment and work, age, education and nationality appear in most, but variables are variously weighted and combined with other more novel variables, so that each algorithm would present a different assessment of the same person. Unsurprisingly, each algorithm reports a different stylised accuracy rate – usually a single percentage. Despite almost 30 years' experience of these algorithms, the technology has not achieved incumbent status, there is no dominant design – each is unique.

What is perhaps more interesting in our review is what goes unsaid, and what is undiscoverable to the public and even the expert managers who implement these algorithms – whether these algorithms are deterministic or non-deterministic. Algorithms that follow a precise formula are deterministic and their workings can be known, understood and replicated, whereas non-deterministic algorithms can never be known as they use heuristics to guess at their answers. As the working of non-deterministic algorithms is never clear, they require close human supervision and oversight.

Hampering the understanding of these algorithms is a dearth of methods statements or reporting that would allow oversight and auditing of their effectiveness (Gallagher and Griffin, 2023). Indeed, our approach here in uncovering the histories of the algorithms (Glaser et al, 2021) is more patchwork (Seaver, 2017) detective work, than normal social policy or sociology. While we report on the public and surviving algorithms, there is evidence that most OECD PES, at one time or another, have examined, altered, aborted or abandoned systems (Matty, 2013). Indeed, many of the surviving systems are problematic, with several countries modifying their existing systems due to problems with acceptance by PES workers and concerns over accuracy – typically emphasising the advisory, non-enforceable nature of the algorithms' decision-making.

Mathematical visions of a person

The following sections briefly outline the different statistical models currently deployed, interrogating them within their administrative context.

Logit and probit models are the most common technique for ASPAs, and are used to produce binary predictions. Logit models use the logistic function to estimate the probability of a certain event happening, while probit models use the cumulative distribution function of the standard normal distribution. The strength of both models is their brutal simplicity – they take complex situations, where multiple complex and chaotic variables relate, and offer a definitive and flat answer that is easy to interpret. In contrast, *random forest and decision trees* are machine learning algorithms that use a collection of decision trees to make predictions, with the random forests approach combining multiple decision trees to improve accuracy and reduce overfitting. Random forests and decision trees are robust and can handle non-linear relationships well. *Neural networks* are another form of machine learning algorithm inspired by the structure of the human brain, where interconnected nodes are organised in layers, with each performing a mathematical operation to produce an output.

Gathering and analysing data has traditionally had problems of quantity and being able to visualise and explain certain situations succinctly. For any given situation there is unending amounts of data that can be collected. So, to make it manageable data is sorted and categorised into easy to understand variables. Additionally, in the input data used for many of the PES algorithms and statistical systems the variables selected for analysis differ from system to system. There are, more often than not, certain standard questions that are asked of subjects (gender, age, marital/co-habitation status) both in the PES systems and in general questionnaires. Grouping individuals into demographics indicates an assumption of similarity in circumstances, needs and so on. Despite the knowledge that unemployed are a heterogeneous group (Cutuli and Grotti, 2020).

This is a generally accepted way of administering large human datasets. However, in the era of big data and increased computing power these categories should not matter. It should be possible to gather every variable and sub-variable and provide an individual profile of circumstances, needs and desires around employment. A technology which recognises and embraces heterogeneity rather than the existing system which attempts to force square pegs into round holes, by presupposing the homogeneity of unemployment. In practice the unemployed are a diverse group – no two cases are the same because no two people are the same.

There also appears to be a desire to keep data simple and uncomplicated when mapping networks. Models which focus primarily on the individual and their skills or characteristics would need to gather data on large numbers of disparate variables that are often very personal to individuals. There is a danger that the data feeding some of these models is limited, such as using data from LinkedIn, which may result in certain segments of the labour market being excluded, particularly the most vulnerable participants in the labour market (for example, those whose economic circumstances limit their ability to access the internet and, as such, LinkedIn).

Generic structure long-term unemployed sorting/profiling algorithms

Strikingly, despite the variation in data infrastructure, variables and statistical method, and being embedded into markedly different PES processes and workflows, each algorithm nevertheless does a remarkably similar job, identified in Figure 3.1. The alchemy of the algorithms is to distinguish between individuals at risk of becoming LTU and those more likely to be frictionally unemployed, so PES can ration access to expensive, intensive ALMPs. Beyond their internal workings, most are reported as being advisory, prepared as a backdrop to support a human PES counsellor's classification, but some are digital first (such as Australia's Job Seeker Classification Instrument), with limited, if any, human oversight. Other studies (Lustig and Nardi, 2015) have shown that people defer to algorithms, even when they know they are error prone and shown to be ineffective.

Figure 3.1: An archetypical model of profiling algorithms

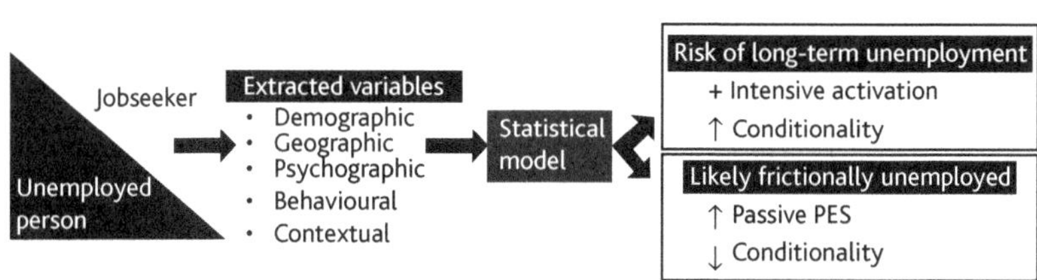

Inaccuracy

The potential for ASPAs to fulfil the promise of increased efficiency, cost effectiveness and tailoring of services to individual needs hinges on their ability to correctly identify those most at risk of LTU. Considering the distributed roles within decision-making between people and things such as algorithms raises important questions about accidents. While in a purest sense, algorithms, like all sciences, have no accidental properties (Aristotle, 1994), a technology cannot exist without its accident (Virilio, 2007). The invention of the ship is the invention of the shipwreck and, similarly, PES algorithms contain the possibility of mistakes.

Algorithms that categorise individuals produce four distinct results (see Table 3.2) and are vulnerable to two types of classic mistakes. First, false positives are the incorrect assignment of a label. For example, when someone is labelled as a terrorist when they are not, when someone is categorised as having cancer when they do not, or when someone is labelled as being unlikely to gain work in six months when they are not. False positives are when the algorithmic decision scans the universe of individuals and mistakenly labels the individual as within the preferred category. Alternatively, false negatives incorrectly exclude someone from a category. For example, identifying someone as not a terrorist when they are, or not identifying someone who becomes LTU. False negatives entail the algorithmic decision scanning the universe of individuals and not labelling them as the preferred category when the label may actual fit. Both false positive and negatives are present in human and machine categorisation practices, what is important to know is the rate of both, and the implications of misclassification.

Table 3.2: Contingency table showing the four results generated by automated statistical profiling algorithms

Risk scores ↓		LTU group	Frictional group
100	High risk group	True positive	False positive
.			
.			
.			
.			
Cut off .	Low risk group	False negative	True negative
.			
.			
1			

Source: Gallagher and Griffin (2023)

The legitimacy of PES algorithms comes from the perception of accuracy, the sense that the tools are successful at capturing those at risk of LTU, a sense that is not borne out by examinations of the complex efficacy of these algorithms (Riipinen, 2011; McGuiness et al, 2014.

Although Table 3.1 also reports accuracy rates, in each case what accuracy means and how it is calculated are not reported, and so without a standardised concept and measurement it is simply not possible compare operational accuracy. Such data would normally be reported with a method statement, and more significant effort to accessibly explain to non-expert users at the point of reporting what this accuracy measure actually means. Without this, the measure is meaningless and comes over as a political gesture to appear accurate, while being opaque and obtuse about actual accuracy.

In order to develop a clear picture of the real-world function of ASPAs it is necessary to delve into the terminology which surrounds the various measures used to quantify accuracy in the world of data science. Data scientists have a range of precise terms and approaches to address the terrain of accuracy, error, sensitivity, specificity around the real-world function of algorithms.

In the little methodological literature reported on the UK, Austrian, Belgian and Danish tools, it appears that what is being reported is a measure called 'forecast accuracy', which is the percentage of an overall target group that the tool captures. Therefore, Table 3.1 only reports the percentage of LTU that the algorithm classifies correctly while omitting the corresponding, unavoidable error rate. The term 'forecasting accuracy' (Tashman, 2000) usefully has the modifier 'forecasting' which serves to moderate the perception of certainty conveyed in terming the measure accuracy. The omission of the term forecasting in the reporting of accuracy means a layperson or even an experienced social policy researcher is likely to think that 80 per cent accuracy means that two in every ten people that are profiled are misclassified. This is far from the truth, because forecast accuracy ignores false positive results. So while the ASPA may well identify 80 per cent of the LTU, there is a corresponding, unavoidable error rate that implies an enormous dead weight cost of unnecessary expenditure on expensive ALMPs for the frictionally unemployed (false positives).

Our research on the accuracy of ASPAs revealed that they tend towards high false positive rates. For example Table 3.3 outlines the results from an empirical study by the Department of Work and Pensions (Matty, 2013) that followed 1,085 people for 12 months. The real-world labour market outcomes of this group were then checked against the predicted outcome generated by the algorithm, uncovering an error ratio of 4:1. Meaning that, for every individual correctly classified, the ASPA misclassified four frictionally unemployed as high risk (Matty, 2013; Gallagher and Griffin, 2023).

In addition, empirical data available on the testing of other ASPAs such as the Belgian (Desiere and Struyven, 2021), Finnish (Riippen, 2011),

Table 3.3: Results of testing the Job Seeker Classification Instrument

	Size of target segment	
	Top 8%	Top 30%
Number of target segments that reach LTU	29	64
Number of target segments that are frictional	58	262
Total number of LTU	91	91
Total number of frictional	994	994
Proportion of all LTU captured	32%	70%
Proportion of all frictional misclassified	6%	26%
Model applied to test dataset (n=1,085)		

Source: Matty (2013)

Danish (Rosholm et al, 2004), Irish (O'Connell et al, 2009) and Swedish (Arbetsförmedlingen, 2014) systems suggest a high false-positive error rate is ubiquitous to all of these ASPAs. For example, the results from empirical testing of the Danish job barometer show the total number of errors – false positives = 171,291 and false negative = 346,270. Therefore, to correctly predict 270,953 LTU, it was necessary to misclassify 517,561 individuals or a ratio of roughly two errors to each correct prediction. Additionally, a study outlining accuracy results for the Irish Probability of Exit model compares accuracy rates with the Danish job barometer and finds only a marginal improvement in the accuracy rate.

The high false positive rate identified in at least four of the 16 ASPAs currently deployed across the OECD calls into question the true administrative purpose of the technology. ASPAs in their current form imply an enormous dead weight cost by providing unnecessary support (expensive ALMPs) to the frictionally unemployed. Raising the question, why do various PES depend on a technology that is so often wrong and results in wasteful spending? A possible explanation lies in the often underplayed administrative background to ASPAs.

Administrative context

The underplayed background of profiling algorithms is the limited capacity of PES to service clients. The need to profile is an affordance of most PES's fixed capacity. The OECD recommend sustaining the ratio of caseworker to unemployed people at 1:150 (Hainmueller et al, 2016; Böheim et al, 2023). Certainly, within a European public sector context it is not possible to rapidly modulate service provision to sustain PES service provision at a 1:150 ratio, and this creates pressure to ration services. Thus, rather than maintain universal service provision and modulate the extent of effort, rationing through profiling is introduced. Given the lag time for deploying such systems, they often arrive after the necessity for them has abated given the cyclical nature of labour market supply and demand flows. Encoded into profiling techniques are thresholds to generate a segment of those who need additional services in and around the fixed capacity of PES.

Profiling systems of any type are always problematic but one generated by an algorithm to assign a 'score' to a human individual inevitably raises questions of algorithmic bias, especially so when it is a government deploying an algorithm to ration resources to citizens. Were they to work as envisaged, at the heart of these various PES projects is an ambition to positively discriminate against those who are likely to thrive in the labour market without intervention. The attraction to algorithmic profiling is that it dehumanises the discrimination, eliding personal responsibility, thereby throwing the unpleasant business of sorting citizens into a black box. Using probabilistic causation around existing discrimination within the labour market gives rise to natural justice concerns around formally encoding discriminatory practices, echoing or even amplifying them.

Designers often removed certain characteristics from the final models either to simplify the processing or for political reasons such as selecting a marker that is too sensitive. Evaluative research done on algorithmic profiling has explored its functional qualities – effectiveness, compliance and consequences – but there has been little in the way of concern over the prurient nature of the questions on the profiling questionnaires. This lack of curiosity might reflect the limited technical knowledge around how such algorithms work, and so, a reluctance to open the black box, instead trusting the hard-to-comprehend mathematical modelling. For many non-mathematicians who seek out ASPAs it is easier to understand what they do on the surface – their purpose, their actions, their consequences – but rarely their inner workings, networks of dependence and independence or their mathematical nuances. Despite this, the profiling algorithm passed into usage with minimal fuss or examination by third parties (Desiere et al, 2019).

Sociological impacts

This final section draws together and parses the deeper ethical issues that the development and deployment of ASPAs raise. ASPAs categorise the unemployed and provide support to turn them into jobseekers. We start by looking into the 'black box', before exploring their larger social life. Critical data scientists tend to focus on the ethical challenges of current systems – algorithmic bias, fairness, data privacy, transparency, scrutable, accountability – rather than taking on the more philosophical and ethical challenge about the moral significance of algorithmic systems. To aspire to fix bias misses the ethics of larger transformation wrought by a limited number of data scientists, functional managers and statisticians charged with redesigning welfare.

There is a deeper consideration of the rationalities and logics that animate how a democracy, the public realm and the state adopt these mathematical-digital technologies to administer, govern and construct welfare and care. As we plunge ethnographically into the world of the algorithm, we necessarily encounter the moral and ethical foundations encoded into the objective, cold and absurdist formula. Going further, we explore the telos of calculability (Callon, 1998) that digital knowledge produces in theological terms as a new iteration of purgatory.

It is unclear if ASPA designers know the vital role of unemployment in preventing social unrest and ensuring political stability. As least since Machiavelli's *Florentine Histories*, politicians and policy makers have used welfare to pacify society and preserve the economic status quo. This vision of the utility of welfare is somewhat forgotten in the current wave of welfare reforms, activation and conditionality, which reflects Calvinist approaches, rooted in Christian and Jewish traditions. ASPAs, as a shared programme, hard-code this moral judgement over the workless into the welfare system, in such a way that the moral and ethical sides are no longer visible. In separating those who need to be reformed, and those who can recover work themselves, the policy machinery of 'reform' is considered 'apolitical', as though state interventions were a purely scientific, disinterested, evidence-based governance of society in order to optimise individual and collective life – and always in balance with individual choice. These algorithms raise profound questions about their role in social solidarity and democracy.

Buried in and around the objectivity of the formula is a deep cultural code of work as a vocation and capitalist enterprise – as the grace of god (Weber, 1958) and the hand of providence or the hand of the market (Agamben, 2011). Furthermore, poverty, unemployment and job seeking can be interpreted as a purgatory on earth, an edifying punishment to purge sins (especially sloth and pride). This journey of unemployment, not unlike Dante's *Divine Comedy*, begins with judgement, as penitents are directed along a path and must yield to the assistance of their guides in order to make them suitable to re-enter the labour market. In suggesting such a radical interpretation, we aspire to expand the vista of ethnographic inquiry into imagined logics of the techno-utopias from which bureaucratic sorting algorithms emerge. In short, PES algorithms have curious theologies, which continue to exert an influence that is the more powerful because it goes unacknowledged.

Towards some concluding reflections

Inside the ASPA black box are ethical and philosophical concerns that ASPA designers are largely oblivious towards. In rushing to ration care with a blunt and inaccurate instrument, PES risk ripping the fabric of welfare. These algorithms are designed by a narrow sect of experts who do not understand welfare, those in welfare are unclear what is inside the algorithms – the perfect recipe for technological accidents (Virilio, 2007). By outsourcing the moral judgement between the deserving and undeserving (Whelan, 2023) to a mechanism, a biased, discriminatory algorithm, and then focusing our concerns on the bias rather than the whole effort of making distinctions between the unemployed, we forget history and the purpose of welfare. We present this as a terrain of inquiry, opening up the field, rather than imposing unity, a single theoretical framework, or even a single list of principles and values to aid algorithmic welfare design. ASPAs may be a salvageable technology for the public good, but not as a private decision-making system, a Kafkaesque trail, where the subject of algorithmic judgement is not even aware of their crime.

References

Agamben, G. (2011) *The Kingdom and the Glory: For a Theological Genealogy of Economy and Government.* Stanford, CA: Stanford University Press.

Allhutter, D., Cech, F., Fischer, F., Grill, G. and Mager, A. (2020) Algorithmic profiling of job seekers in Austria: How austerity politics are made effective. *Frontiers in Big Data*, 3: 5.

Arbetsförmedlingen (2014) *Arbetsförmedlingens Återrapportering: Insatser för att förhindra långvarig arbetslöshet* [Arbetsförmedlingen Reports 2014: Efforts to Prevent Long-term Unemployment].

Aristotle (1994) *Metaphysics* (vols 1–6). Cambridge, MA: Harvard University Press.

Böheim, R., Eppel, R. and Mahringer, H. (2023) The impact of lower caseloads in public employment services on the unemployed. *Journal for Labour Market Research*, 57(1): 31.

Bolin, G. and Andersson Schwarz, J. (2015) Heuristics of the algorithm: Big Data, user interpretation and institutional translation. *Big Data & Society*, 2(2): 2053951715608406.

Callon, M. (1998). Introduction: The embeddedness of economic markets in economics. *The Sociological Review*, 46: 1–57.

Card, D., Kluve, J. and Weber, A. (2018) What works? A meta analysis of recent active labor market program evaluations. *Journal of the European Economic Association*, 16(3): 894–931.

Cutuli, G. and Grotti, R. (2020) Heterogeneity in unemployment dynamics: (Un)observed drivers of the longitudinal accumulation of risks. *Research in Social Stratification and Mobility*, 67: 100494.

Delpierre, A., Demazière, D. and El Fatihi, H. (2024) The stealth legitimization of a controversial policy tool: Statistical profiling in French Public Employment Service. *Regulation & Governance*, 18(2): 499–512.

Desiere, S. and Struyven, L. (2021) Using artificial intelligence to classify job seekers: The accuracy-equity trade-off. *Journal of Social Policy*, 50(2): 367–385.

Desiere, S., Langenbucher, K. and Struyven, L. (2019) *Statistical Profiling in Public Employment Services: An International Comparison*. Paris: OECD. https://doi.org/10.1787/b5e5f16e-en

Dourish, P. (2016) Algorithms and their others: Algorithmic culture in context. *Big Data & Society*, 3(2): 2053951716665128.

Flyvbjerg, B. (2020) The law of regression to the tail: How to survive COVID-19, the climate crisis, and other disasters. *Environmental Science & Policy*, 114: 614–618.

Gallagher, P. and Griffin, R. (2023) (In) accuracy in algorithmic profiling of the unemployed: An exploratory review of reporting standards. *Social Policy and Society*. doi:10.1017/S1474746423000428

Georges, N. (2008) Le profilage statistique est-il l'avenir des politiques de l'emploi? *L'emploi, nouveaux enjeux*: 117–124.

Glaser, V.L., Pollock, N. and D'Adderio, L. (2021) The biography of an algorithm: Performing algorithmic technologies in organizations. *Organization Theory*, 2(2).

Griffin, R., Boland, T., Tuite, A. and Hennessy, A. (2020) Electric dreams of welfare in the 4th industrial revolution: An actor-network investigation and genealogy of an algorithm. In V. Bobkov and P. Herrmann (eds) *Digitisation and Precarisation: Redefining Work and Redefining Society* (pp 181–203). Cham: Springer Nature.

Hainmueller, J., Hofmann, B., Krug, G. and Wolf, K. (2016) Do lower caseloads improve the performance of public employment services? New evidence from German employment offices. *The Scandinavian Journal of Economics*, 118(4): 941–974.

Ingold, T. (2018) *Anthropology: Why It Matters*. Cambridge: John Wiley & Sons.

Jupp, V. and Norris, C. (1993) Traditions in documentary analysis. In M. Hammersley (ed) *Social Research: Philosophy, Politics and Practice* (pp 37–51). London: SAGE.

Knabe, A. and Rätzel, S. (2011) Scarring or scaring? The psychological impact of past unemployment and future unemployment risk. *Economica*, 78(310): 283–293.

Kotler, P. (2009) *Marketing Management*. Hoboken, NJ: Pearson Education.

Lindsay, C. (2010) In a lonely place? Social networks, job seeking and the experience of long-term unemployment. *Social Policy and Society*, 9(1): 25–37.

Loxha, A. and Morgandi, M. (2014) Profiling the unemployed: A review of OECD experiences and implications for emerging economics. Technical report, Social Protection and Labour No 1424.

Lustig, C. and Nardi, B. (2015) Algorithmic authority: The case of Bitcoin. In *2015 48th Hawaii International Conference on System Sciences* (pp 743–752). IEEE.

Malinowski, B. (1922) *Argonauts of the Western Pacific.* Abingdon: Routledge.

Matty, S. (2013) *Predicting Likelihood of Long-term Unemployment: The Development of a UK Jobseekers' Classification Instrument.* London: Corporate Document Services.

Mauss, M. (1925) *The Gift,* trans I. Cunnison. London: Cohen & West.

Mayer-Schoenberger, V. and Cukier, K. (2013) *Big Data: A Revolution That Will Transform How We Live, Work, and Think.* London: John Murray Publishers.

McGuinness, S., Kelly, E. and Walsh, J.R. (2014) Predicting the probability of long-term unemployment in Ireland using administrative data. *Economic and Social Research Institute Research Series,* 51: 1–29.

O'Connell, P., McGuinness, S., Kelly, E. and Walsh, J. (2009) *National Profiling of the Unemployed in Ireland.* Dublin: ESRI. https://www.esri.ie/system/files/media/file-uploads/2015-07/RS010.pd

Pentzold, C. and Fischer, C. (2017) Framing big data: The discursive construction of a radio cell query in Germany. *Big Data & Society,* 4(2): 2053951717745897.

Pignatti, C. and Van Belle, E. (2018) Better together: Active and passive labor market policies in developed and developing economies. *IZA Journal of Development and Migration,* 12(1).

Sztandar-Sztanderska, K., and Zielenska, M. (2020). What makes an ideal unemployed person? Values and norms encapsulated in a computerized profiling tool. Social Work & Society, 18(1).

Riipinen, T. (2011) Risk profiling of long-term unemployment in Finland. In *Power Point Presentation at the European Commission's 'PES to PES Dialogue Dissemination Conference',* Brussels, September (pp 8–9).

Rosholm, M., Svarer, M. and Hammer, B. (2004) *A Danish Profiling System.* Bonn: Institute for the Study of Labor. http://ssrn.com/abstract=628062

Seaver, N. (2017). Algorithms as culture: Some tactics for the ethnography of algorithmic systems. *Big Data &Society,* 4(2): 2053951717738104.

Sztandar-Sztanderska, K. and Zielenska, M. (2020) What makes an ideal unemployed person? Values and norms encapsulated in a computerized profiling tool. *Social Work & Society,* 18(1).

Tashman, L.J. (2000) Out-of-sample tests of forecasting accuracy: An analysis and review. *International Journal of Forecasting,* 16(4): 437–450.

Virilio, P. (2007) *The Original Accident.* Oxford: Polity.

Weber, M. (1958) *The Vocation Lectures.* Indianapolis, IN: Hackett Publishing.

Whelan, J. (2023) Hidden in statistics? On the lived experience of poverty. *Journal of Social Work Practice,* 37(2): 137–151.

4

The making of an unemployed population

Antoinette Jordan, Zeta Dooly and Ray Griffin

Introduction

Unemployment is not a natural category, rather it is one made by institutions, in policy documents, in application forms and most meaningfully in national statistics (Salais et al, 1986). More particularly, unemployment is made in the complex thicket of National Statistics Institutions (NSIs) and infrastructures. This chapter explores the practices of producing statistical knowledge about unemployment, drawing on an ethnographic study of the census data collection and labour force data collection practices of a national statistical agency. Here, we follow the action, tracing ethnographically the moment in which complex messy and unique people are flattened into their data. This process of extraction forecloses the individual, as it moves the analogue to the digital, where vaguely similar and comparable people are forced to be the digital same. Thus it is the core technique that allows clumps of problem people to emerge as categories that float away from the context from which they are extracted into administrative use. Informed by philosophers of science and technology, particularly Ian Hacking, this chapter explores the emergence of unemployment in practice, as an active practice of the technique of turning people into data. Once the data is extracted, cleaned and processed, the person becomes far removed from their data through this process. Through further refinements, the individual experience of unemployment becomes a statistical sample of the unemployed population.

Unemployment is *sui generis*, emerging from nowhere before 1900, to come to dominate how we think about economic vitality, poverty (Whelan, 2023) and human wellbeing. Although the term was in use before the 20th century, it started to take on its contemporary use as a social policy problem in the early 1900s (Rowntree and Lasker, 1911; Brown, 1971; Card, 2011). In the aftermath of the First World War, during the Treaty of Versailles negotiations, the term came to define a national social problem, with the foundation of the International Labour Organization (ILO). The ILO, in its 1919 constitution, explicitly set out to prevent unemployment and developed rubrics for the production and communication of statistical information around unemployment, the setting up of public employment agencies in Member States and the establishment of social insurance schemes to provide for the unemployed. Indeed, it is the 1954 definition of unemployment established by the ILO – 'a person not working, available for work and seeking work' – that establishes unemployment as a precise statistical concept, which can then be measured and administered across the ILO's 175 Member States.

Following the creation of unemployment as a concept, national statistics offices were established with responsibility for producing unemployment statistics. Before modern censuses, even before the concept of the nation state, political entities have traditionally established a register of property and people in their domain – mentioned in the bible and the Domesday Book (1086). As the bureaucratic nation state took on its form, particularly with colonies and dominions, direct surveys or censuses of population became more regularised and standardised across multiple different countries (Ruppert, 2012). With this standardisation, the quality of data improved, thus initiating cycles of comparative data. Academic theory, for example, *An Essay on the Principle of Population* (Malthus, 1798), legislative basis and the establishment of statistical offices of government advanced across the world since the Enlightenment (Desrosières, 1998), taking on an ever-more regular form supported by supranational institutions in the post-war era.

Initiatives such as the ILO, Eurostat (the Statistical Office of the European Communities) and United Nations Statistics Division formed in the 1940–1950s served to coordinate, standardise and thus globalise the production of national statistics. With an agreed classification of society, driven by standardised collection and distribution of statistical knowledge about a society and economy, contextual differences were overlooked and similarities came to the fore. This effort is undergirded by considerable and ongoing organisational effort to standardise and coordinate the production of data, for example, the Integrated European Social Statistics (IESS) Framework Regulation (EU 2019/1700) established a common framework for European statistics relating to persons and households for data collected from January 2021. Data collected by European Union (EU) Member States (27) and transmitted to the European Commission (Eurostat) inform datasets including the EU Statistics on Income and Living Conditions instrument, the Labour Force Survey (LFS) and Monthly Unemployment Estimates (MUE), in ways that are comparable between countries. The IESS governs the production of the LFS and MUE. Standard EU classifications are used for economic activity (NACE), occupations (ISCO), education (ISCED) and European regions (NUTS).

This chapter aspires to explore the social life of national statistical data production, starting with the citizen to see how data is produced in the field, through to how it is aggregated and processed. It traces the process of how populations come to be built, and in turn how these populations are known and understood through data and statistics. Given the multiple data collection activities which fall under the heading of unemployment, it is important to understand how the census, LFS, MUE and registry data collected by public employment services (PES) all exist as statistical datasets, but how the LFS is seen as the true measure of unemployment by statistical agencies.

In taking up this question, the chapter builds on anthropological and science and technology studies work that explores population making (Ruppert and Scheel, 2021; Biruk, 2022; Cool, 2022). As a process, this ethnography follows the action (Dourish, 2001), starting with an ethnographic study of national census statistical data collection. From there the transposition of this survey material into aggregate data is traced (Ingold, 2023), paying particular attention to the process and coordination methodologies, reporting and communication activities and some near-field uses of this data. In this way the social life of labour market data produced by a nation state is revealed. Generating this ethnography allows for a consideration of the complicated entanglement of a person and their data, where this process traduces the individual, as it moves from the analogue to the digital, with vaguely similar and comparable people becoming the digital same, and thus is the core technique that allows clumps of problem people to emerge as categories that float away into administrative use. Informed by philosophers of science and technology, particularly Ian Hacking's seminal paper (1968), 'Making up people', this chapter explores the emergence of unemployment in practice, as an active practice of the technique of turning people into data.

Within the rubric of national statistic systems, the starting point is always data collection. With its ubiquity and familiarity undisputed, a census of population is still worthy of attention. Many individuals first encounter the census as part of the Catholic story of Christmas. Since almost every country in the world has been encouraged to conduct a census since the end of the 19th century (only five countries did not from 2005 to 2014), it is now a naturalised feature of social life globally. In many regions, smaller censuses have been used to survey land, property and people for various reasons, for example, the Domesday Book, Griffith's Valuation of Ireland and landlord surveys of tenants during the Irish famine (Griffith, 1874; Vesey, 2008).

EU political goals envision a European public service which is online and digital. Along with digitising historical census records, these digital aspirations extend to future census data collection. This EU vision to automate encompasses new data collection techniques such as mobile devices for fieldworkers and online census forms for citizens. As this move towards digital data collection changes the nature of census data collection, recording of paper-based fieldwork-intensive census practices is an exercise in salvage ethnography, tracing practices which are at risk of disappearing (Gruber,

1970). Online census data collection has been shown to improve data quality, with data quality for the Northern Ireland census improved overall through the use of online census returns, attributed to automated question routing, the presentation of one question at a time and online validation (NISRA, 2022). Therefore, future census data collection methodologies are expected to focus on digital techniques for collection and processing.

This chapter explores the creation and evolution of the statistical category of unemployment, in a social policy space where numbers and statistics influence political intervention and shape government responses (Hacking, 1982; Desrosières, 1998; Kopper and Knox, 2024). The ethnographic method is described, focusing on the census of population. Findings show unemployment data is extracted in detail from citizens during the mandatory census process, through a voluntary sample during the LFS, and through a combination of both the census and registry data in the calculation of the MUE. The unemployed population in each dataset is different, collected in a different way and used for different purposes, where the findings show that each dataset fails to fully capture the individual experience of unemployment. Therefore, researchers and policy makers benefit from an awareness of what data is being presented through each dataset, what experiences of unemployment are revealed through each and what experiences are lost through digital data collection and flattening of individuals into data.

Method

This chapter uses ethnographic methods to trace the social life of population making. In developing this ethnographic study, the data collection practices of a national census of population and a sample survey (the LFS) were examined. The dataset includes public documents and archival material produced by the Central Statistics Office (CSO), the NSI in Ireland and Eurostat, the Statistical Office of the European Communities. In taking up this novel approach to studying the making of statistical categories of unemployment, this chapter reflects the new concerns for ethnography (Augé and Colleyn, 2006; Ingold, 2016), moving away from comparative fine-grained and well-bounded studies of cultural diversity in a globalised world, as it tackles new lived experiences (O'Doherty and Neyland, 2019) without methodological sensibilities (Ingold, 2014). Ethnography is traditionally a technique deployed in closed identifiable communities (Geertz, 1973), but this new response to grand challenges and emerging phenomena is influenced by Ingold's call to 'encounter the world' and write 'about the people' (Ingold, 2011; 2014). In this, we follow the considerable body of work that repurposes ethnography for how we live now entangled in complex administrative systems and statistics (Latour, 1988; Strathern, 1999; Mol, 2002; Law, 2004; Holmes and Marcus, 2008; Maurer, 2016; Knox and Nafus, 2018).

This study shows that data is collected from unemployed populations at many times, but the LFS is noted as the primary indicator of unemployment by EU Member States, in collaboration with Eurostat. Therefore we see there are several unemployed populations in statistical datasets. Tracing the social life of data production led to an in-depth study of census data collection, an examination of the processing and coordination methodologies of the census and LFS, then the LFS transposition of sample surveys into aggregate data.

Extracting data from people: censusing people

A census of population takes place every five years in Ireland, collecting statistical data from every citizen on a range of topics from education, health and economic status to the type of house they live in. The census involves a person from the government visiting every household, presenting a form, explaining how to fill it out and the legal obligation to complete it, then returning to collect it. Fieldworkers operate within strict codes of conduct, with statutory duties to be performed while conducting fieldwork. But, the role of census enumerator is an embodied walking activity (Ingold, 2023), where the calibration of invasiveness is highly regulated – so enumerators can never cross a threshold, are trained in bias and appropriate questioning, but equally assert the legal right of the state to enforce data collection. This is a very human activity of meeting people, often engendering very positive feelings towards the state of pride and community, and equally can feel to some like a gross invasion of privacy.

The census is a large logistical operation. In Ireland it involves the production of a short-lived, specific purpose organisation, drawn together for this specific purpose every five years. In 2022 this comprised 5,100 temporary field enumerators, administered by 466 supervisors. Above and around this temporary organisation sits the technical, administrative and production activities that define and deliver the statistical programme of work of the NSI. Planning starts almost as soon as the results are reported for the last census, first more conceptually redesigning the questions and format, piloting and testing, before the formal enumeration organisation is brought up in the months before the census campaign is conducted. In the 2022 census, fieldwork was supported by a new phone application, a case management system introduced following a successful pilot (Central Statistics Office Ireland, 2021).

A national media campaign informed the public of the census date, known as census night. Publicity material assured citizens that 'it's quick, it's confidential and it's compulsory'. Fieldwork staff started delivering census forms four weeks before census night. Three main paper forms were distributed – a household form, a listing form for communal establishments such as hospitals, hotels and prisons or an individual form as appropriate;

as well as other more specialist forms such as Irish language forms, large print and braille forms. Delivery of a census form is a ceremonial activity, highly orchestrated by census protocols. The enumerator formally recorded delivery with a handheld case management system and followed the scripted handover explanation. Each household gathered to complete the form on census night. The form collection phase began the day after census night and ran for four weeks. Census forms were received from 96 per cent of the population of Ireland in 2022, a similar rate to other Organisation for Economic Co-operation and Development countries.

Extracting data from people: the Labour Force Survey

Despite collecting data from the entire population, explicitly asking questions that reflect the 1954 ILO definition of unemployment, the census is not the definitive measure of unemployment and a further data collection process takes place through the LFS. In reporting census data on unemployment, a warning notes that it is not the official measure of unemployment and the LFS must be consulted instead. Therefore the formal rate of unemployment is determined from the quarterly LFS, a nationwide survey of households in Ireland, reflecting a shared methodology with all Eurostat countries. The LFS was introduced by the EU in 2017, replacing the quarterly national household survey (QNHS, undertaken from 1998 to 2017) – this is indicative of the significant institutional background to generating a shared, agreed and universal method of determining unemployment.

The EU Labour Force Survey (EU-LFS) is conducted in all EU countries, four candidate countries and three European Free Trade Association countries, and is a large household sample survey, providing quarterly results. It provides data on labour participation across all industries and occupations on persons aged 15 and over who live in private households, which excludes institutional or collective households and those doing military or community service. Data collection is done by NSIs, who select the sample, prepare the questionnaires, conduct surveys and interviews, and forward the data to Eurostat. Each NSI must use the same concepts and definitions, follow the guidelines of the ILO, use common classifications (NACE, ISCO, ISCED, NUTS) and record the same set of characteristics in each country, yet there is always some localisation. Following this protocol, NSIs can send broadly comparable data to Eurostat to provide a European overview, with the quarterly EU-LFS in 2021 comprising survey data on 1.1 million people.

In Ireland, the LFS uses around 11,000 observations gathered in mixed mode – some face-to-face and some phone interviews, with respondents traced over five waves (one and a quarter years), with respondents selected to model the structure of the census. Complicating matters is that the Central Statistics Office in Ireland do not use the raw data collected in the survey, called 'primitive data', to report unemployment. Rather, the data is processed in three ways – seasonally adjusted, inflated for non-response and back-casted. Seasonal adjustment is done using a smoothing algorithm (titled X-13-ARIMA methodology, developed by the US Census Bureau) 'to correct for seasonal patterns'. This algorithm is revised periodically, with X-13 replacing X-12 in 2017. Beyond seasonal adjustments, the model is also adjusted for non-response by estimating non-response rates and weighting data to inflate for non-responses. Finally, the primitive data is adjusted to ensure coherence of the historic data series, where changes in the structure of the data are scaled into reporting to allow long-term trends to use comparable data structures.

Indeed, the LFS survey data provides a very different vision of unemployment from the registry data collected by PES. Registry data, of people in receipt of an unemployment social transfer, is also produced monthly, and similar to the census is a whole of the population approach. Nonetheless, registry data is not the official measurement of unemployment. The NSI in Ireland also produces the MUE, which bridge the two datasets using a Proportional Denton method, which is little more than a smoothing technique between the quarterly observations of the LFS, forecasting forward based on live registry data.

Unemployment is precisely defined and refined in a series of resolutions of the International Conference of Labour Statisticians, a conference convened by the ILO, as being not in work, available for work and seeking work. Beyond that broad guideline, the age range of unemployment is important: age 15 to 89 is the current Eurostat range. However in Ireland the age ranges of unemployment are distinguished between 15–74 and 15–64; as is the technical delimitation between work and unemployed as expressed in hours of work per week (typically less than 20 hours in administrative data, and one hour in ILO survey definitions). In practice, at the point of data collection, data is extracted and cleaned, extruded from individuals and their complex lives into similar categories of administrative use. An individual's data is almost immediately aggregated, they join types of people, and this data is wrangled into statistical sense through a range of data management practices.

Addressing the labour market through census questions

Despite the LFS being the key measure of unemployment, the census collects significant unemployment-related data from citizens. The census household form is a substantial 24-page booklet. It contains space to record details of six people and one dwelling place, with each person required to complete three pages of personal questions, numbered in sections from 1 to 38. Labour market activity is queried in question 28, where a person must describe their present principal status by ticking only one of the available nine options. Options include working, looking for a first job, long-term unemployed, short-term unemployed, student, retired, unable to work due to illness or looking after home and family. Many people would categorise themselves with several of these labels, in particular those in part-time work, on maternity leave, undertaking part-time study or seeking work. Therefore, many instances of labour market activity cannot be recorded on this form, on the assumption that people fit into only one category.

Personal questions cover three pages of the household census form. A full biography is taken – name, sex, date of birth, place of birth, citizenship, marital status, address, ethnic background, religion, education. Then more detailed questions begin to build a personal history, from relationships to other household members, migration experiences, to language skills, health evaluations, caring responsibilities and volunteering activities. Then the form turns to principal status and labour market activity, directing students, retired people, unemployed or working people to different questions depending on their main status. The cumulative effect is a confrontation of a personal life story with an official form, explicitly confronting the often difficult topics of illness, disability, emigration, poor English language skills and caring duties. Each question takes the rich, complex and long-form lived experience of a person, and flattens this person into a number (Verran, 2001). Once cleaved from the person and enumerated, the individual is now rendered statistically, in a mode that allows them to be added, subtracted, or indeed a range of mathematical operations, as part of the population.

Despite an explicit question on principal status (question 28), initial enquiries into labour market activity begin in question 16, which asks if as a result of a long-lasting condition, the person has difficulty working at a job or business or attending school or college. This question lies between other health questions, to identify which long-lasting condition a person might have and how they would categorise their health. Several questions link health and labour market activity before the individual must define their principal status. A further enquiry into labour market participation occurs in question 19, which asks how a person usually travels to work, school, college or childcare. Follow-up questions ask what time a person leaves home in the morning and leaves work in the evening, how long the journey takes and how many days they work from home. The person may not take part in these activities, yet must answer questions on it.

A person whose principal status is a student is not permitted to enter any employment data on the form. Question 29 directs students to enter the name and address of their educational institution, bypassing four employment questions then exiting the form. Therefore no student employment data is captured, such as whether they are working full- or part-time, are employees, entrepreneurs or working from home. Young people under the age of 15 are asked which type of childcare they are in, which follows the ILO definition of an unemployed person being aged 15 or over. Similarly a young person not in employment, education or training could not accurately reflect their situation through their answers, instead leaving large sections blank as they are directed to exit the form. Again, the lived experience of many people is not captured by the census form.

The LFS approach to determining unemployment status, as a survey conducted by an expert interviewer (in-person or by phone), is more faithfully oriented to complying with the precise definition from the International Conference of Labour Statisticians and ILO, and so is somewhat confounding to the non-expert.

The census and LFS are the primary modes of assembling the labour market to be seen by economists, planners and others. They work as an entanglement, with the LFS built on the universe of data generated by the census – particularly in the operation of sampling and non-respondent inflation, so that data, extracted from individuals, is statistically pasteurised in terms of gender, education and other markers against some form of whole. In this way the census echoes in the years after its collection through a hidden emulation in data infrastructure such as the LFS. Indeed, censuses themselves, as well as the QNHS and LFS, become aggregated into long-term trends and those trends become filled in between data collection to show things such as population growth, economic cycles and the changing relations between gender and politics. The second mode is that the census is a universal survey of the total labour market, the definitive classification of people defined by definitive properties (Hacking, 1968). Within policy, and more specifically, in developing digital policies, these classifications become firmer and more powerful the further from the site of production they become.

Data extraction and cleaning

The classification of people in the census questions, a form of species segmentation and nominalism, is always something of an artificial activity. People are dynamic between these categories, moving from work to unemployment, from one gender or marital status to another, but beyond boundary cases people are sometimes not one thing nor particularly the other. Cleaning up this messiness begins with the individual confronting the form (Goffman, 1990), where they categorise themselves into a 'pure description of discursive events' (Foucault, 1970). For many this is unproblematic and even self-evident, but for others the questions are confounding and perhaps force them to articulate for the first time a specific status in harsh binary terms.

When individuals fail to categorise themselves in a census, it falls to the fieldworker when checking the form to clarify missing data – the starting point of data cleaning and scrubbing. This ambiguous process, between the fieldworker and the individual, discretely involves the state (manhandling into categories) in resolving the messy subjectivity of people into categories. This marks the shift in the politics of data—when "datum," once meaning a given thing in the world, transforms into "data" that is extracted or taken (Ingold, 2011). This data in many ways stands as a cipher for the individual, indeed beyond the micro-resistance to individual questions, as non-completion is a legal offence and non-compliance ultimately is underwritten by state sanctions.

Making a population out of data

From the very public-facing collection of census and LFS, extracting data from people, the data almost immediately starts to be aggregated. As national statistical offices move away from paper data collection to streamlined electronic systems, this aggregation is increasingly black-boxed, hidden from view in digital systems. To give a sense of this process, paper data collection at scale has increasingly adopted optical character recognition – a process of scanning and processing completed census forms. Forms are physically collected into a central processing facility, one site which is a brute form of aggregation, with thousands of forms physically scanned each day. This process involves stacking, guillotining, feeding an ImageTrac-Lite 6000 machine that then automatically reads forms, converting them into digital formats, first as digital images, and then the handwritten text extracted into type. Daily 80 CSO staff turn 15,000 census forms into 360,000 digital images, and onwards into making a population. The physical forms are, by law, stored for 100 years, but in practice there is little possibility of them ever being consulted again – the digital replaces the analogue, a cipher or avatar of the original.

Data on scanning mishaps, accidental destruction of forms or other challenges of data wrangling and storage are not shared by the CSO in their census background information, although they presumably have physical manifestations in the office where the forms are turning into data. For computer-assisted data collection, it is no longer visible what data handling mishaps, errors, deletions and duplications corrupt the transmission of people into data. Nonetheless, it is apparent that there is a hidden world of data extraction, homogenising, cleaning, wrangling and pasteurising now accomplished out of view before the production of a statistical fact. This process disintermediates individuals, and their agency and discretion from the supranational efforts of Eurostat, ILO, the United Nations and NSIs to the citizen providing or having data extracted from themselves, into 'readable data' to interact with standardised data infrastructures. Through a range of coordinating activities, consultations, conferences, project designs, tenders, machinery from third party suppliers, fieldworker selection and training, a huge human effort is assembled to construct the accomplishment of an unimpeachable scientific fact about a population such as an unemployment rate.

Discussion

The chapter demonstrates how unemployment is not a natural nor a particularly old category of public administration (O'Brien and Griffin, 2015). Our genealogy of the term, its emergence as a precisely defined statistical concept and the significant contemporary efforts to precisely measure the category, suggest that unemployment is an accomplishment of the state. That accomplishment is the outcome of a massive and complex administrative effort in enumerating the whole population through forced-choice questions, a process in which withdrawal, refusal, resignation or non-completion are simply not allowed. The mandatory census entangles everyone and even further refusal in other surveys models non-participation and thus enmeshes them in the data. As such, every person in the state is co-opted into the measurement of the labour market and is either one thing or another – a worker, a student, unemployed, a carer, sick or unwell.

The ethnography shows the massive effort to collect data, a process we term extraction after Ingold (2011). Traditionally data is understood in contemporary empirical science, with origins in Enlightenment constructs of objective, rational knowledge production and the legacy of the British empiricism of Bacon, Locke, Berkeley and Hume, as encoded information about one or more target phenomena, however it has a more archaic meaning in the Latin term – datum. Datum, from dare to give, means a thing given – literally a gift, a thing given from the natural world which naturally entangles us in cycles of generosity, exchange and reciprocity (Ingold, 2016). In contemporary empirical science, data is extracted, rather than received. It is extracted clinically without contaminating the field. This usually means numerical data that is severed from context, meaning and web of social relations, this data is extracted rather than given. For the scientist even to admit to a relationship of give and take with the things in the world with which they deal would be enough to disqualify the inquiry and any insights arising from it. And yet, from exploring data collection ethnographically, the extraction process, underwritten by order of the state and its powers – it is clear that unemployment data is produced by forced extraction.

Much of this is hidden, black-boxed as this data is severed from the collection site, with little to no relationship between those who collect it and those who use it. Instead, emphasis and attention is brought to the rubrics of coordination – such as the standardisation approaches of Eurostat, the carefulness of sampling approaches in elaborate method statements and the earnestness of the various methods – from census to MUE, to registry data to LFS, none of which can be made to align, but are explained away in a fog of complexity. Buried in the black box are the micro-practices of data cleaning, forcing individuals into one box or another, massive efforts at data wrangling to impute coherence to data, for example in smoothing algorithms, such that the actual data is as much synthetic as it is an echo of the real. It is from the careful assembly of all this, first in aggregation nationally, but also comparatively across and within countries, and then on to the policy and practice domain. These processes of looking inside the black box of data collection and reconnecting it to the use of data suggests that, at best, the data emulates or even simulates rather than presents it. As a result, the individuals whose traces remain in the data are more ciphers than avatars.

This data infrastructure produces signals to politics and policy makers, constructing problems that call up action, affirming a set of labels such as unemployed, long-term unemployed, not in employment, education or training (NEETs), bogus self-employment, precarious workers, women returning to work, discouraged jobseekers or a range of other populations that can be rendered statically through mathematical operation on the labour market data. Of course these communities can exist, but for the expert social policy makers they can only exist when presented in the numbers. Thus, a social change requires new categories of people produced in statistics, labelled and problematised by experts, an activity Ian Hacking (1968) memorably describes as 'making up people to create a new reality embedded in practices and lives'.

Unemployment, while institutionally durable since at least the 1960s, is neither stable nor a static category. The massive changes in our labour market from male breadwinner structures, established around the nuclear family, no longer reflect the blended and complex family and income structures of our society. And yet, the construct of unemployment weaves an enduring and seamlessly complete dataset that reaches back generations. Transformations in the algorithms such as seasonal adjustment (moving from X-ARIMA-12 to 13), or larger changes in data structure such as the move from the QNHS to the LFS, subtly remake the entire construction of unemployment while keeping the façade of durability. And yet, it is these new descriptions of populations that bring new possibilities for action – increasingly digital action.

References

Augé, M. and Colleyn, J.P. (2006) *The World of the Anthropologist.* Oxford: Berg.

Biruk, C. (2022) Assembling population data in the field: The labour, technologies, and materialities of quantification. In M.H. Bruun, A. Wahlberg, R. Douglas-Jones, C. Hasse, K. Hoeyer, D.B. Kristensen, et al (eds) *The Palgrave Handbook of the Anthropology of Technology* (pp 309–329). Singapore: Springer Singapore.

Brown, K.D. (1971) Conflict in early British welfare policy: The case of the Unemployed Workmen's Bill of 1905. *The Journal of Modern History*, 43(4): 615–629.

Card, D. (2011) Origins of the unemployment rate: The lasting legacy of measurement without theory. *The American Economic Review*, 101(3): 552–557.

Central Statistics Office Ireland (2021) *Report on the Public Consultation on Content of Census 2021 and the Census Pilot Survey 2018*. https://www.cso.ie/en/media/csoie/census/census2021/Census_Pilot_Survey_Report_2018_V1.pdf

Cool, A. (2022) Peopled by data: Statistical knowledge practices, population-making, and the state. In M.H. Bruun, A. Wahlberg, R. Douglas-Jones, C. Hasse, K. Hoeyer, D.B. Kristensen, et al (eds) *The Palgrave Handbook of the Anthropology of Technology* (pp 331–353). Singapore: Springer Singapore.

Desrosières, A. (1998) *The Politics of Large Numbers: A History of Statistical Reasoning*. Cambridge, MA: Harvard University Press.

Dourish, P. (2001) *Where the Action Is: The Foundations of Embodied Interaction*. Cambridge, MA: MIT Press.

Foucault, M. (1970) The archaeology of knowledge. *Social Science Information*, 9(1): 175–185.

Geertz, C. (1973) *The Interpretation of Cultures*. New York: Basic Books.

Goffman, E. (1990) *The Presentation of Self in Everyday Life*. London: Penguin.

Griffith, R.J. (1874) *Griffith's Valuation of Ireland 1847–1864*. Dublin: Alex Thom and Sons [National Library of Ireland].

Gruber, J.W. (1970) Ethnographic salvage and the shaping of anthropology. *American Anthropologist*, 72(6): 1289–1299.

Hacking, I. (1968) Making up people. In T.C. Heller, M. Sosna and D.E. Wellbery (eds) *Reconstructing Individualism: Autonomy, Individuality, and the Self in Western Thought* (pp 222–236). Stanford: Stanford University Press.

Hacking, I. (1982) Biopower and the avalanche of printed numbers. *Humanities in Society*, 5: 279–295.

Holmes, D.R. and Marcus, G.E. (2008) Para-ethnography. In L.M. Given (ed) *The SAGE Encyclopaedia of Qualitative Research Methods* (pp 26–27). London: SAGE.

Ingold, T. (2011) *Being Alive: Essays on Movement, Knowledge and Description*. London and New York: Routledge.

Ingold, T. (2014) That's enough about ethnography! *HAU: Journal of Ethnographic Theory*, 4(1): 383–395.

Ingold, T. (2016) *Lines: A Brief History*. London: Routledge.

Ingold, T. (2023) On not knowing and paying attention: How to walk in a possible world. *Irish Journal of Sociology*, 31(1): 20–36.

Knox, H. and Nafus, D. (eds) (2018) *Ethnography for a Data-Saturated World*. Manchester: Manchester University Press.

Kopper, M. and Knox, H. (2024) Introduction: Number politics after datafication. *The Cambridge Journal of Anthropology*, 42(1): 1–22.

Latour, B. (1988) The politics of explanation: An alternative. In S. Woolgar (ed) *Knowledge and Reflexivity: New Frontiers in the Sociology of Knowledge* (pp 155–176). London: SAGE.

Law, J. (2004) *After Method: Mess in Social Science Research*. London and New York: Routledge.

Malthus, T.R. (1798) *An Essay on the Principle of Population*. London: J. Johnson.

Maurer, B. (2016) *Mutual Life Limited: Islamic Banking, Alternative Currencies, Lateral Reason*. Princeton: Princeton University Press.

Mol, A. (2002) *The Body Multiple: Ontology in Medical Practice*. Durham, NC: Duke University Press.

NISRA (Northern Ireland Statistics and Research Agency) (2022) *Census 2021: Statement about Data Quality*. Belfast: NISRA. https://www.nisra.gov.uk/system/files/statistics/census-2021-statement-about-data-quality.pdf

O'Brien, J. and Griffin, R. (2015) Statistics: On the statistical composition of unemployment. In T. Boland and R. Griffin (eds) *The Sociology of Unemployment* (pp 209–211). Manchester: Manchester University Press.

O'Doherty, D. and Neyland, D. (2019) The developments in ethnographic studies of organising: Towards objects of ignorance and objects of concern. *Organization*, 26(4): 449–469.

Rowntree, S. and Lasker, B. (1911) *Unemployment: A Social Study*. New York: Macmillan.

Ruppert, E. (2012) Seeing population: census and surveillance by numbers. In K. Ball, K. Haggerty and D. Lyon (eds) *Routledge Handbook of Surveillance Studies* (pp 209–216). London: Routledge.

Ruppert, E. and Scheel, S. (2021) *Data Practices: Making Up a European People*. London: Goldsmiths Press.

Salais, R., Baverez, N. and Reynaud, B. (1986) *L'invention du chômage*. Paris: Presses universitaires de France.

Strathern, M. (1999) *Property, Substance and Effect: Anthropological Essays on Persons and Things*. London: Athlone Press.

Verran, H. (2001) *Science and an African Logic*. Chicago: The University of Chicago Press.

Vesey, P. (2008) *The Murder of Major Mahon, Strokestown, County Roscommon, 1847*. Dublin: Four Courts Press.

Whelan, J. (2023) Hidden in statistics? On the lived experience of poverty. *Journal of Social Work Practice*, 37(2): 137–151.

5

Open inquiry into disruptive digital services

Aisling Tuite

This chapter lays out the practices, networks and tensions that emerge around the development of a disruptive digital system for deployment in a public service that placed citizen experience at the centre of its design. The digital system was co-developed with stakeholders from social sciences, data and technical sciences and users in a collaborative and open innovative (Chesbrough, 2003) setting. The principles guiding the development of the digital system was to draw on sociological and social science disciplines to lead a user-centred approach to designing a decision support technology that was ethical, useful and meaningful.

The research draws on deep ethnographic immersion in the development and deployment of disruptive technologies (DT) for use in public employment services (PES), designed, built and deployed by a collaborative team, each with different baseline positions and expert knowledge. This chapter pulls apart and analyses the interdisciplinary practices and methods that emerged instinctively across this collaborative research project. The innovative working method captures the complexities of coupled processes of innovation that are enhanced through the expertise and knowledge within and across the consortium disciplines. The methods of co-production successfully led to the development and deployment of a DT platform with three tools for career and job search decision-making. While the chapter analyses a specific case, the HECAT framework for user-centred DTs (Griffin et al, 2023) has value to all user-centred technological design projects, especially those designed for a public good and for ensuring embedded public services.

The HECAT project brought together a carefully curated group of experienced researchers to explore the landscape of PES and the street-level experiences of access and interaction with this service. The aim was to produce tools for labour market decision-making that would disrupt existing service technologies and logics by allowing both caseworkers and unemployed people to see personalised labour markets. The overriding ethos of HECAT was to *work with and not on* unemployed people, an ethos that had to unconditionally translate into a digital technology. To address societal challenges related to digital transformation, the research was led from the sociological register, where each partner had deep knowledge and experience of researching unemployment and the labour market, although from different perspectives, methodologies and analytical skills. The technology partners were equally experienced in data science and applying novel techniques to explore existing phenomena and in creating user-centred interfaces. In between, the PES partners went beyond being just a pilot site, their experienced project analysts were deeply involved in the development of the technology and opened pathways for in-depth research into technological advances across European and global PES. The challenge that this chapter outlines is one of bringing all these moving parts together to ensure that an ethical, useful and meaningful DT could be developed and deployed in a live setting.

The chapter presents the contextual basis for this open inquiry into DT; what it means to be disruptive in the prevailing landscape of digital PES, how to place the users at the centre of design and how to overcome translation between social scientists and technologists, while addressing biases inherent in technology to ensure that statistics, algorithms and artificial intelligence (AI) technologies were employed ethically and transparently – returning data to, and building trust with, users.

Background and context

Digital disruption and government services

Governments, for at least the past 20 years, increasingly think of radical transformational change in terms of disruption. In PES and other social welfare services ongoing economic and demographic challenges place a strain on resources, compelling them to do more with less – to reduce costs, improve quality and develop new services to meet new challenges (Eggers and Gonzalez, 2012). Citizens, policy makers and PES managers are looking for ever more capable, responsive, resilient, adaptable and efficient public services. Increasingly, disruptive technologies are believed to be the panacea that will square that circle.

To disrupt is to set aside existing ways of thinking and acting. The etymology of the term arises from the Latin *disruptus*, from *disrumpo*, commonly to break or burst asunder, and so the term follows the logic of Schumpeter's creative destruction, itself a form of radical social change. Technology here is the generative creative replacement of what is broken in change processes, with a Greek etymology in *tekhnē* meaning art, craft or system. More recently, the term *disruptive technology* emerged through observations of the way in which both established industries and new entrants approach innovation towards new technologies or business models (Bower and Christensen, 1995; Christensen, 1997; Chesbrough, 2006). Disruptive innovations from new entrants, although less advanced initially, access markets through serving consumers who are removed from accessing the higher performing, and often more expensive, incumbent products or services (Christensen, 1997; Christensen et al, 2018). Seminal commercial examples are mobility apps disrupting taxis and car ownership (Uber and Lyft), media firms with no content (Facebook and Twitter), communication companies with no physical infrastructure (WeChat and Skype), and retailers without stores (Alibaba and Amazon). All of which open up business opportunities, services and communications with low input costs, low risk and limited access discrimination.

Relevant for many contemporary public services is that the very process of disruption makes forms of organisation change inevitable, often resulting in incumbents avoiding engagement with DTs (Christensen et al, 2018). Although, at the outset public services have been at the forefront of disruption – think of the development of mass healthcare, education and welfare as well as scientific programmes that led to the internet, space discovery and cures for multiple diseases. Nonetheless, once established, public service organisations tend to prioritise stability, capability, procedural justice and the status quo, so tend to follow the mode of classical Weberian hierarchical bureaucracy (De Vries et al, 2018), often considered adverse to change, innovation and disruption.

PES have long made use of technologies to deliver their increasingly complex services; form filling and gathering data, statistics and categorising have been the default methods that organise their clients for targeted resource allocation. In more recent times these logics have transferred into digital technologies. The promise of digital technologies is that services will be more accessible and convenient for citizens, available at any time, and provide information in ways that are easier, more flexible, more transparent and of a higher quality. In this way, digital services can foster greater civic engagement, compliance and participation. In the back office of government services, the promise of digital advances is for more efficient, more productive, rule-based self-service administration.

When digital disruptions and transformations happen to government services, they can, in turn, gently, recompose society. As forms of creative destruction, it is important to examine the dynamics that are displacing institutional apparatuses, and how they, in turn, re-form the assemblage of government. In this, the relational and performative impacts of digital change cascade outward from the technology to the citizen and how they relate to the state. As a result, the starting point for any analysis of digital disruptions is a deep understanding of the institutional context of change and the underlying processes that are being recomposed digitally.

Early advances into digital public employment services

Antecedent to the current turn to advanced digital technologies in PES has been the use of statistical and algorithmic methods to sort and organise administrative work and clients. Algorithms are best described as an unambiguous procedure – a step-by-step set of instructions for solving a particular problem (Hill, 2016: 47). Their structured pathway approach is attractive to rule-based systems, such as social welfare provision, as they 'integrate the certainties of mathematics with the objectivity of technology' (Seaver, 2013: 2). European countries have been employing algorithmic techniques in the back-office work of PES since the late 1990s and early 2000s, following on from their nascent use in Australia since 1994 and the United States in 1995 (O'Connell et al, 2009; Boland et al, 2020). Many of the algorithms are used for the purpose of profiling unemployed people and aim to make predictions about the length of time they will remain unemployed. Profiling algorithms are adopted in the hope that they will improve efficiency and better meet the complex and individual needs of jobseekers, particularly those most distanced from the labour market (Desiere et al, 2019). Analysis of these systems show that there is limited success in long-term integration and have mixed levels of system accuracy (Gallagher and Griffin, 2023) in their predictions. The challenges and problems associated with first-generation algorithmic profiling include concerns over accuracy, usefulness, increase in the administrative burden, use of limited sample data, static data and the General Data Protection Regulation (Rosholm and Hammer, 2004; O'Connell et al, 2009; Larsen and Jonsson, 2011; Riipinen, 2011; Loxha and Morgandi, 2014; Wijnhoven and Havinga, 2014; Boland et al, 2020).

The continued adaptation of profiling algorithms and the digital tools that surround them have made little progress, particularly disruptive progress, since the 1990s. This is especially evident regarding 'best practice' in designing and deploying such technologies and lack of 'across the board' metrics that can be used to explore just how well such systems operate in working scenarios (Scoppetta and Buckenleib, 2018). It is in this landscape of existing technology and the logics of efficient use of resources that the HECAT consortium took up the challenge of developing a DT, a transparent and ethical decision support system, for unemployed people and their caseworkers.

Call to action

The HECAT project was funded under an EU Horizon 2020 *Transformative Impact of Disruptive Technologies in Public Services* call for proposals on the topic of the transformative impact of DTs in public services. The call text outlined areas where the use of DTs is growing and where it can be beneficial, such as in public administrations, public goods, public governance, public engagement, public–private partnerships, public third sector partnerships and policy impact assessment. However, it acknowledged that the real potential impact of such technologies are the ways in which they can disrupt the existing landscape of public services. The call challenged projects to develop and pilot disruptive technologies, to engage with multidisciplinary partners, stakeholders and users to examine how emerging technologies impact the public sector (including the impact on public servants and the relation between public services and citizens) and explore in a wide-ranging fashion the issues surrounding the use of these technologies. The goal was to develop pathways for the introduction of DTs, while addressing the societal challenges raised by such technologies, based on a thorough understanding of users' needs, to enhance knowledge on digital democracy and develop new ways of providing public services.

The Horizon 2020 call was itself disruptive in that it called for social scientists to lead the challenge, placing at its centre concern for how technological advances often emerge through limited interaction with the complexity of needs of human end users. Interdisciplinary research is not new, neither is collaborative and user-centred product design, but the HECAT consortium set out with a strong position to ensure that often-vulnerable citizens were provided with tools, and not solutions, that are useful, ethical, transparent and respectful to individual needs.

A HECAT framework for user-centred disruptive technologies

Inspired by Chesbrough's (2003) exploration of open innovation, the research ethos was to draw in, develop and disseminate expert knowledge from each discipline and externally pass on that knowledge to the end users through the DT platform. The development cycle was central for understanding and addressing the challenges and risks that would determine the success or failure of the planned DT. While respecting the expertise of each discipline, methods needed to be developed to inform and learn horizontally across each discipline.

To kick off the project each partner outlined their vision for the research with an overarching agreement that to be disruptive the new digital technology should visualise the labour market, provide accessible data that was useful, understandable, neutral and trusted, so as to allow for decision-making on labour market participation based on individual needs and desires.

Design process

The main objective of the HECAT project was to develop DTs to support PES and citizens in evidence-based decision-making around unemployment, work readiness and job seeking. HECAT achieved this objective through deployment of the My Labour Market (MLM) platform, a co-designed and piloted set of decision support tools that values the experience of being unemployed, job seeking, and being on the front line of PES services.

Contributing to the success of the project are the working methods set out here.

Phase 1: Scoping and benchmarking the digital landscape of public employment services

The first task for the HECAT project was to gather extant knowledge within the consortium on digital and disruptive technologies in PES along with benchmarking exercises to establish the state-of-the-art of those technologies. The benchmarking study included collating literature (n=146 documents) identifying and analysing the 25-year development of profiling algorithms used by PES and attending workshops where PES and developers outlined the current advances and challenges. This work was carried out in two streams.

Sociological investigation

The sociological investigations explored the historical context of algorithms, profiling, policy, AI, categorising technologies and digital systems in PES. To support the development of the DT it mapped studies that surfaced insights into complex user needs to form a deep understanding of the contemporary experience of unemployment. Exploring the human and digital relations that define the micro-practices of PES (policy, politics and systems) included experiences from caseworkers/counsellors, unemployed people and PES management. In essence it aimed to develop a vision of the human in the labour market. Moving from this central position the investigations dispersed outwards and pieced together the broader interconnectedness of each stakeholder within society and the governing systems of the political economy. To complement this work the consortium PES partners organised a series of a Technical Assistance and Information Exchange instrument of the European Commission (TAIEX) and Organisation for Economic Co-operation and Development briefings from PES administrators and technology developers (France, Australia, Croatia, Slovenia, Austria) to explore current developments and challenges around digital systems, AI and data.

Technological investigation

The teams from the technological partner cohort explored both existing and emerging digital algorithmic and AI PES systems with a particular focus on forms, types and sources of data employed. The past and existing statistical modelling of the labour market, labour force and labour flows included variables, regression models, hazard models and random forest models. The team additionally investigated emerging technologies around decision support systems and the potential for use of AI modelling. This investigation mapped their findings and the potential for each model to address the DT contribution of the research. Building on the explorative study, advanced work included experimenting with various technological modelling approaches (regression, classification and neural network approaches) based on the expected PES and publicly available data.

Identifying challenges

The findings from the scoping and benchmarking study produced a number of reports for the consortium which served as the foundation for the overarching design of the HECAT platform, the point of departure for entering the explorative and innovative design stage. The study identified a number of gaps, limitations and conditions in the PES and general public service ecosystem that had potential to create barriers to deploying and implementing DT in PES, particularly for algorithmic profiling and forecasting. These challenges present both risk and opportunity for creating innovative technologies. The main challenges are discussed in the following sections.

Closed innovation

Innovation is described as 'the capacity to generate ideas or products that are both novel and useful' (Chan et al, 2011: 1). Closed innovations tend to be vertical within organisations, closed off for a variety of reasons such as protection of intellectual property or organisational inertia. Public service digitalisation projects are heavily contingent on existing structures and resources (Veale et al, 2018), mediated through competing priorities across all government services. Narrowing this down to PES, advances and innovations across 25 years of implementation have made limited impact on the efficiency or effectiveness of social welfare services. The research reveals that there is limited desire to innovate or move from existing PES practices, such as active labour market policies or to collaborate with regard to design and development, often emerging through individualised approaches which have failed to contribute to best practice across states (Scoppetta and Buckenleib, 2018). While third-party specialists are often engaged to design and develop digital systems for PES, they have not, as yet, created technologies that are disruptive or could fit into the category of open innovation. In this way, the development of many digital systems can be considered to be closed-loop innovation based on inertia, limited desire to innovate and limited resources.

Limited user engagement

Despite a growing body of works that call for more user-centred design, benchmarking of the antecedent and extant forms of digital and algorithmic technologies in PES have revealed that there is limited co-design and development with end users. Eichhorst et al stress that, for PES, 'approaches to profiling should progress towards more holistic profiling methods, moving away from simply gathering information about a jobseeker's work experience and formal qualification to information on his/her generic and soft skills' (2015: 18). Caseworkers, counsellors, PES management and PES organisations have large bodies of both tacit and explicit knowledge and data around user requirements. This is valuable information that is used in technological design to describe persona scenarios – imagined sets of unemployed people, categories of users and their needs. While theoretical sense is made in the desire to build algorithms with their data subjects in mind, the stark reality reveals an almost oppositional case. As a consequential effect of limited user engagement, many existing systems stop at profiling broad categories of users as a way to determine allocation of resources and interventions.

Data availability

The most common data approach for digital systems employed by PES is to use state statistical agencies and data gathered by local PES, such as registry data. At a broader scale and to produce a technology that is scalable, the differences in data availability and completeness is a limiting factor in accuracy of systems. Statistical offices globally have different methods of gathering data and for allowing third parties access to this data, as do private organisations, such as LinkedIn, which have large amounts of job search behavioural data. Limited standardisation, structures and anonymisation protocols are challenges for applying more sophisticated data analysis tools, that would lead to the creation novel digital systems for use in PES.

Overcoming the challenges

To overcome the challenges highlighted in benchmarking, the consortium took on a holistic approach in the development stages, aiming to rectify the failings of past profiling attempts to produce user-centric labour market decision-making tools built with stakeholder engagement and sociological insights at the heart. The approach to user design was to understand the needs of users (unemployed people, caseworkers, counsellors) and PES management who strive to deliver efficient and effective services. By way of example, the *algorithm imaginary* was considered to explore 'spaces where people and algorithms meet' (Bucher, 2017: 42), moving from benchmarking to observation and lived experiences surfacing not just where and when algorithms are deployed or, indeed, their functionality, but delving into the role individual subjects play in advancing the very tools under consideration (Büchi et al, 2021).

The result of this phase of the interdisciplinary research process was a series of seven conceptual functionalities that would be the backbone of the first iteration of the MLM platform. These functionalities address the gaps and conditions that emerged and were informed by the overriding ethos of the HECAT consortium to work with and not on unemployed people.

Phase 2: Ideation and discovery

The ideation and discovery phase is broadly divided into two movements. It begins with further exploration of the phase 1 findings where both the sociological team and the technological team analysed the initial findings as separate groups, allowing for expertise to develop as the process moves between conceptual wishes and practical reality. Again, following Chesbrough's (2006) model of open innovation which calls for 'the purposive use of inflows and outflows of knowledge to accelerate innovation', the consortium viewed it as necessary to supplement internal knowledge with external expertise in the co-development of the tools.

Over time, to bridge between the sociological foundations of the research and the technological development of the tools an iterative cycle of information flows emerged. To achieve agile working arrangements and open innovation three taskforce groups were convened: a *sociological taskforce*; a *data taskforce*; and a *functionalities taskforce*. These were narrow groups consisting of workpackage team leads, pilot case analysts and technical experts. The taskforce groups investigated the merits of each of the seven functionalities, working iteratively to develop working prototypes, while feeding back to the whole consortium on a monthly basis.

Iterative process

To maintain the overarching aim of leading a DT development from the sociological imagination, the sociological taskforce led the formal working arrangements of the iterative cycle of development. This structure consisted of a series of 'memo' based interactions on a standard template. In this format, for each of the conceptual functionalities, the sociological lead sent a memo to the data taskforce and the functionality taskforce describing the theoretical and technical interpretation of the concept, the current situation (based on existing and past PES systems), the desired situation and the challenges of achieving this. A longer form explanation followed which outlined the importance to the PES context and job search, how it is normally calculated or represented, and the data objects and points that would inform its analysis and integration into the platform. In this way the process moves beyond merely informing the technological teams but enabled the development of knowledge in lay form to generate understanding as to why particular sociological and market concepts are valuable. It allowed the data scientists to determine which forms of data and data modelling were most useful to achieve a desired outcome and how this should be presented visually on a digital platform.

With the knowledge provided in the memo, the data taskforce investigated and responded with available data, possible analytics and modelling outcomes, this was then communicated to the functionalities taskforce to determine the user interface, text, language and visualisations that could accompany the functionality. The iterative process continues with the sociological team investigating and agreeing on the design and potential usability of each conceptual functionality.

This design and development cycle continued to work systematically through all of the conceptual functionalities. Recommendations were made as to the feasibility of functionality based on available data, technical capability or usefulness for end users. The functionalities iterative process was the most creative experience of the project, where small groups worked interactively across the disciplinary divides in an agile and interactive mode.

Phase 3: Piloting 1

Once the functionalities of the platform had been agreed the prototype version of MLM was made ready for piloting. Piloting was organised with the PES partners who selected two locations, the capital of Slovenia, Ljubljana (population c. 288,359) and Ptuj (population c. 17,972) a large town in the northeast of the country.

The piloting team developed a detailed piloting document that ensured all researchers collected similar data. The purpose of interactive piloting interviews was to:

- assess the usefulness of the platform tools in decision-making around job search and visualisation of labour market data;
- discover if there were functions missing from the platform that would assist with job search;
- check the technical functionality of the system; and
- assess if users felt that they would use the platform on an ongoing basis, including trust in the data.

The piloting participants were given access to explore MLM before the interviews, which were one-hour-long interactive sessions where participants led researchers through the functionalities and tools and provided feedback based on the structured piloting brief.

In addition to the piloting sessions, interviews also took place with the managers of each office in Ljubljana and Ptuj to assess the wider landscape, needs and concerns within PES in Slovenia. A focus group of eight unemployed people yielded further information on the particularities of job search and careers in Slovenia, the use of digital tools and concerns with data protection.

Piloting highlighted a number of areas for improvement, including: the number of functionalities, visual presentation, variances in understanding of the graphical visual representations, user digital skills, technical glitches and optimisation, and responsiveness to multiple device platforms.

Expert panels

Running concurrently with the piloting, but over a more prolonged period, the consortium engaged in focus groups with expert panels. Three expert panels (unemployed people, policy makers/stakeholders and caseworkers) were convened in Ireland, France, Denmark and Slovenia and took place over a one-year period. The format of the expert panel focus groups was repeated in each location. These were formatted as scenario vignettes to instigate open panel discussion, and early versions of MLM were also demonstrated.

Phase 4: Iterative refinement

Following the first phase of piloting, and with initial feedback from the expert panels, the consortium engaged in a series of meetings to discuss the findings and set out plans for improving and altering the HECAT MLM platform. The evidence-based findings from piloting included technical functionalities and user feedback.

To expedite the cycles of refinement, three cross-discipline working groups were established to examine elements of the platform:

- WG1: platform landing page and integration of job quality metrics.
- WG2: Advanced tools (Probability of Exit, job preparedness).
- WG3: Job progression routes.

Each working group met concurrently, analysing the feedback from piloting and the expert panels. Their purpose was to make recommendations for changes, improvements and alterations to the platform. At points across the refinement cycle each working group reported to the consortium to evaluate their recommendations and agree a way forward for the second version of the platform. Using data from piloting and expert panels, the functionality was refined into three tools for job seeking and longer-term career planning. During the iterative cycles of refinement, a number of functions were removed or replaced with more appropriate forms of data representation for the users. Version 2.0 of the MLM platform was launched and determined by the consortium to be ready for piloting.

Phase 5: Piloting 2

The second iteration of piloting mirrored the format of the first phase, using the same two PES offices in Ljubljana and Ptuj. As before, each participant was observed using the MLM platform, where they were free to move through the three refined tools and to give their opinion and feedback on usability and functionality. Following this phase of piloting, the MLM platform and tools were presented to the PES management team at the Employment Service of Slovenia for review, while the consortium made adjustments and outlined requirements for future use and development of the platform.

Results and observations

The working methods used by the HECAT consortium to design and deploy a sociologically led disruptive technology were based on the principles of open innovation. The model employed for interdisciplinary, agile and open discovery emerged as a process based on preserving the ethos of the HECAT project to create an ethical and transparent decision support system that would allow unemployed people and their caseworkers to see the labour market. Ultimately from ideation to deployment of version 2 of MLM the functionalities were narrowed down from seven to three tools, all which meet the definition of being disruptive.

This approach uses three core principles to guide the development, each of which align with the HECAT core principles:

- *See the labour market*: to render visible the labour market for all market participants. Making the labour market fairer by overcoming informational asymmetries and ensuring high-quality information flow.
- *Data-driven*: to return data extracted by national statistics offices, by creating a reciprocal flow of data back to the citizen, breaking the singular direction of data from citizens to policy makers.
- *Transparent*: to provide a visual representation of the labour market that is accessible to both unemployed people and caseworkers or counsellors. The use of the term tool rather than solution captures a device that assists, rather than leads, people into forms of action.

PES are not new to using digital platforms to assist with supporting unemployed people and jobseekers, the quality and impact of the disruption from this research, achieved through the open inquiry working methods, is located within the functions of the tools. The three DT tools specific to PES that emerge into the final version of MLM are:

- *DT1 Reconceptualising profiling*: development of two distinctive algorithmic models for estimating return to the labour market. Here new statistical constructs about the labour market are introduced (such as liquidity and volatility) to offer deeper insight into how the market functions.
- *DT2 Moving from job first to sustainable high-quality work*: avoiding job-first approaches by exploiting underused data on job quality and integrating it into a job search decision model that allows individual to explore the job quality trade-offs in their personal labour market.
- *DT3 Moving from job title search to a skills and preference-matching job search*: recognising that 'job titles' are ambiguous and limiting for job search and career decisions, the tool asks users for skills, experience and particular job needs before presenting a number of options for occupation choices.

A framework for next generation user-centred disruptive technologies in public employment services

In answering the call to develop DTs for public services, the HECAT consortium emerged with an overarching ethos to use algorithms, statistics and AI for the public good. The consortium successfully led technological development from the social sciences by listening to the experience and needs of the users and embedding it in a novel and innovative digital platform with a range of tools to support labour market decision-making.

As with any multi-stakeholder research, the working arrangements developed organically as we faced decisions and challenges around developing the platform as well as our working methods. Through embedding the whole consortium in the landscape of social welfare, PES and international labour markets, each researcher developed a better understanding of the perspectives and technical work that other partners brought to the consortium. The working practices of the consortium have contributed to developing a framework for interdisciplinary design of user-centred DTs.

The successful pathway for integrating DTs into PES required novel and agile working practices across the interdisciplinary consortium which was greatly enhanced by the bottom-up approach of co-creating the platform with users and having PES partners, the Employment Service of Slovenia, integrated into the consortium as design and development partners. The HECAT Framework for User-Centred DTs in Public Services (see Figure 5.1) is a significant output of this research that can potentially guide continued development and deployment of disruptive technologies in PES and other public services.

Figure 5.1: Disruptive technology from existing PES to next-generation PES

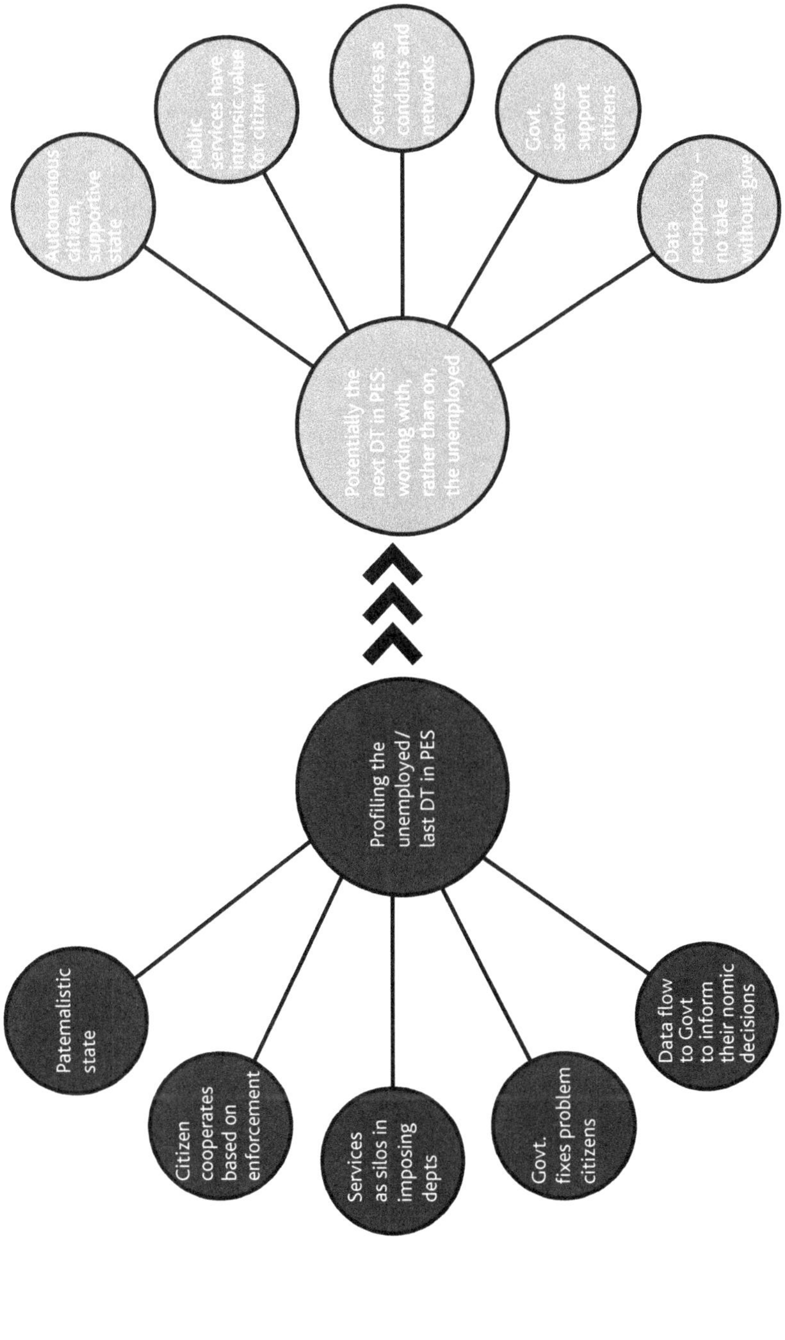

Conclusion

The HECAT framework for user-centred DTs encompasses the consortium's principles of creating value through provision of useful, transparent and reciprocal information for all users. While this framework is centred on PES it has many elements that are generalisable to any open inquiry that seeks to develop innovate disruptive technologies, especially those led from the social sciences. The framework represents the possibilities for engaged user-centred design of technology through harnessing single discipline expertise which moves towards knowledge sharing in an interdisciplinary consortium that engaged with principles of open innovation and agile work. This is particularly useful where the technology being developed is for the public good and for use by public services that are human-centred and play a significant role in providing care for citizens.

References

Boland, T., Griffin, R., Tuite, A. and Hennessy, A. (2020) Electric dreams of welfare in the 4th industrial revolution: An actor network investigation and genealogy of an algorithm. In V. Bobkov and P. Herrmann (eds) *Digitisation and Precarisation: Redefining Work and Redefining Society* (pp 181–204). np: Springer.

Bower, J.L. and Christensen, C.M. (1995) Disruptive technologies: Catching the wave. *Harvard Business Review*, 73(1): 43–53.

Bucher, T. (2017) The algorithmic imaginary: Exploring the ordinary affects of Facebook algorithms. *Information, Communication & Society*, 20(1): 30–44.

Büchi, M., Fosch-Villaronga, E., Lutz, C., Tamò-Larrieux, A. and Velidi, S. (2021) Making sense of algorithmic profiling: User perceptions on Facebook. *Information, Communication & Society*, 26(4): 809–825.

Chan, J., Fu, K., Schunn, C., Cagan, J., Wood, K. and Kotovsky, K. (2011) On the benefits and pitfalls of analogies for innovative design: Ideation performance based on analogical distance, commonness, and modality of examples. *Journal of Mechanical Design*, 133(8): 081004-1–081004-11.

Chesbrough, H.W. (2003) *Open Innovation: The New Imperative for Creating and Profiting from Technology*. Boston: Harvard Business School Press.

Chesbrough, H.W. (2006) *Open Business Models: How to Thrive in the New Innovation Landscape*. Boston: Harvard University Press.

Christensen, C.M. (1997) *The Innovator's Dilemma: When New Technologies Cause Great Firms to Fail*. Boston: Harvard Business School Press.

Christensen, C.M., McDonald, R., Altman, E.J. and Palmer, J.E. (2018) Disruptive innovation: An intellectual history and directions for future research. *Journal of Management Studies*, 55(7): 1043–1078.

Desiere, S., Langenbucher, K. and Struyven, L. (2019) *Statistical Profiling in Public Employment Services: An International Comparison*. Paris: OECD. https://doi.org/10.1787/b5e5f16e-en

De Vries, H.A., Tummers, L.G. and Bekkers, V. (2018) The diffusion and adoption of public sector innovations: A meta-synthesis of the literature. *Perspectives on Public Management and Governance*, 1(3): 159–176.

Eggers, W.D. and Gonzalez, R. (2012) Disrupting the public sector. *Harvard Business Review*. https://hbr.org/2012/03/disrupting-the-public-sector

Eichhorst, W., Neder, F. and Tobsch, V. (2015) *A European Perspective on Long-Term Unemployment. IZA Discussion Papers No 9321.* Bonn: Institute for the Study of Labor (IZA).

Gallagher, P. and Griffin, R. (2023) (In) accuracy in algorithmic profiling of the unemployed: An exploratory review of reporting standards. *Social Policy and Society*, 3.

Griffin, R., Tuite, A., Hayes, O. and Jordan, A (2023) Report and model for developing pathways for disruptive technologies into public services. HECAT D5.4. https://zenodo.org/records/11210213

Hill, R.K. (2016) What an algorithm is. *Philosophy & Technology*, 29(1): 35–59.

Larsen, A. and Jonsson, A.B. (2011) *Employability Profiling Systems: The Danish Experience.* Brussels: European Commission.

Loxha, A. and Morgandi, M. (2014) *Profiling the Unemployed: A Review of OECD Experiences and Implications for Emerging Economies. Social Protection and Labor Discussion Paper, No. SP 1424.* Washington, DC: World Bank. https://www.openknowledge.worldbank.org/handle/10986

O'Connell, P.J., McGuiness, S., Kelly, E. and Walsh, J. (2009) *National Profiling of the Unemployed in Ireland.* Dublin: The Economic and Social Research Institute.

Riipinen, T. (2011) *Risk Profiling of Long-Term Unemployment in Finland.* Dialogue Conference, Brussels. ec.europa.eu/social/BlobServlet?docId=7583&langId=en

Rosholm, M. and Hammer, B. (2004) *A Danish Profiling System.* Bonn: Institute for the Study of Labour.

Scoppetta, A. and Buckenleib, A. (2018) *Tackling Long-Term Unemployment through Risk Profiling and Outreach.* Brussels: European Commission, Directorate General for Employment, Social Affairs and Inclusion.

Seaver, N. (2013) Knowing algorithms. *Media in Transition*, 8: 1–12.

Veale, M., Van Kleek, M. and Binns, R. (2018) *Fairness and Accountability Design Needs for Algorithmic Support in High-Stakes Public Sector Decision-Making.* Proceedings of the 2018 CHI Conference on Human Factors in Computing Systems.

Wijnhoven, M. A. and Havinga, H., 2014. The Work Profiler: A digital instrument for selection and diagnosis of the unemployed. *Local Economy*, 29(6–7): 740–749.

6

Legal considerations
for algorithm development

Ayo Næsborg-Andersen

Introduction

The introduction of algorithms in the administration is often justified by claims of the algorithm being 'fair' and 'objective', or at least *more* fair and objective than the individual caseworker. While the individual caseworker may very well be biased, and decisions made will invariably vary from one case to another as long as some degree of discretion is allowed, these are not unknown or indeed un-tackled issues. In fact, general principles of administrative law have been developed to counter exactly these problems, ensuring as fair and unbiased decisions as possible, while providing citizens with the opportunity to seek redress where the safeguards fail. Such principles have yet to be developed to counter the specific issues, such as 'black box' decisions, or algorithmic bias, raised by the introduction of algorithms. Administrative law in general has developed over centuries, while the introduction of algorithms is a very recent development. Therefore, there is a particular need to be thorough when developing and implementing algorithms in the (public) administration, as many different aspects need to be considered, and no authoritative 'roadmap' has been developed yet on which aspects to consider, or when.

Algorithms made by combining data sources to glean new information about individuals can be considered an interference in their privacy, according to the European Convention on Human Rights (ECHR), Article 8, and the European Union (EU) Charter for Fundamental Rights (CFR), Articles 7 and 8. Such an interference is not necessarily illegal per se but needs to be carefully considered before being put into action, to justify its use. This consideration is necessitated both by the General Data Protection Regulation (GDPR), and by the case law of the European Court of Human Rights (ECtHR) as well as the Court of Justice of the European Union (CJEU), whereby a measure – such as the introduction of potentially privacy-violating profiling – needs to be shown to be both necessary and proportional in order to be in accordance with human rights law. If these considerations are not met, then the project runs a severe risk of being later found to be illegal, with, at best, changes required to the algorithm and/or the implementation, and, at worst, the entire algorithm being shut down because it is impossible to make it legal. See, for example, the Austrian algorithm for profiling jobseekers which was shut down before it was put into use (Szigetvari, 2020), or the Dutch SyRI algorithm for detecting social benefit fraud which was found illegal by the Dutch courts (Appelman et al, 2021).

This chapter interprets and collects principles from the GDPR, human rights law and general administrative law, as well as EU's AI Act, to sketch out the beginnings of such a roadmap. Where possible it relates these principles to data use and data practices in public employment services (PES), particularly with a view to statistical profiling. As of the writing of this chapter, February 2024, the EU's Proposal for a Regulation on Artificial Intelligence (AI Act) has been politically agreed upon, but has not been finalised (European Parliament, 2024). As such, all mentions of the AI Act must be considered preliminary and should be held against the final text.

Proposal for a model for ensuring legality

First, it is important to note, that neither the GDPR nor the AI Act holds any checklists for which data can be used, nor which algorithms can be implemented, with the exceptions of the few prohibited types of algorithms in the AI Act. A proposed model for relevant considerations when designing an algorithm could look like Figure 6.1.

The model is circular to illustrate that the considerations are ongoing and should be continually updated to reflect the outcome of both the algorithm and the different steps of the considerations. Most of the steps should also happen more or less concurrently. The four steps are expanded upon in the following sections.

Legal requirements

In order for an algorithm to be considered legal, it has to both have a legal basis in law, and fulfil the requirements of said law, as well as all other relevant regulations.

AI Act

The AI Act is a regulation primarily aimed at the developers of artificial intelligence (AI). According to the preliminary text, an AI system is 'a machine-based system designed to operate with varying levels of autonomy and that may exhibit adaptiveness after deployment and that, for explicit or implicit objectives, infers, from the input it receives, how to generate outputs such as predictions, content, recommendations, or decisions that

Figure 6.1: A proposed model for designing algorithms

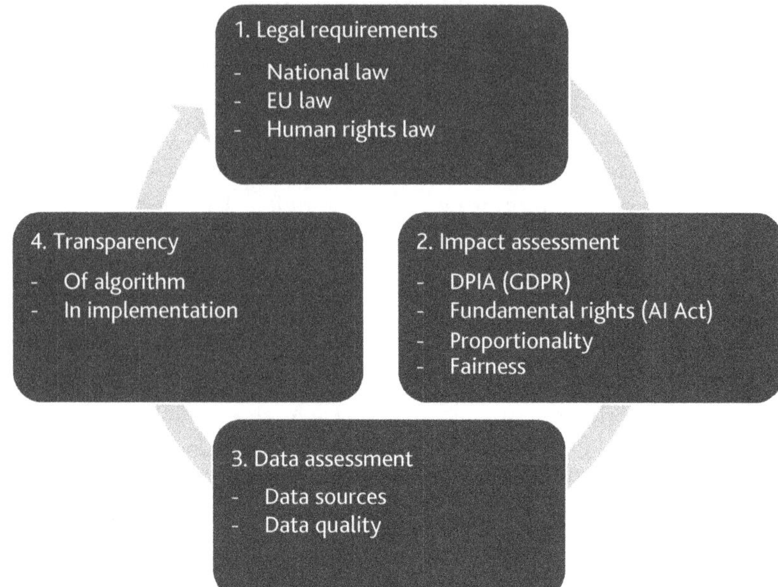

can influence physical or virtual environments' (Article 2.5g.1, Full Draft Text, 2024).

The pivotal component thus seems to be the fact that the system *infers* an output, which would be the case if the system is, for example, used to profile jobseekers. If that is the case, the system next needs to be classified according to the risk categories of the AI Act.

Prohibited systems (Article 5): systems using subliminal techniques; exploiting vulnerabilities of persons with, for example, a disability; biometric categorisation; social scoring; or biometric surveillance. These are all prohibited, with explicit exceptions for law enforcements in particular situations, provided national or EU legislation specifically allows them.

High-risk systems (Article 6 and Annex III): including, but not limited to, profiling of natural persons, and systems 'intended to be used by public authorities or on behalf of public authorities to evaluate the eligibility of natural persons for essential public assistance benefits and services, including healthcare services, as well as to grant, reduce, revoke, or reclaim such benefits and services'. A profiling algorithm intended for allocating public resources would potentially fall within this category.

The AI Act sets out a long list of requirements for extensive documentation for high-risk systems such as a risk management system; data and data governance; technical documentation; automated logs; transparency and provision of information to the deployers of the system; human oversight;

and accuracy, robustness and cybersecurity. All high-risk systems must also be registered with relevant authorities (yet to be defined), and a fundamental rights impact assessment must be performed.

Limited risk systems: systems the use of which do not inherently pose harm, but which require transparency in that the user should know they are interacting with AI. Use-cases are, for example, chatbots and deepfakes.

Minimal risk systems: everything which does not fall under the previous categories, excepting general-purpose AI. Minimal risk systems are not regulated in the AI Act.

General-purpose AI: including generative AI models. Must, among other requirements, be clearly labelled, and use of such to make decisions must be communicated to the people whom the decisions concern.

Since the AI Act is not yet final, this chapter does not expand upon the requirements of it, but encourages anyone working on a system which might be high-risk to follow the developments on that front.

Regardless of whether or not the AI Act requires particular considerations or documentation, however, the GDPR still applies when an algorithm using personal data is developed. Likewise, both human rights law and administrative law remains relevant.

GDPR

All systems must be designed to uphold the demands of the GDPR (data protection by design, Article 25). Therefore, any potential algorithm must be mapped against the GDPR, preferably in the planning stages, but certainly before it is put into use, to ensure the GDPR is upheld. The following outlines the overarching principles and the choice of legal basis, while other parts of the GDPR are touched upon in later sections, as relevant.

Principles of data protection

Article 5 of the GDPR describes the principles which all processing of personal data must uphold. These are all, in some way or form, relevant for the development of algorithms when utilising personal data.

Lawfulness refers to the fact that the processing must be in accordance with national law, as well as the GDPR. Therefore, there is a need to ensure the processing has basis in national law.

Fairness is both a question of the processing being non-discriminatory, but also not going beyond the reasonable expectations of the persons whose data is being processed. The requirement of impact assessments can be seen as a consequence of this principle, and the principle of fairness also necessitates proportionality.

Transparency is a matter of the registered persons being able to understand and follow what is happening to their personal data.

Purpose limitation entails not using data for purposes which they were not originally intended to be used for. In the context of profiling this usually entails ensuring there is a legal basis for using the data specifically for profiling.

Data minimalisation means you can only use the data which is actually necessary for fulfilling the purpose of the processing. Conversely, it also means you must use the data you deem necessary (provided it does not violate other principles such as fairness). 'Need to have, not nice to have' is a popular way of phrasing this principle.

Accuracy is also sometimes referred to as data quality. This is the demand both that you know how accurate your data is, and that you do not rely on data of questionable quality (see the 'Data assessment' section).

Storage limitation means not keeping data for longer than necessary. This is usually a question of setting up schedules for automatic or manual deletion.

Integrity and confidentiality as a principle demands of the controller that data is sufficiently protected, both from security breaches or accidental damage.

And finally, but perhaps most importantly, the principle of *accountability* demands that the controller is able to demonstrate compliance with all these principles. For this reason, all considerations on, for example, what data to use, how to use it and when to delete it, must be *documented*.

Choice of legal basis

According to Article 5.1.a of the GDPR (see Næsborg-Andersen et al, 2019, appendix A2.b), processing of personal data needs to be lawful, that is, have a legal basis. The various legal bases can be found in Article 6 (and Article 9 if processing sensitive data).

The relevant legal basis for profiling in the context of unemployment would be either Article 6.1.c, whereby processing is necessary for compliance with a legal obligation to which the controller (in this case the public authority) is subject, such as the obligation to provide a legally mandated service to the jobseeker, or 6.1.e, where processing is necessary for the performance of a task carried out in the public interest or in the exercise of official authority, such as the tasks necessary to run a PES. Which of the two is relevant will depend on the national law of the country where the profiling is implemented.

If an algorithm targeting vulnerable citizens is considered necessary, then the implementation of it should be supported by national law. The greater the democratic legitimacy, the easier it is to argue that a measure can be considered to be necessary in a democratic society. Vice versa, the more influence an algorithm has on individual citizens, the greater the need for specific legislation (see also Datatilsynet, 2023).

One common misunderstanding is the idea that consent can be used as a legal basis in the context of unemployment services, as consent is one of the legal bases covered in Article 6. Consent must be 'freely given', according to the GDPR (Article 4.11). This means that the registered person must be in a position where the choice is actually free, and a lack of consent will not have negative consequences. In practice, in most institutional settings jobseekers are systematically profiled and consent is not ensured. But even in cases where profiling is not mandatory for the jobseeker authorities will almost always hold power over citizens, which creates an unequal relationship, meaning the choice is not actually free. An authority can use consent for inconsequential things such as subscription to a newsletter, but not for things that will almost inevitably impact a case, such as with unemployment profiling, where the outcome of the profile will inevitably influence the caseworker, as will the lack of a profile due to the citizen not giving consent. This situation, therefore, cannot be based on consent according to the GDPR (European Data Protection Board, 2020: points 16–20).

Profiling done on an 'opt-in' basis would not be considered consent in terms of the GDPR, meaning the profiling would still have to have a legal basis in law under the Article 6.1.c or 6.1.e.

Consent would potentially be a relevant legal basis if the resulting profile was made available exclusively to the citizen as a tool for self-assessment, and not to the caseworker and/or the authorities. This would to a large extent depend on how the tool was presented to the citizen.

Human rights law and administrative law

Article 13 of the ECHR provides the right to an effective remedy. Therefore, the citizen has the right to challenge an administrative decision. There is not currently any case law from either the ECtHR or the European Court of Justice on what, exactly, the right to an effective remedy entails as regards assessments made by algorithms. Based on previous case law on effective remedies, however, some guidelines can be proposed. These are also in line with general principles of administrative law, applicable to all European countries (Næsborg-Andersen, 2015).

In order for the right to be effective, the citizen about whom a decision was made must be able to assess whether the decision was correct, and whether they want to appeal it. Therefore, it follows that the citizen must have access to enough information to make this assessment. If an algorithm formed all or part of a decision this needs to be communicated. The question then becomes which information, exactly, should be provided. Access to the underlying codes of any algorithm does not in-and-of itself provide useful information to anyone who is not trained in programming languages. Instead, an explanation of the underlying logic of the algorithm, as well as the deciding factors, would be more useful (more on this in Burrell, 2016; Goodman and Flaxman, 2017).

An explanation for all factors considered would also be relevant, as that enables the citizen to point out any omissions. Likewise, the importance attached by the administration to the outcome of an algorithm would be a useful explanation. These explanations must show a complete picture of the way the algorithm is implemented, and which data it assesses. In order to ensure that the citizen is given the complete picture the administration must also be able to verify that the explanations are in accordance with the truth and it would probably, as a consequence hereof, need access to the underlying algorithm. In other words, the right to an effective remedy, as regards the use of algorithms in administrative decisions, first and foremost requires transparency.

The administration must also stop the continuation of any violations of human rights. Therefore, if an algorithm is found to be in violation of human rights in one decision, the administration must be able to make corrections before it is used in other decisions. The right to an effective remedy thus requires the ability of the administration to make continuous changes to any algorithm used. This requirement is also reflected in the AI Act in the demand for human oversight of high-risk AI systems.

Impact assessment

To determine what data an algorithm can use, and how the algorithm can be implemented by the administration, the all-important first step is to make an impact assessment. This requirement follows directly from GDPR Article 25, whereby data protection, including considerations for the citizens affected by the algorithm, must be built into the system from the start. This should be carried out ideally prior to development of the algorithm, and then updated concurrently with any changes. If the algorithm is developed as part of a research project, then at the very least the assessment must be made before the algorithm is implemented in administrative practice. If the algorithm is considered high risk, then a Fundamental Rights Impact Assessment must also be conducted before the algorithm is deployed, according to the AI Act.

The assessment should focus on two different aspects: First of all ensuring the requirements of the GDPR and (potentially) the AI Act, namely both the safety and *proportionality* of using the data, as well as the *necessity* of using the algorithm, including the impact of the algorithm on the citizens in question. Relevant aspects are both human rights (as considered in a Data Protection Impact Assessment, GDPR Article 35, and a Fundamental Rights Impact Assessment according to the AI Act), and the administrative impact of the algorithm on the citizen whom the decision concerns (Motzfeldt and Næsborg-Andersen, 2018). These aspects are somewhat overlapping, but it is important to keep track of both sides of the assessment, that is, the data and the citizens.

To be able to perform an impact assessment, it is necessary to determine first how the algorithm will be used, as this determines the level of impact on the citizen. If, as in the Belgian case, the purpose is to prioritise which jobseeker gets a phone call from the unemployment agency first (Desiere and Struyven, 2020), the impact is likely to be very low. After all, all jobseekers will get the same call, it is only a matter of timing. If, on the other hand, the purpose of the algorithm is to sort jobseekers into different categories with correspondingly vastly different types of services and/or differentiated access to active labour market measures, like in the Austrian case (Allhutter et al, 2020), the impact is likely to be moderate or high, depending on the various safeguards built into the system, and what, exactly, the consequences are. The higher the impact, the greater the requirement on the development and use of the algorithm.

Proportionality

To assess proportionality, the importance of the overall objective must be considered, as well as whether the included measures meet the objective. In short, the ends must justify the means. For predictive analytics, as used in labour market profiling systems, the 'means' are twofold: (1) the algorithm learning to map specific inputs to predicted outcomes; and (2) the historical data providing examples of inputs and outcomes. Both the opportunities and threats of using different types and sources of data must be evaluated. If a type of variable infringes upon fundamental rights, it must be strictly necessary for the functioning of the model to be included. If a variable infringes upon fundamental rights and does not substantially contribute to the functioning of the model, it should be removed from the training data.

This raises the following questions: when is a variable considered to contribute substantially, and likewise, when is a variable considered to be too sensitive for inclusion? This motivates the establishment of a clearly defined balancing point between these thresholds of predictive contribution and sensitivity. For predictive analytics, the added value of utilising sensitive data is generally measured in terms of a model's ability to correctly predict a chosen outcome, as judged by a chosen evaluation metric. Therefore, to evaluate the added value of including sensitive or risky data, it is necessary to consider both the definition of the outcome which the model is tasked with predicting, as well as how the models' predictions of this outcome are evaluated. Further evaluation on the impact of the programme (for example, how effective is the use of the algorithm in helping jobseekers to find a new job of decent quality) should also be taken into consideration.

Fairness

It is well-known that algorithms contain bias, which can lead to discrimination. According to human rights law (ECHR Article 14 and CFR chapter III) discrimination means treating somebody:

1. in comparable situations;
2. differently;
3. based on certain characteristics; and
4. without legitimate aim or proportionality.

So, there are four criteria to assess when considering whether something is discriminating. First of all, *comparable situations*. In this case, that would be people who are unemployed. *The certain characteristics* could be all kinds of things but are typically the classical causes for discrimination; race, gender, sexuality and so on – all personal characteristics, which cannot be changed (such as race), or which it is not reasonable to ask people to change (such as religion).

If these characteristics are used as grounds for decisions without good reason, it is considered to be discriminatory, but non-discriminatory if the reason is good. In the context of jobseekers this would mean you can make a distinction between, for example, levels of education, as that is directly relevant to the types of job they can apply for. Likewise, an argument could be made for making a distinction on the grounds of previous work or unemployment experience, as someone with many years of experience will present a different value for an employer than someone with no experience. It is, however, important to consider whether the reason you are distinguishing two persons or groups from each other is due to prejudice, as prejudice is never an acceptable reason for discrimination. Employers being reluctant to employ a certain category of people due to prejudice does not qualify, as a public authority must work against, instead of amplifying, any prejudice. In this case discrimination would be grounded in a personal characteristic, which has no influence on whether or not the person can fulfil the job and is therefore in violation of human rights law.

You are allowed to treat people differently based on certain characteristics if you are trying to correct factual inequalities (sometimes you are even required to do so). You must, however, (a) be very certain there is an inequality (that is, needs to be documented), and (b) be fairly certain the differential treatment will actually help correct the inequality (so follow-ups and course-corrections to the algorithm/implementation and use of the algorithm would be expected). In this context, it matters greatly what the differential treatment consists of. If, as was intended in the Austrian case, falling in the category with highest employment barriers leads to a 'moral training' course, it is highly doubtful such a course actually corrects anything.

This would therefore be considered discriminatory and in violation of human rights law. There is also the question of whether the differential treatment attaches a stigma to the groups you are trying to help, which singling people out based on characteristics such as race invariably does, to some degree. This kind of *positive discrimination* needs to be considered very carefully, before it is put into action. Preferably, the national parliament needs to be making this decision, as this would give it the most democratic legitimacy possible, although this is not a guarantee it will not be found discriminatory at a later time. If the main problem is prejudice on the employer side, then singling out the potential employees which the employers discriminate against is probably not going to help, unless you also (predominantly) actively work on challenging and changing the underlying prejudice. You need to attack the root cause of the discrimination, not the people being discriminated against, for positive discrimination to be considered positive (Desiere and Struyven, 2020).

In cases where statistics are used for decisions (or support for decisions), the question of *indirect discrimination* invariably poses an issue. If a measure can be shown to proportionally affect certain groups more than others, it is considered to be indirectly discriminating, regardless of whether that was the intent. This is especially the case if the affected group is traditionally considered a minority, on the basis of, for example, ethnic origin, gender or sexuality. Therefore, if some proxies correlate strongly with protected characteristics, their inclusion must be considered very thoroughly, and if so, what measures can be taken to counteract the correlation. Some data may need to be excluded on this account, even if this makes the algorithm less precise. One consideration here is whether the data reflects the information which one seeks in a precise enough way. If, say, country of residence is included, this poses a high risk of being discriminatory data. If the reason for including the information about country of residence is that it reflects whether the jobseeker has a temporary work permit or not, then that information should be the input instead. The information about the status of a work permit may still indirectly discriminate against jobseekers of other nationalities, but the justification for including it is much higher, as (a) it is more accurate, (b) it runs less of a risk of discriminating against specific nationalities, and (c) it is directly relevant to the jobseeker's situation. The country of residence may also serve as a proxy for language skills, in which case the country of residence conflates two different issues, resulting in less precision, and less actionable information. Language skills can be worked on, but only if the jobseeker and/or the caseworker are aware of the potential problem. Therefore, using the input of country of residence instead of language skills and/or status of work permit will disguise the relevant issues, leaving the jobseeker and the caseworker ignorant of potential areas for improvement. To completely ensure the inclusion of a parameter such as country of residence is not discriminatory a final assessment of the relevance and necessity of including the information would need to be weighed against the measures imposed, to ensure proportionality.

The stronger the impact on the persons affected, the stronger will be the need to demonstrate the necessity of sorting people according to personal characteristics which have no impact on their ability to fulfil a job, such as ethnic origin. A measure which has next-to-no impact, such as the ranking of which jobseeker will get a phone call from the unemployment agency first within a short timeframe, does not need strong justifications. In contrast, a measure such as sorting the jobseekers into different categories determining both whether they get specific assistance from the public authority and which type, needs stronger justification.

On a more practical note, the predictions of profiling algorithms can be linked to differential administrative treatment by caseworkers, such as whether a client is to be referred to interventions focused on job training or job-seeking motivation (Allhutter et al, 2020). Therefore statistical disparities in data can have direct impact for the treatment of individuals in job centres, leading to discrimination and lack of fairness.

Data assessment

Any time data about citizens are gathered, this is a considered an interference with their right to privacy (ECHR Article 8; CFR Article 7). In a democratic society, for an interference with the right to privacy to be considered legal, it must be *necessary*. Likewise, according to GDPR Article 5.1.c, usage of personal data must be limited to the strictly necessary data. Necessity is only justified on the basis of objective evidence. In turn, the option which is least intrusive while still obtaining the goal must be used. Basing the development of an algorithm on, for example, literature reviews identifying relevant theoretical paradigms may be one such justification, as may basing it on other kinds of research (see, for example, Wijnhoven and Havinga, 2014). Using all kinds of available data to develop a predictive model, on the other hand, would require a strict examination of the resulting model both in terms of accuracy, and ensuring, for example, non-bias.

According to the GDPR, the project should only collect and use data that is up to date and relevant. This therefore calls for an assessment of the quality of data at the core of profiling models. The frameworks recognised useful for such assessment are few. An interesting example was published by Smith et al (2018). In short, they distinguish five dimensions to assess the quality of administrative data.

1. *Accuracy*: gives account of the completeness (how important are missing values), correctness (how important are values wrongly formatted,

impossible values, or outliers), measurement error (wrong answers), level of bias (of the reported values relative to the real values) and consistency (would repeated measures provide the same table?) of the database.

2. *Internal validity*: measures the extent to which values of two different fields of the dataset are compatible (over time or across variables at a given time).
3. *External validity*: measures the extent to which elements of the dataset contradicts other data sources.
4. *Timeliness*: refers to whether the data is up-to-date and, for databases including waves, how quick it is to update.
5. *Interpretability*: measures how easy it is to understand the content of the database, including with its documentation.

Further principles should be evaluated regarding the data. In particular, one should only use data necessary to sufficiently serve the quality of the profiling or model, and in a way compatible with the specific purpose for which the data was collected in the first place.

One consideration is how much of the jobseekers' (employment) history should be included in the model; that is, is there a point where it is no longer useful to 'go further back in time'? For example, according to Frid-Nielsen (2019) information pertaining to the individuals' most recent occupation contributes a high level of accuracy for predicting the next occupation, with diminishing returns when using information on occupations further in the past. Limiting the data in terms of the time scope may not only help comply with the legal basis, but also offer an avenue to prune data and improve the model outcomes in the case of profiling.

In the case of profiling, the outcome variable of interest is typically whether a given person who has entered unemployment will remain in this state for a long enough period to be classified as long-term unemployed. The definition of the outcome variable has substantial importance because the influence of input variables will likely vary depending on the time scale. The individual characteristics, personal skills, experiences and external labour market conditions that hinder or expedite returning to the labour market in the short term will likely differ greatly from those that are at play for extended periods of unemployment. For example, research has found that besides age, socio-professional variables such as allowances, loans and training can correctly predict employment status at six months in 74 per cent of cases (Meyers and Houssemand, 2010). In turn, demographic variables such as age and gender, combined with psychological variables, such as openness, self-efficacy, symptom-reduction coping, social anxiety and intelligence, allow the model to correctly predict employment status at 12 months in 75 per cent of cases. These findings illustrate that there are different time-dependent factors at play depending on the chosen operationalisation of long-term unemployment. The implication for proportionality is that the marginal utility of sensitive data may fluctuate over time, complicating the justification of the use of sensitive data. This might be less of an issue with regard to a decision support system where jobseekers receive recommendations for relevant occupations given their profile (for example, previous occupation, skills, geographic constraints) and expectations (for example, wages, working time, type of contract). These factors might, however, come into play if the tool works at a very detailed level including conditioning on the time a jobseeker has spent in unemployment.

In addition to considering how to define the desired predictions of a model, it is relevant to consider how to evaluate the quality of these predictions. There is no 'golden rule' for the choice of *evaluation metric* by which to assess predictive models. In fact, certain evaluation metrics may favour certain algorithms, where some may favour prediction, recommendation or utility maximisation tasks (Gunawardana and Shani, 2009). Therefore, the choice of evaluation metric should depend on, for example, the characteristics of the problem at hand, the distribution of the data, or the needs of stakeholders and end-users. As we see in much of the pre-existing reporting on statistical profiling (Desiere et al, 2019), 'accuracy' is the golden standard for evaluating model performance. In predicting a binary or multiclass outcome, as is generally the case in statistical profiling of long-term unemployment, accuracy is simply defined as the share of correctly predicted outcomes.

Accuracy as an evaluation metric has some serious shortcomings, urging a move 'beyond accuracy' within the decision-support systems literature (McNee et al, 2006; Cremonesi et al, 2010; Ge et al, 2010; Kaminskas and Bridge, 2016; Nilashi et al, 2016). For example, accuracy does not take into account differences between false positives and false negatives in the assessment of predictions. If there are different costs associated with false negatives and positives, this can have serious impacts for the individual-level outcomes generated by the interaction with a model. In terms of labour market profiling, for example, false negatives would imply individuals who are categorised as low-risk of long-term unemployment, who actually become long-term unemployed. Conversely, false positives would imply individuals categorised as high-risk of long-term unemployment, who actually return to work quickly. While overinvesting in the low-risk group will lead to inefficiency at the administrative level, underinvesting in the high-risk group may fail to reduce unemployment durations, thereby missing to reduce caseworkers' load and to improve the fate of the jobseekers most likely to be trapped in negative feedback loops involving poor mental health due to long-term unemployment (Oberholzer-Gee, 2008; Paul and Moser, 2009; Strandh et al, 2014). Therefore, the costs associated with false negatives and false positives within unemployment profiling are not symmetrical, and should be taken into careful consideration when developing and implementing a model.

Transparency

It is a basic, and central, principle of general administrative law, that all decisions adversely affecting a citizen shall be adequately explained. This must enable the citizen to both understand the decision, and to evaluate whether the decision was correct, and if not whether to make an appeal. This principle does not change with the digitalisation of the administration, but requires careful consideration of which algorithms to implement, and how. If a decision is made by a so-called 'black box' (Pasquale, 2015), then it is all but impossible to provide a relevant and correct statement of the reasons underlying the decision. If, on the other hand, an algorithm has only provided insight into, for example, the current waiting period to acquire specific documentation, the citizen does not need to be told of the algorithm's existence (Næsborg-Andersen et al, 2023).

Equally important are considerations on how the caseworker receiving the algorithm output is trained. The AI Act requires AI literacy, both of caseworkers and of persons affected by the algorithms (Article 4). In case of high-risk AI systems, this includes awareness of automation bias and the ability to detect flaws and override the system.

Finally, the ECHR Article 13 requires the existence of efficient remedies in cases decided by the administration. A remedy can only be efficient if the administration can explain the working of the algorithm, both in the initial training phase, in implementation and in later corrections.

While the requirements of the administration when using various algorithms have yet to find their final form, many of the relevant considerations are, however, already known, as shown here.

Conclusion

This chapter has presented the legal considerations that one should take when using data and algorithms for profiling jobseekers in PES. Many of the considerations are also relevant with regard to use of individual-level data in PES beyond profiling, for example, for the purpose of data-driven decision support systems. These considerations matter per se if we believe in the control of privacy by the judiciary. They are also important on a more pragmatic level, as it regularly happens that experimentations are aborted or challenged for non-respect of the legalese presented here. To give but one example, in 2020, the Austrian algorithmic profiling tool intended to classify jobseekers was shut down by the data protection authority due to a lack of a sufficient legal basis, even before it was rolled out. It had previously been highly criticised on grounds of potential discrimination and lack of transparency. Likewise, the fully automated decision system SyRI, intended to detect social welfare fraud, was shut down by the Dutch courts in 2020, due to severe lack of transparency and infringement of several human rights (Appelman et al, 2021).

The most important conclusion from this analysis is that any algorithm needs to be continuously assessed with a view to the right to privacy of the jobseeker. Such impact assessment is relevant both for the design as well as the implementation phase of the project. Crucially, the requirements for administrative safeguards and restrictions to the underlying data will vary with the expected impact of the algorithm – the higher the expected impact on the jobseeker the stricter the requirements. Legal requirements to consider are to be found in national (administrative) law, in EU law, particularly the GDPR, as well as human rights law. Importantly, all considerations vis-à-vis the data and the algorithm need to be documented and there needs to be a legal basis for the algorithm and the underlying data. The legal requirements will shape the subsequent impact assessment of the algorithm. As administrations such as the PES need to make decision that are both proportional and fair, these two principles need to be at the core of such an assessment.

References

Allhutter, D., Cech, F., Fischer, F., Grill, G. and Mager, A. (2020) Algorithmic profiling of job seekers in Austria: How austerity politics are made effective. *Frontiers in Big Data*, 3: 5.

Appelman, N., Fathaigh, R.Ó. and van Hoboken, J. (2021) Social welfare, risk profiling and fundamental rights: The case of SyRI in the Netherlands. *Journal of Intellectual Property, Information Technology and E-Commerce Law*, 12(4).

Burrell, J. (2016) How the machine 'thinks': Understanding opacity in machine learning algorithms, *Big Data & Society*, 3(1): 2053951715622512.

Cremonesi, P., Koren, Y. and Turrin, R. (2010) Performance of recommender algorithms on top-n recommendation tasks. Proceedings of the Fourth ACM Conference on Recommender Systems. New York: Association for Computing Machinery, pp 39–46.

Datatilsynet (2023) *Udtalelse om behandlingsgrundlag til udvikling og drift af AI-løsning inden for sundheds- og omsorgsområdet.* https://www.datatilsynet.dk/afgoerelser/afgoerelser/2023/nov/udtalelse-om-behandlingsgrundlag-til-udvikling-og-drift-af-ai-loesning-inden-for-sundheds-og-omsorgsomraadet

Desiere, S. and Struyven, L. (2020) Using artificial intelligence to classify jobseekers: The accuracy-equity trade-off. *Journal of Social Policy*: 1–19.

Desiere, S., Langenbucher, K. and Struyven, L. (2019) Statistical profiling in public employment services: An international comparison. OECD Social, Employment and Migration Working Papers, No. 224. Paris: OECD Publishing.

European Data Protection Board (2020) Guidelines 05/2020 on consent under Regulation 2016/679. Guidelines 05/2020 on consent under Regulation 2016/679, Version 1.1. https://www.edpb.europa.eu/sites/default/files/files/file1/edpb_guidelines_202005_consent_en.pdf

European Parliament (2024) Artificial intelligence act. Legislative Train Schedule. https://www.europarl.europa.eu/legislative-train/theme-a-europe-fit-for-the-digital-age/file-regulation-on-artificial-intelligence

Frid-Nielsen, S.S. (2019) Find my next job: Labor market recommendations using administrative big data. Proceedings of the 13th ACM Conference on Recommender Systems. New York: Association for Computing Machinery, pp 408–412.

Ge, M., Delgado, C. and Jannach, D. (2010) Beyond accuracy: Evaluating recommender systems by coverage and serendipity. Proceedings of the Fourth ACM Conference on Recommender Systems. New York: Association for Computing Machinery, pp 257–260.

Goodman, B. and Flaxman, S. (2017) European Union regulations on algorithmic decision-making and a 'right to explanation'. *AI Magazine*, 38(3): 50–57.

Gunawardana, A. and Shani, G. (2009) A survey of accuracy evaluation metrics of recommendation tasks. *Journal of Machine Learning Research*, 10: 2935–2962.

Kaminskas, M. and Bridge, D. (2016) Diversity, serendipity, novelty, and coverage: A survey and empirical analysis of beyond–accuracy objectives in recommender systems. *ACM Transactions on Interactive Intelligent Systems*, 7(1): 1–42.

McNee, S.M., Riedl, J. and Konstan, J. (2006) Accurate is not always good: How accuracy metrics have hurt recommender systems. CHI '06 Extended Abstracts on Human Factors in Computing Systems. New York: Association for Computing Machinery, pp 1097–1101.

Meyers, R. and Houssemand, C. (2010) Socioprofessional and psychological variables that predict job finding. *European Review of Applied Psychology*, 60(3): 201–219.

Motzfeldt, H.M. and Næsborg-Andersen, A. (2018) Developing administrative law into handling the challenges of digital government in Denmark. *Electronic Journal of e-government*, 16(2): 136–146.

Næsborg-Andersen, A. (2015) *Human Rights in National Administrative Law: Dissemination of Knowledge of Human Rights through Administrative Decisions.* Copenhagen: Djøf.

Næsborg-Andersen, A., Hammerslev, O. and Ullits, J. (2023) Beslutningsunderstøttende algoritmer i det offentlige: påvirkningen af sagsbehandlerens skøn og begrundelse. *Politica*, 55(3): 199–217.

Næsborg-Andersen, A., Frid-Nielsen, S., Leschke, J. and Brébion, C. (2021) Technical report data sources and data protection for algorithm development. *HECAT Deliverable 2.2.* https://zenodo.org/records/7914776

Nilashi, M., Jannach, D., bin Ibrahim, O., Esfahani, M.D. and Ahmadi, H. (2016) Recommendation quality, transparency, and website quality for trust-building in recommendation agents. *Electronic Commerce Research and Applications*, 19: 70–84.

Oberholzer-Gee, F. (2008) Nonemployment stigma as rational herding: A field experiment. *Journal of Economic Behavior & Organization*, 65(1): 30–40.

Pasquale, F. (2015) *The Black Box Society*. Cambridge, MA: Harvard University Press.

Paul, K.I. and Moser, K. (2009) Unemployment impairs mental health: Meta-analyses. *Journal of Vocational Behavior*, 74(3): 264–282.

Smith, M. et al (2018) Assessing the quality of administrative data for research: A framework from the Manitoba Centre for Health Policy. *Journal of the American Medical Informatics Association*, 25(3): 224–229.

Strandh, M., Winefield, A., Nilsson, K. and Hammarström, A. (2014) Unemployment and mental health scarring during the life course. *European Journal of Public Health*, 24(3): 440–445.

Szigetvari, A. (2020) Datenschutzbehörde kippt umstrittenen AMS-Algorithmus. https://www.derstandard.at/story/2000119486931/date nschutzbehoerde-kippt-umstrittenen-ams-algorithmus

Wijnhoven, M.A. and Havinga, H. (2014) The Work Profiler: A digital instrument for selection and diagnosis of the unemployed. *Local Economy*, 29(6–7): 740–749.

7

Labour market data, job matching and job quality

Clément Brébion and Janine Leschke

Introduction

This chapter discusses and operationalises the multidimensional concept of job quality and links it with the relevant European data. This is done with a view on whether and how job quality items can be integrated into an online matching platform that provides the unemployed and jobseekers with a snapshot of their labour market options. We take as a starting point the lessons learned from first generation statistical profiling tools in public employment services (PES) (Desiere et al, 2019), the economic literature on the impact of online matching platforms, as well as the sociological vision of labour market integration and good-quality work (Demazière and Delpierre, 2020: deliverable 1.4). We also take into account fieldwork as part of the HECAT project on the lived experience of unemployed (and caseworkers) in the PES in Slovenia (Hansen and Pultz, 2021: deliverable 1.1; Hansen and Pultz, 2023: deliverable 5.3). In the framework of this project, a job matching tool, MyLabourMarket, was developed.

Underemployment and poor job quality can have substantially negative effects similar to unemployment, they range from more objective indicators (for example, future earnings potential or job performance) to more subjective ones such as job satisfaction or job withdrawal attitude and behaviour (Virick and McKee-Ryan, 2014/2018). Re-employment efforts, including those facilitated by the PES, should thus focus on helping jobseekers to find jobs that offer the prospect of long-term employment, preferably in a job that matches their previous occupation and/or skills and/or their personal needs for career aspirations and location.

State-of-the-art statistical profiling tools in PES have many shortcomings and this includes that they draw on sensitive personal data, have limited accuracy and transparency, can be discriminatory and categorise unemployed persons broadly instead of focusing on their actual and complex situation (for example, Alhutter et al, 2020; Griffin et al, 2020a: deliverable 1.3; Næsborg-Andersen et al, 2021: deliverable 2.2). These limitations have led to the rolling back of several profiling algorithms on legal grounds. Nevertheless, they remain commonly used in PES nowadays and this is why we take them as a starting point with a view to improving the output variable by introducing job quality features. In the light of a more enabling vision of a job matching platform we also discuss how job quality features as part of the matching functionalities of such a platform can be introduced to positively support labour market decision-making.

The first part of the next section discusses a range of job matching platforms currently used by PES with a view to how far they consider job quality dimension. The second part discusses the limitations of online matching platforms and profiling tools with a particular focus on the common output variable that does not consider job quality but rather any exit (to employment) from the benefit record. In the following section we scrutinise the multidisciplinary literature on job quality. We draw on lessons learned from a range of European multidimensional comparative job quality indices and we propose seven dimensions of job quality to consider in our job matching platform. The next section translates these recommendations into practice. We do a census of European comparative data and propose a set of concrete items (variables) for each of the seven job quality dimensions. The subsequent section provides insights into the considerations taken with regard to operationalising job quality features in our prototype MyLabourMarket platform.

Online matching platforms and profiling tools do not take into account job quality

Job matching tools

Table 7.1 describes the type of information available across a selection of online matching platforms in the European Union (EU). It shows that all of these platforms allow jobseekers to look for vacancies in their preferred occupation or industry in a selected geographical area. Most of these platforms complement the search with filters for contract type (typically permanent versus short-term contracts) and working time (either to discriminate between full-time and part-time jobs or according to more precise numbers of working hours). Most of the platforms identified in this research offer barely any further option for filtering vacancies. One should, however, mention the Spanish, French and Wallon cases that offer jobseekers more discriminatory power to identify relevant jobs. Forem, in Wallonia, is the most complete of them. The tool allows jobseekers to filter out positions according to their work experience, potential disability, the language required in the job, whether one needs to work over weekends or at night, and if a driving licence is required. Importantly enough, some of the platforms presented in Table 7.1 suggest vacancies for occupations/

Table 7.1: Variables used in a number of online matching platforms in the European Union (on top of filters for the occupation/industry and geographical area)

	Wage	Contract type	Working time	Level of diploma	Work experience	Disability	Teleworking feasibility	Manager or not	Language	Non-standard working time	Driving licence	EU work permit required	Firm commitments (diversity, equality, and so on)
EURES (UE) Adem (Luxemburg)		X		X	X								
Empleate (Spain)		X	X	X	X	X	X						
Pôle emploi (France)		X	X		X	X		X					
Forem (Wallonia)		X	X	X	X				X	X	X		
Bundesagentur für Arbeit (Germany)			X		X	X		X					
Indeed	X	X	X										
Linked In		X			X		X						X
Eurojobs	X	X										X	
Jobnet (Denmark)		X	X										
Burza rada (Croatia)													
Tyomarkkinatori (Finland)		X	X						X				
vinnumálastofnun (Iceland)			X										
Instituto do Emprego e Formação Profissional (Portugal)		X	X	X									
Arbetsformedlingen (Sweden)		X	X				X				X		

industries that are close to the one searched or are part of a market with labour shortages. Examples are the platforms for Wallonia, Germany, Denmark and Finland as well as Indeed and LinkedIn.

Job ads are not always depicted on a map, which is likely to make it harder for jobseekers to assess commuting time. This is emphasised in Gutiérrez et al (2019) who claim that interactions with visualisation tools may ease users' understanding of complex data. The authors highlight that users' views on the usability and performance of online matching platforms are rarely taken into account. They emphasise for the Belgian context the following three goals that should guide the design of online platforms:

(1) Exploration/control: job seekers should be able to control job recommendations and filter out the information flow coming from the recommender engine; (2) Explanations: recommendations and matching scores should be explained, and details should be provided on-demand; (3) Actionable insights: the interface should provide actionable insights to help job-seekers find new or more job recommendations from different perspectives. (Gutiérrez et al, 2019: p 64)

Using focus groups to test a prototype, the authors uncover the importance of a location-based overview as well as clear explanations of concepts that are used on the platform.

Building on this background, we offer to develop an online matching platform tool that:

1. shows selected vacancies on a map that users can navigate;
2. includes a large number of filtering options to discriminate between vacancies according to their level of job quality; and
3. takes into account the feedback received from jobseekers and caseworkers in dedicated focus groups.

Profiling tools

The output variable of current profiling tools, first drawbacks

Algorithms that profile jobseekers have developed since the 1990s with the objective of increasing the efficiency of PES expenditures in a context of budget constraints (Griffin et al, 2020a). They aim at identifying individuals that have little counselling needs, and those for whom intensive counselling and active labour market policies (ALMPs) are expected to have the largest returns. The ultimate goal is to target expenditures towards the latter. A consensus has developed to proxy needs for counselling and for ALMPs by the expected length of unemployment spells. Thus, Table 7.2 shows that all but two countries (Austria and Estonia) use the probability to remain

Table 7.2: Output variables of different profiling tools

Country	Ambition	Source
Ireland – PEX	Identifying those at risk of LTU (12 months)	O'Connell et al (2009); Griffin, Boland, Tuite and Hennessy (2020b)
Austria – AMAS	Build three groups: • High probability to find a non-subsidised work lasting more than 3 months in the following 7 months • Low probability to work in a non-subsidised job lasting more than 6 months in the next 2 years • The rest	Allhutter et al (2020)
Denmark – Job Barometer	Identifying those at risk of LTU (6 months)	Roshol et al (2004); Madsen (2014); Larsen et al (2011)
France – Intelligence Emploi	Identifying those at risk of LTU (6 months)	Ponomareva and Sheen (2013)
Australia – JSCI	Identifying those at risk of LTU (12 months)	Ponomareva and Sheen (2013); Lipp (2005)
Croatia – StAP	Identifying those at risk of LTU (12 months)	Botrić (2017); Flesicher (2016)
Finland – Risk Profiling Tool	Identifying those at risk of LTU (12 months)	Riipinen (2011); Behncke et al (2007)
Belgium – VDAB	Identifying those at risk of LTU (6 months)	Desiere et al (2019)
Estonia – Soft Profiling	ALMP effect	Van Ours (2007); Brixiova and Egert (2012)
Italy	Identifying those at risk of LTU (12 months)	OECD (2019a)
Latvia	Identifying those at risk of LTU (12 months)	Desiere et al (2019); OECD (2019b)
Netherlands – WorkProfiler	Identifying those at risk of LTU (12 months)	Wijnhoven and Havinga (2014); Hasluck (2008)
New Zealand – SEM	Identifying those at risk of LTU (6 months)	Ministry for Social Development (2018)
Sweden – AST	Identifying those at risk of LTU (6 months)	Loxha and Morgandi (2014)

Note: LTU = long-term unemployment

Source: Adapted from Griffin et al (2020a)

unemployed over either six or 12 months as an output variable in their profiling algorithm (also addressed as the probability of exit hereafter).

These output variables are seemingly easy to measure, objective, simple to grasp for both the unemployed and the caseworkers and transparent – which matters for such algorithms as discussed in Næsborg-Andersen et al (2021). However, when going into details, things appear to be more complex. Most models in place measure the probability of exiting unemployment for any type of employment rather than for sustainable employment. They fail to consider the revolving door between the unemployment insurance and short-term employment. Individuals who keep going back and forth between employment and unemployment are classified as low risk and are not offered extensive support. This can be dysfunctional and inefficient both from the perspective of the individual (for example, van den Berg and Vikström, 2014) and the PES as unsustainable labour market integration is likely to lead to vicious circles where people circle between (short-term) employment and unemployment (for example, on repercussion of flexible job search behaviour see Vansteenkiste et al [2016]).

Next, important subjective choices are hidden behind an apparently very straightforward and neutral measure. To classify individuals into risk groups, PES must decide upon classification thresholds that divide the distribution of the long-term unemployment (LTU) probability. The value of these thresholds is not neutral and can respond to several concerns. Budget constraints are the first one: the higher the threshold, the lower the number of individuals classified as high risk. Second, accuracy concerns may govern decision-making on classification thresholds too. In their article, Kern et al (2021) identify several types of profiling algorithms (logistic regression, penalised logistic regression, random forest and gradient boosting machines) and highlight that thresholds affect the performance of algorithms. Their review indicates that precision increases with the classification threshold whereas recall (the proportion of correct identifications) decreases. The literature has no clear-cut argument to favour one performance measure over the other and the choice ultimately rests with policy makers and statisticians – with the potential involvement of caseworkers. Third, classification thresholds also have implications on the fairness of algorithms. In their article, Kern et al (2021) find that all the models tested lead to the same conclusion: the threshold allowing to reach the largest accuracy levels (defined as the average between the precision and recall rates) offers poor levels of fairness.

In the same vein, the choice of the time window to define jobseekers has consequences on the classification (O'Connell et al, 2012; Arni et al, 2014).

In a report on the limitations of the Austrian profiling tool, the Ombudsman (2019) states that the definition of the dependent variable is 'purely a matter of labour market policy decisions' and insists on the fact that different individuals will be classified as high risk when the dependent variable changes. The categorisation of jobseekers – and thereby their access to ALMPs and ultimately their chances to find a new job – indeed depends on the integration target (for more information see Allhutter et al, 2020). Unfortunately, despite having great implications, underlying preferences that govern decision-making on the design of the tools are generally concealed (Allhutter et al, 2020).

The need for a platform that considers job quality

In order to overcome the shortcomings of established profiling systems our platform aims to provide an improved probability of exit score and a tool to visualise vacancies. As regards the probability of exit score, the ambition is to implement a more ethical algorithm that respects the General Data Protection Regulation, is less discriminatory in the use of data than some of the previous examples, considers job quality in the output variable and does not focus on specific time windows. This probability appears on our platform as one of several indicators that can be considered by the jobseeker in her job search activities but is not used to profile individuals into groups that would automatically offer different levels of intensity of counselling or of ALMPs. The visualisation tool, in turn, aims to show alternative options in the labour market with a focus on quality employment.

From the current practice to our vision: accounting for multidimensional job quality

One of the important features that emerged from the scrutiny of the lived experiences of unemployment (Demazière and Delpierre, 2020) as well as the in-depth study of the user context in our pilot sites, the Public Employment Services of Slovenia, in the Ljubljana and Ptuj offices (Hansen and Pultz, 2021), is that the situation, wishes and prospects of the unemployed vary substantively within and across national contexts (see also O'Reilly et al, 2019). The platform thus necessarily needs to operate with a set of options regarding dimensions of job quality.

In the spirit of working with and not on the unemployed, job quality should be a multidimensional construct, drawing on the interdisciplinary job quality literature. This will provide options for the unemployed who use the platform to focus on the dimensions that are most relevant for them given their lived experience and current situation.

Job quality: definitions and social sciences traditions

In this chapter we refer to 'job quality', a term which puts emphasis on the job content and work environment whereas quality of employment and decent work tend to have broader definitions, including, for example, labour relations, rights and/or gender gaps (Burchell et al, 2014). We do not limit ourselves to either intrinsic or extrinsic features or, in turn, subjective or objective job quality indicators (Gallie, 2007). This seems a suitable strategy as we aim for a comprehensive yet job-focused scrutiny of the qualitative dimension of paid work.

There is no agreed conceptualisation or operationalisation of job quality but there has been an increasing trend towards depicting job quality in a multidimensional way (Gallie, 2007; Green, 2007; Kalleberg, 2011) including in studies that have constructed European job quality indices (Muñoz de Bustillo et al, 2011b; Eurofound, 2012; Leschke and Watt, 2014). Singular measures such as (subjective) job satisfaction and wellbeing have been shown to have little relation to other objective elements of job quality (for example, Muñoz de Bustillo and Fernández Macías, 2005; Gallie, 2007) and their policy relevance is severely limited.

Capturing multidimensional job quality draws on an interdisciplinary approach including insights from economics, sociology and other social sciences (for example, Warhurst et al, 2017). In this tradition, Green (2007) focuses on five core aspects of job quality, namely skill, work effort, personal discretion, pay and security. Similarly, Muñoz de Bustillo et al (2011b) provide a comprehensive discussion of the traditions in job quality and emphasise how they are structured by various academic disciplines, including economy, sociology, institutional approaches, occupational medicine and health and safety, and work–life balance studies. The traditional sociological approach, for example, emphasises alienation and intrinsic quality (for example, skills, autonomy, meaningfulness, social isolation) (Muñoz de Bustillo et al, 2011b). Institutional approaches often focus on segmentation and quality of employment (for example, contractual status and stability of employment). Approaches to job quality also differ within disciplines. In economics, for example, the orthodox approach focuses on labour compensation (wages) whereas more heterodox approaches are often interested in power relations (for example, collective interest representation), and behavioural economic approaches, in turn, in participation dimensions such as employee representation in the company (Muñoz de Bustillo et al, 2011b).

For the purpose of our platform such a multidisciplinary approach to job quality drawing on various social science disciplines seems most appropriate in view of the varied experiences of the unemployed.

Multidimensional job quality indices as inspirations

Job quality has often featured in second place compared to job quantity (that is, fostering higher employment rates), including on the European agenda. In spite of some EU initiatives, including the 2021 Laeken Indicators of Job Quality (for example, Muñoz de Bustillo et al, 2009) and the EU Lisbon agenda slogan 'more and better jobs (and greater social cohesion)', job quality only permeated the European policy agenda to a limited degree (Bothfeld and

Leschke, 2012). A rather limited set of job quality dimensions – particularly those pertaining to job flexibility and job security – was included in the EU flexicurity agenda from the mid-2000s onwards and was thereby also part of EU policy coordination in employment (Smith et al, 2019). The subordination of job quality is also evident in the core EU data collections in the field of labour market and social policy, namely the European Labour Force Survey (EU-LFS) and the EU statistics on income and living conditions. The European Working Conditions Survey (EWCS), in turn, though with smaller case numbers, contains comprehensive information on subjective and objective job quality across countries, sectors and occupations (see 'the Wish list of job quality dimensions and data sources for the MyLabourMarket tool section). Similarly, academic research has over-emphasised quantitative re-employment outcomes (for example, speed of re-employment, number of job offers) rather than focusing on qualitative aspects (for example, job satisfaction or fit with job) (for example, Wanberg et al, 2002; Virick and McKee-Ryan, 2014/2018).

We scrutinised comparative multidimensional European job quality indices for inspiration. Naturally, they differ slightly in the denomination of the sub-dimensions of job quality and the different variables (indicators) that make up the different sub-dimensions. Leschke et al (2008) (on the latest version of this indicator see Piasna, 2023) is based on aggregate data drawing on Eurostat data and the EWCS. Muñoz de Bustillo et al (2011b) (latest version Antón et al, 2015) and Eurofound (2012) (latest version Eurofound, 2017) are both exclusively based on individual level EWCS data, as revised from time to time. Warhurst et al (2017) conducted a thematic literature review on understanding and measuring job quality (see also Stefana et al, 2021) and highlighted the lack of an agreed definition and measure, yet substantive overlap in job quality dimensions that researchers identify. Accordingly, Warhurst et al (2017: 21) condensed the following key job quality dimensions:

- *Pay and other rewards* (wage level, non-wage fringe benefits and subjective aspects including satisfaction with pay).
- *Intrinsic characteristics of work* (objective aspects including skills, autonomy and control and subjective aspects including meaningfulness and social support).
- *Terms of employment* (objective aspects including contractual stability and career development opportunities and subjective aspects including perceptions of job security).
- *Health and safety* (physical and psycho-social risks).
- *Work–life balance* (including working time arrangements and work intensity).
- *Representation and voice* (including employee consultation and involvement and trade union representation).

This list served as a starting point for identifying relevant dimensions and indicators for the matching platform.

The job quality wishes of unemployed and job quality at re-employment

Ideally, we would additionally draw on in-depth information on what different groups of unemployed value in terms of job quality at re-employment. However, the academic literature on this is sparse. Abraham et al (2017) draw on a survey experiment on a large German population survey (Panel Study Labour Market and Social Security) which asked respondents to evaluate their willingness to accept (hypothetical) job offers with varied characteristics such as expected income, the career prospects and the difficulties of finding adequate housing at a new place of work. Unemployed were more likely to make concessions with regard to job quality, for example being willing to accept fixed-term jobs. With the same data, Auspurg and Gundert (2015) demonstrated that higher qualifications, a higher social class position and better financial resources all have strong negative impacts on the likelihood of accepting a fixed-term job. Unemployed, in turn, were more likely to accept fixed-term jobs and they required lower financial compensation for accepting such contracts than those permanently employed. Using a field experiment in the United States, Mas and Pallais (2017) study workers' willingness to pay for non-traditional work arrangements. They show that most workers: are not seeking scheduling flexibility (measured as the ability to set one's own days and times of work or to choose the number of hours one works); have preferences against employer discretion in scheduling; and value work-from-home arrangements. Interestingly enough, women are shown to have stronger preferences for flexible work arrangements. Feld et al (2020) use a discrete choice experiment separately for men and women inside a job matching centre in Cairo (Egypt). Their results show that men have a 30 per cent higher baseline wage than women. Women, in turn, require almost double the compensation than men for accepting jobs further away from their homes. Women are more sensitive to work on weekends than men.

Studies assessing job quality in re-employment outcomes commonly focus exclusively on earnings (for example, Hijzen et al, 2010). Some go beyond earnings. Brand (2006) scrutinises occupational status, job authority (supervisory position or not), employer-offered pensions and health insurance for the US context. Dieckhoff (2011) considers type of contract, job authority, job satisfaction and satisfaction with job security for selected EU countries. OECD (2013) studies earnings, non-standard work, working arrangements, job authority and fringe benefits for selected Organisation for Economic Co-operation and Development countries. Damaris and Haya (2019) focus on financial and job security as well as skills-match for the German context and Vossemer (2019) scrutinise occupational status, autonomy and job security for 34 European countries. These studies provide us with some hints as to which factors besides earnings might be relevant to include in the online matching platform.

Job quality in the context of unemployment and job seeking

When considering relevant job quality dimensions, indicators and measurement the context of the MyLabourMarket digital platform, namely (unassisted) job search processes of unemployed, need to be put centre-stage.

First, there are dimensions that are not central in the job quality literature but which are highly relevant for the specific setting. *Geographic distance of the job offer* is such an example. Geographic location is common dimension in job recommender systems (for example, Gutiérrez Hernández et al, 2019). Also, what is an acceptable geographic distance of a job offer is often laid out in job search requirements of PES as quid pro quo for unemployment benefit receipt and it can vary with the specific situation of the jobseeker (for example, dependent children and thereby constraints to geographic mobility) or get stricter with time in unemployment (Venn, 2012).

Second, there is a high likelihood that wishes for a quality job are not independent of *previous labour market experience*. To provide a simple example, when judging the adequacy of a specific wage linked to a job offer, the jobseeker will likely take a starting point in his/her previous job. Jobs which are located in the same or a similar occupational category and thus require skills close to the ones of the jobseeker are likely more relevant to be visualised than other occupations. Note, however, that occupational mobility varies according to the extent of occupational regulation in a given welfare state and occupation (for example, Longhi and Brynin, 2010; Damelang et al, 2018). The functionalities of the platform should be set in a way that unemployed who are interested in shifting occupation (which might require skills-upgrading) can easily retrieve information on jobs located in other occupations. The platform could potentially even be used to flag up relevant ALMP measures geared at skills-upgrading. Ideally, the platform would also take a starting point in the previous wage of the unemployed, however in the current setting this is not possible due to data restrictions.

Third, the *concrete situation of the unemployed* will impact his/her assessment of what is a good job. Gutiérrez Hernández et al (2019) have shown that there is a great variation in the type of information that jobseekers consider the most important. Rather than pre-setting certain dimensions by simple proxies such as gender or migration background as is commonly done in profiling models (for example, Allhutter et al [2020] for Austria; Desiere and Struyven [2020] for Belgium), an online matching platform should allow for the users to adapt the relevant functions to their perceived needs. Some users might, for example, not wish for a permanent job but rather for a trainee or apprenticeship position or a fixed-term project assignment. Some users – for example those with limited prior labour market experience, no or low education level and/or long spells of unemployment – might even be interested in jobs with characteristics that are not usually deemed as high quality.

This implies that jobseekers should have a range of options regarding job quality dimensions (user-driven approach). This consideration is particularly relevant for the labour market context of our pilot sites as precarity is a challenge particularly for young persons and migrants (see Hansen and Pultz, 2021). In some instances, precarious jobs may act as stepping stones to more favourable future labour market outcomes, though this is by no means the rule (for example, Mattijssen and Pavlopoulos, 2019).

Wish list of job quality dimensions and data sources for the MyLabourMarket tool

Informed by the job quality literature and the available European indices, we provide in Table 7A.1 in the Appendix a wish list of 24 job quality items that we view as the most important for the HECAT platform. The table also includes information on relevant data sources and where relevant variables for the respective items.

We drew both on recommendations put forward by Muñoz de Bustillo et al (2011a) and challenges outlined by Leschke and Watt (2014). These included the need to provide clear definitions of the job quality items and to be transparent with regard to data and methods used. We limited attributes to those directly related to the job itself and focused as much as possible on results rather than procedures. Also, we carefully considered the *relevance* of the single *sub-dimensions* and the *indicators* from the viewpoint of the specific users. A broad approach to job quality had to be carefully weighted by the necessity to provide a platform that is manageable and not overwhelming for the users (thus the prioritisation of items suggested below). The challenge of comparability of job quality items over time and space is relevant as the overall HECAT project's ambition was to design a platform that uses up-to-date data and is transferable to other European settings. We therefore preferred EWCS data, complemented only where strictly necessary by Slovenian register and process data from the PES. While the five-yearly rhythm of the EWCS seems appropriate as job quality is a slow moving target in 'normal times', the COVID-19 pandemic prevented a full data collection in 2020/ 2021 and the MyLabourMarket platform is currently sourced with 2015 data. A number of decisions also had to be taken on how to code response categories for categorical variables (where to pre-set cut-off points, for example, when focusing on user wishes for work intensity) and how to deal with missing values. Transparency is key here.

The items displayed in Table 7A.1 in the Appendix fall under seven job quality sub-dimensions: pay and other rewards; intrinsic characteristics of work; terms of employment; health and safety; work–life balance; representation and voice; and distance to work. We classified the items on a three-level scale, according to their importance. The first level can be referred to as 'need-to-have' information, the second and third levels as 'nice to have'. This initial choice was based on the job quality literature and indices, but also certainly uncovers some arbitrary preferences from a researcher's perspective and impacted by specific academic discipline. The jobseekers' and counsellors' perspective on job quality was assessed to some degree as part of the focus groups and interviews (Hansen and Pultz, 2023, deliverable 5.3). The next section reports on the final choice of dimensions and indicators for the prototype platform which was also driven by data availability.

Because the HECAT platform should be transferable across EU countries, we use EU survey data (Table 7A.1). Ideally, one would like to match these databases with the jobs at stake at the most disaggregate ISCO (occupation) × NACE (sector) levels. ISCO refers to the international standard classification of occupations, supported by the ILO, whereas NACE refers to the statistical classification of economic activities prepared by the EU and EUROSTAT. However, the low case numbers impede this. We recommend to privilege matching on occupations (that is, ISCO codes). Note that MLM ISCO codes are only available at the two-digit level in the EU-SILC and the EWCS.

Operationalisation through MyLabourMarket platform

This section describes our vision for the prototype platform. We allow jobseekers to identify the most relevant vacancies according to a number of filters that were selected based on our reading of the literature and in line with the wish list presented in the previous section. For the sake of simplicity, we use two levels for the filters. On the upper level, jobseekers must fill in their current location, the occupation in which they are willing to work and whether they prefer full-time or part-time work. They can search vacancies on a map using these filters only. Jobseekers also have the option to refine their search by applying additional filters based on the job quality dimensions they consider most crucial. The following options are then offered:

- autonomy and control over working tasks;
- meaningful work;
- training opportunities at work;
- career advancement;
- limited physical risks;
- limited psycho-social risks;

- standard working time;
- flexible working time; and
- worker representation.

A simply worded explanation clarifies the meaning of each of these explanations and, for General Data Protection Regulation reasons, users may click on an information button (i) to gather further information on the data work we put together to classify the vacancies.

The literature has emphasised the relevance of opening jobseekers' perspectives on online platforms similar to ours (Altmann et al, 2022; Belot et al, 2022). Building on this, we show vacancies in occupations neighbouring the one selected by the jobseeker – but still applying the relevant filters.

Figures 7A.1, 7A.2 and 7A.3 in the Appendix give an overview of how the platform may look. We use the prototype available on www.mylabourmarket. com developed in the context of the H2020 Hecat project. The map shows vacancies for the selected occupation and neighbouring ones using a colour code to highlight those that fit best the series of filters selected by the user. When clicking on a vacancy, users may see details on the advertising firm, statistics on wages to expect for this position as well as a link to apply. Some important limitations relating to data availability should be mentioned here. Job quality data mostly comes from the EWCS that provides information on ISCOs at the two-digit level. Likewise, information on wages is only available at a somewhat aggregate level. As a result, variation in job quality across vacancies is limited, which shows on the current version of the platform.

With regards to the tool tackling jobseekers' probability of exit, we provide individuals with the whole predictive curve assessing their likelihood to find a job according to the length of their unemployment spell. The interest of such tool is to provide the largest quantity of information to individuals. The downsides are that individuals need guidance to fully grasp it. The limited number of open-ended and full-time contracts in Slovenia complexified the conditioning of exits according to the type of jobs and this is left for further research.

Conclusion

Drawing on accounts of the lived experience of the unemployed in Europe and Slovenia, this chapter discusses dimensions of job quality and how they can be integrated into a platform that combines a prediction of jobseekers' probability of exit into good jobs and an individualised tool to identify relevant vacancies. We address the limitations of current online matching platforms and state-of-the-art profiling systems by proposing a multidimensional perspective on job quality. Building on the literature, we put forward a list of job quality dimensions to consider for our tool: pay and other rewards, intrinsic characteristics of work, terms of employment, health and safety, work–life balance, representation and voice and distance to work. We then offer a census of the relevant datasets in view of filling these job quality dimensions with meaning. Further, we include a subjective prioritisation of the different items ('need to have' and 'nice to have' using three different priority levels). Such a prioritisation is necessary in order not to render the platform options on job quality so complex that they will impede the easy use of the platform. Our subjective prioritisation was reviewed by the unemployed and caseworkers in the Slovenian context. Last, we operationalise this discussion and our findings into a platform that includes both a job visualisation tool and a tool allowing one to assess a time frame to secure a new job.

References

Abraham, M., Auspurg, K., Bähr, S., Frodermann, C., Gundert, S. and Hinz, T. (2017) Unemployment and willingness to accept job offers: Results of a factorial survey experiment. *Journal for Labour Market Research*, 46: 283–305.

Allhutter, D., Cech, F., Fischer, F., Grill, G. and Mager, A. (2020) Algorithmic profiling of job seekers in Austria: How austerity politics are made effective. *Frontiers in Big Data*, 3. https://doi.org/10.3389/fdata.2020.00005

Altmann, S., Glenny, A., Mahlstedt, R. and Sebald, A. (2022) The direct and indirect effects of online job search advice. *IZA Discussion Paper* No. 15830. https://ssrn.com/abstract=4310239

Antón, J.-I., Fernández-Macías, E. and Muñoz de Bustillo, L.R. (2015) *Job Quality in Europe in the First Decade of the 21st Century*. Economics Working Papers 2015–09, Department of Economics, Johannes Kepler University.

Arni, P., Caliendo, M., Künn, S. and Mahlstedt, R. (2014) *Predicting the Risk of Long-Term Unemployment: What Can We Learn from Personality Traits, Beliefs and Other Behavioral Variables*. Working Paper.

Auspurg, K. and Gundert, S. (2015) Precarious employment and bargaining power: Results of a factorial survey analysis. *Zeitschrift für Soziologie*, 44(2): 99–117.

Belot, M., Kircher, P. and Muller, P. (2022) How wage announcements affect job search: A field experiment. *American Economic Journal: Macroeconomics*, 14(4): 1–67.

Bothfeld, S. and Leschke, J. (2012) 'More and better jobs': Is quality of work still an issue – and was it ever? *Transfer: European Review of Labour and Research*, 18(3): 337–353.

Botrić, V. (2017) LTU recommendation implementation in Croatia. Presentation, Zagreb.

Brand, J.E. (2006) The effects of job displacement on job quality: Findings from the Wisconsin Longitudinal Study. *Research in Social Stratification and Mobility*, 24: 275–298.

Brixiova, Z. and Egert, B. (2012) Labour market reforms and outcomes in Estonia. Technical report, OECD, University of Paris West – Nanterre La Deefense, CESifo and WDI.

Burchell, B., Sehnbruch, K., Piasna, A. and Agloni, N. (2014) The quality of employment and decent work: Definitions, methodologies, and ongoing debates. *Cambridge Journal of Economics*, 38(2): 459–477.

Damaris, R. and Haya, S. (2019) The skill divide in post-unemployment job quality. *Social Science Research*, 82: 105–112.

Damelang, A., Stops, M. and Abraham, M. (2018) Occupations as labour market institutions: Occupational regulation and its effects on job matching and occupational closure. *Soziale Welt*, 69(4): 406–426.

Demazière, D. and Delpierre, A. (2020) Interim report on User Vision Statement. *HECAT Deliverable 1.4*. https://zenodo.org/records/7914249

Desiere, S. and Struyven, L. (2021) Using artificial intelligence to classify jobseekers: The accuracy–equity trade-off. *Journal of Social Policy*, 50(2): 367–385.

Desiere, S., Langenbucher, K. and Struyven, L. (2019) Statistical profiling in public employment services: An international comparison. *OECD Social, Employment and Migration Working Papers*, No. 224. Paris: OECD Publishing. https://doi.org/10.1787/b5e5f16e-en

Dieckhoff, M. (2011) The effect of unemployment on subsequent job quality in Europe: A comparative study of four countries. *Acta Sociologica*, 54(3): 233–249.

Eurofound (2012) *Trends in Job Quality in Europe*. Luxembourg: Publications Office of the European Union.

Eurofound (2017) *Sixth European Working Conditions Survey – Overview Report*. Luxembourg: Publications Office of the European Union.

Feld, B., Nagy, A. and Osman, A. (2020) What do jobseekers want? Estimating reservation wages and the value of job attributes. *Economic Research Forum*.

Fleischer, K. (2016) Statistically assisted profiling: Client support by appropriate tools. Presentation, Zagreb.

Gallie, D. (2007) Employment regimes and the quality of work. *Oxford Scholarship*.

Green, F. (2007) *Demanding Work: The Paradox of Job Quality in the Affluent Economy*. Princeton, NJ: Princeton University Press.

Griffin, R., Tuite, A., Roche, Z. and Gallagher, P. (2020a) Report ethical, social, theological, technical review of 1st generation PES algorithms and data use. *HECAT Deliverable 1.3*. https://zenodo.org/records/7913459

Griffin, R., Boland, T., Tuite, A., and Hennessy, A. (2020b) Electric dreams of welfare in the 4th Industrial Revolution: An actor-network investigation and genealogy of an algorithm. In *Digitisation and Precarisation* (pp 181–203). Wiesbaden: Springer VS.

Gutiérrez, F., Charleer, S., De Croon, R., Htun, N.N., Goetschalckx, G. and Verbert, K. (2019) Explaining and exploring job recommendations: A user-driven approach for interacting with knowledge-based job recommender systems. In *Proceedings of the 13th ACM Conference on Recommender Systems* (pp 60–68).

Gutiérrez Hernández, F., Charleer, S., De Croon, R., Htun, N.N, Goetschalckx, G. and Verbert, K. (2019) Explaining and exploring job recommendations: A user-driven approach for interacting with knowledge-based job recommender systems. *Proceedings of the 13th ACM Conference on Recommender Systems* (pp 60–68), Copenhagen.

Hansen, M.P. and Pultz, S. (2021) Detailed user context document Slovenia. *HECAT Deliverable 1.1.* https://zenodo.org/records/7908567

Hansen, M.P. and Pultz, S. (2023) Report on data collected during and after piloting including benchmarking: Sociological report. *HECAT Deliverable 5.3.* https://zenodo.org/records/11210171

Hijzen, A., Upward, R. and Wright, P. (2010) The income losses of displaced workers. *The Journal of Human Resources*, 45(1): 243–269.

Kalleberg, A. (2011) *Good Jobs, Bad Jobs: The Rise of Polarized and Precarious Employment Systems in the United States, 1970s–2000s.* New York: Russell Sage Foundation.

Kern, C., Bach, R.L., Mautner, H. and Kreuter, F. (2021) 'Fairness in Algorithmic Profiling: A German Case Study': ArXiv:2108.04134.

Leschke, J. and Watt, A. (2014) Challenges in constructing a multidimensional European job quality index. *Social Indicators Research*, 118(1): 1–31.

Leschke, J., Watt, A. and Finn, M. (2008) Putting a number on job quality? Constructing a European job quality index. *Working Paper, 2008.03.* Brussels: European Trade Union Institute.

Lipp, R. (2005) Job seeker profiling: The Australian experience. EU-Profiling Seminar.

Longhi, S. and Brynin, M. (2010) Occupational change in Britain and Germany. *Labour Economics*, 17: 655–666.

Loxha, A. and Morgandi, M. (2014) Profiling the unemployed: A review of OECD experiences and implications for emerging economics. Technical report, Social Protection and Labour No 1424.

Mas, A. and Pallais, A. (2017) Valuing alternative work arrangements. *American Economic Review*, 107(12): 3722–3759.

Mattijssen, L. and Pavlopoulos, D. (2019) A multichannel typology of temporary employment careers in the Netherlands: Identifying traps and stepping stones in terms of employment and income security. *Social Science Research*, 77: 101–114.

Ministry of Social Development (2018) *Implementation Plan: Client Service Matching Effectiveness Model.* Wellington City: Ministry of Social Development.

Muñoz de Bustillo, L.R. and Fernández Macías, E. (2005) Job satisfaction as an indicator of the quality of work. *The Journal of Socio-Economics*, 34(5): 656–673.

Muñoz de Bustillo, L.R., Fernández Macías, E., Antón, J.E. and Esteve, F. (2009) *Indicators of Job Quality in the European Union*. Study prepared for the European Parliament, Department of Employment and Social Affairs.

Muñoz de Bustillo, L.R., Fernández Macías, E., Esteve, F. and Antón, J.E. (2011a) E pluribus unum? A critical survey of job quality indicators. *Socio-Economic Review*, 9(3): 447–475.

Muñoz de Bustillo, L.R., Fernández Macías, E., Esteve, F. and Antón, J.E (2011b) *Measuring More Than Money: The Social Economics of Job Quality*. Cheltenham: Edward Elgar.

Næsborg-Andersen, A., Frid-Nielsen, S., Leschke, J. and Brébion, C. (2021) Technical report data sources and data protection for algorithm development. *HECAT Deliverable 2.2*. https://zenodo.org/records/7914776

O'Connell, P.J., McGuinness, S. and Kelly, E. (2012) The transition from short- to long-term unemployment: A statistical profiling model for Ireland. *The Economic and Social Review*, 43(1): 135–164.

OECD (2013) Back to work: Re-employment, earnings, and skill use after job displacement. In *OECD Employment Outlook* (ch 4). Paris: OECD.

OECD (2019a), *Strengthening Active Labour Market Policies in Italy, Connecting People with Jobs*. Paris: OECD Publishing. https://doi.org/10.1787/160a3c28-en

OECD (2019b), *Evaluating Latvia's Active Labour Market Policies, Connecting People with Jobs*. Paris: OECD Publishing. https://doi.org/10.1787/6037200a-en

O'Reilly, J., Leschke, J., Ortlieb, R., Seeleib-Kaiser, M. and Villa, P. (eds) (2019) *Youth Labor in Transition: Inequalities, Mobility, and Policies in Europe*. Oxford: Oxford University Press.

OWAL Group (2019) *Artificial Intelligence in Employment Services: A Mapping Final Report*. Helsinki: Ministry of Economic Affairs and Employment.

Piasna, A. (2023) Job quality in turbulent times: An update of the European Job Quality Index. *Working Paper 2023.05*, European Trade Union Institute.

Ponomareva, N. and Sheen, J. (2013) Australian labor market dynamics across the ages. *Economic Modelling*, 35: 453–463.

Smith, M., Leschke, J., Russell, H. and Villa, P. (2019) Stressed economies, distressed policies, and distraught young people: European policies and outcomes from a youth perspective. In J. O'Reilly, J. Leschke, R. Ortlieb, M. Seeleib-Kaiser and P. Villa (eds) *Youth Labor in Transition: Inequalities, Mobility and Policies in Europe* (pp 104–131). Oxford: Oxford University Press.

Stefana, E., Marciano, F., Rossi, D. and Cocca, P. (2021) Composite indicators to measure quality of working life in Europe: a systematic review. *Social Indicators Research*, 157: 1047–1078.

van den Berg, G. and Vikström, J. (2014) Monitoring job offer decisions, punishments, exit to work, and job quality. *The Scandinavian Journal of Economics*, 116(2): 284–334.

Van Ours, J. (2007) Compulsion in active labour market programmes. *National Institute Economic Review*, 202(1): 67–78.

Vansteenkiste, S., Verbruggen, M. and Sels, L. (2016) Flexible job search behaviour among unemployed jobseekers: antecedents and outcomes. *European Journal of Work and Organizational Psychology*, 25(6): 862–882.

Venn, D. (2012) Eligibility criteria for unemployment benefits: Quantitative indicators for OECD and EU countries. *OECD Social, Employment and Migration Working Papers* No. 131. Paris: OECD.

Virick, M. and McKee-Ryan, F. (2014/2018) Reemployment quality, underemployment, and career outcomes. In U. Klehe and E. van Hooft (eds) *The Oxford Handbook of Job Loss and Job Search* (pp 359–376). Oxford: Oxford Library of Psychology.

Vossemer, J. (2019) The effects of unemployment on non-monetary job quality in Europe: The moderating role of economic situation and labor market policies. *Social Indicators Research*, 144(1): 379–401.

Wanberg, C.R., Hough, L.M. and Song, Z. (2002) Predictive validity of a multidisciplinary model of reemployment success. *Journal of Applied Psychology*, 87(6): 1100–1120.

Warhurst, C., Wright, S. and Lyonette, C. (2017) Understanding and measuring job quality: Part 1 – thematic literature review. *IER Research Report*. Coventry: Institute for Employment Research, University of Warwick.

Wijnhoven, M.A. and Havinga, H. (2014) The Work Profiler: A digital instrument for selection and diagnosis of the unemployed. *Local Economy*, 29(6–7): 740–749.

Table 7A.1: Classifying and measuring the characteristics of jobs in the HECAT platform

	Notes under the table	Indicator	Value	Order of importance	Database (1st best)	Variables	Database (2nd best)	Variables	Database (3rd best)	Variables
	(1)	(2)	(3)	(4)	(5)	(6)	(7)	(8)	(9)	(10)
Pay and other rewards	(a)	Wage compared to previous occupation	Low; similar (+/- 10 %); high	1	National register data		EU-LFS – match at the ISCO 3 digit level	INCDECIL	EU-SILC – match at the ISCO 2 digit level	PY010G, PY020G
Intrinsic characteristics of work	(b)	Skills matching	ISCO code compared to the previous occupation	1	National register data		EU-LFS – match according to a transitional graph (see comment)	ISCO3D	EU-SILC – match according to a transitional graph (see comment)	PL051
	(c)	Educational requirement	Underqualified; qualified; overqualified	2	National register data		EU-LFS – match at the ISCO 3 digit level	HAT11LEV	EU-SILC – match at the ISCO 2 digit level	PE040
	(d)	Autonomy and control	Such as perceived by workers in the same ISCO	3	EWCS – match at the ISCO 2 digit level	Q54A-C; Q42; Q53B-C; Q61C; Q61N				
	(e)	Meaningfulness of the job	Such as perceived by workers in the same ISCO	3	EWCS – match at the ISCO 2 digit level	Q61H-J				
Terms of employment	(f)	Type of contract	Self-employed or dependent work. If dependent, then (i) permanent standard contract; (ii) fixed standard contract; (iii) trainee; or (iv) apprenticeship	1	National register data		EU-LFS – match at the ISCO 3 digit level	STAPRO, TEMP, TEMPREAS	EU-SILC – match at the ISCO 2 digit level	PL040, PL140, PL031

Table 7A.1: Classifying and measuring the characteristics of jobs in the HECAT platform (continued)

Notes under the table	Indicator	Value	Order of importance	Database (1st best)	Variables	Database (2nd best)	Variables	Database (3rd best)	Variables
(1)	(2)	(3)	(4)	(5)	(6)	(7)	(8)	(9)	(10)
(g)	Job security (objective)	Probability to remain employed for more than 12 months	2	Computed using the register data		EU-LFS – match at the ISCO 3 digit level	WSTAT1Y		
(h)		Probability that the establishment closes in the next 6 months	3	Computed using the register data					
(i)	Job security (subjective)	Job security – such as perceived by workers in the same sector	3	EWCS – match at the ICSO 2 digit level	Q89G-H				
(j)	Career advancement opportunities (Objective)	Sum of expected earnings over 5 years	3	Computed using the register data (average earnings over 5 years of individuals in the same isco)					
(k)	Career advancement opportunities (Subjective)	Career advancement opportunities – such as perceived by workers in the same ISCO	3	EWCS – match at the ISCO 2 digit level	Q89 – B				

(continued)

Table 7A.1: Classifying and measuring the characteristics of jobs in the HECAT platform (continued)

	Notes under the table	Indicator	Value	Order of importance	Database (1st best)	Variables	Database (2nd best)	Variables	Database (3rd best)	Variables
	(1)	(2)	(3)	(4)	(5)	(6)	(7)	(8)	(9)	(10)
	(l)	Training opportunities	Employers normally offer training courses	3	EU-LFS – match at the ISCO 3 digit level	COURATT, COURWORH	EWCS – match at the ISCO 2 digit level	Q66		
Health and safety	(m)	Physical risks	Sector with a high incidence of work accidents	3	European statistics on accidents at work – only available at the NACE 1 digit level	HSW_N2_01, HSW_N2_02	EU-LFS – adhoc module 2013 – match at the ISCO 2 digit level	AWNUMBR, AWDOFF, PHYSRISK	EWCS – match at the ISCO 2 digit level	Q83A, Q83B, Q29 A-I, Q30 A-C
	(n)	Psycho-social risks	Work negatively affects mental health	3	EU-LFS – adhoc module 2013 – match at the ISCO 2 digit level	MENTRISK	EWCS – match at the ISCO 2 digit level	Q81 A-C, Q80 A-D, Q45A		
Work–life balance	(o)	Working time	Full-time (> 30 hours a week or number of hours not provided in the contract); Part-time (16–30 hours) or Marginal (< 15 hours)	1	Register data		EU-LFS – match at the ISCO 3 digit level	VARIABLE HWUSUAL	EU-SILC	PL060
	(p)	Non-standard working time	Work at night or during weekends	1	EU-LFS – match at the ISCO 3 digit level	NIGHTWK, SATWK, SUNWK	EWCS – match at the ISCO 2 digit level	Q37A, Q37B, Q37C		

Table 7A.1: Classifying and measuring the characteristics of jobs in the HECAT platform (continued)

	Notes under the table	Indicator	Value	Order of importance	Database (1st best)	Variables	Database (2nd best)	Variables	Database (3rd best)	Variables
	(1)	(2)	(3)	(4)	(5)	(6)	(7)	(8)	(9)	(10)
	(q)	Involuntary part-time work	Yes/No	2	EU-LFS – match at the ISCO 3 digit level	FTPTREAS	EU-SILC – match at the ISCO 2 digit level	PL120		
	(r)	Flexibility of working time	Important/limited	3	EU-LFS – adhoc module 2019 – match at the ISCO 3 digit level	VARIWT	EWCS – match at the ISCO 2 digit level	Q42		
	(s)	Home office	Frequency	3	EU-LFS – match at the ISCO 3 digit level	HOMEWK				
Representation and voice	(t)	Collective bargaining coverage	Share of workers that are covered in the occupation	2	Register data					
	(u)	Trade union density	Share of workers that are covered in the occupation	2	Register data					
	(v)	Representation at the firm level	Share of workers that are covered in the occupation	2	Register data					

(continued)

Table 7A.1: Classifying and measuring the characteristics of jobs in the HECAT platform (continued)

	Notes under the table	Indicator	Value	Order of importance	Database (1st best)	Variables	Database (2nd best)	Variables	Database (3rd best)	Variables
	(1)	(2)	(3)	(4)	(5)	(6)	(7)	(8)	(9)	(10)
	(w)	Self-assessed quality of employer–employee relations	Share of workers that are covered in the occupation	2	EWCS – match at the ISCO 2 digit level	Q70 B,C,F				
Distance to work	(x)	Distance to work	Distance in kilometres between home and work	1	Register data					

Note: (a) EU-LFS and EWCS provide net wages; EU-SILC provides gross wages. Note that the variation +/- 10 per cent does not have the same implications for the bottom and the top of the distribution.

(b) Skill matching should be assessed by using a transitional graph highlighting the most usual job-to-job transitions.

(d), (e), (m), (n), (p) inspiration for the EWCS data partly comes from Muñoz et al (2011b).

(m) Regarding the EU-LFS data, one should either use q83a and q83b OR q29 and q30. We see the former as strongly dependent on the institutional setting (due to a variation in the ease of access to health insurance, in whether self-employed workers have access to sick leave, and so on) to the extent that figures could artificially be very low in some settings. We would therefore privilege q29 and q30 over q83a and q83b.

Regarding the European statistics on accidents at work, the data can be found on the Eurostat website. More information here.

(m), (n) EU-LFS data come from the 2013 adhoc module on Health and Safety at Work (the adhoc module was also run in 2020 but the data is not available at the time of writing). It is run on a subsample of observations – that is larger than the EWCS database.

(q) We define involuntary part-time jobs with reference to individuals who state that they could not find a full-time job, thereby excluding childcare or family reasons which might also underlie involuntary part-time. This is the most conservative measure, and we acknowledge that households act within institutional constraints that can limit their ability to take on full-time jobs.

(t), (u), (v) No EU survey data provide detailed measure of these variables at a disaggregate level.

Source: Authors' computations

Figure 7A.1: Example of a search

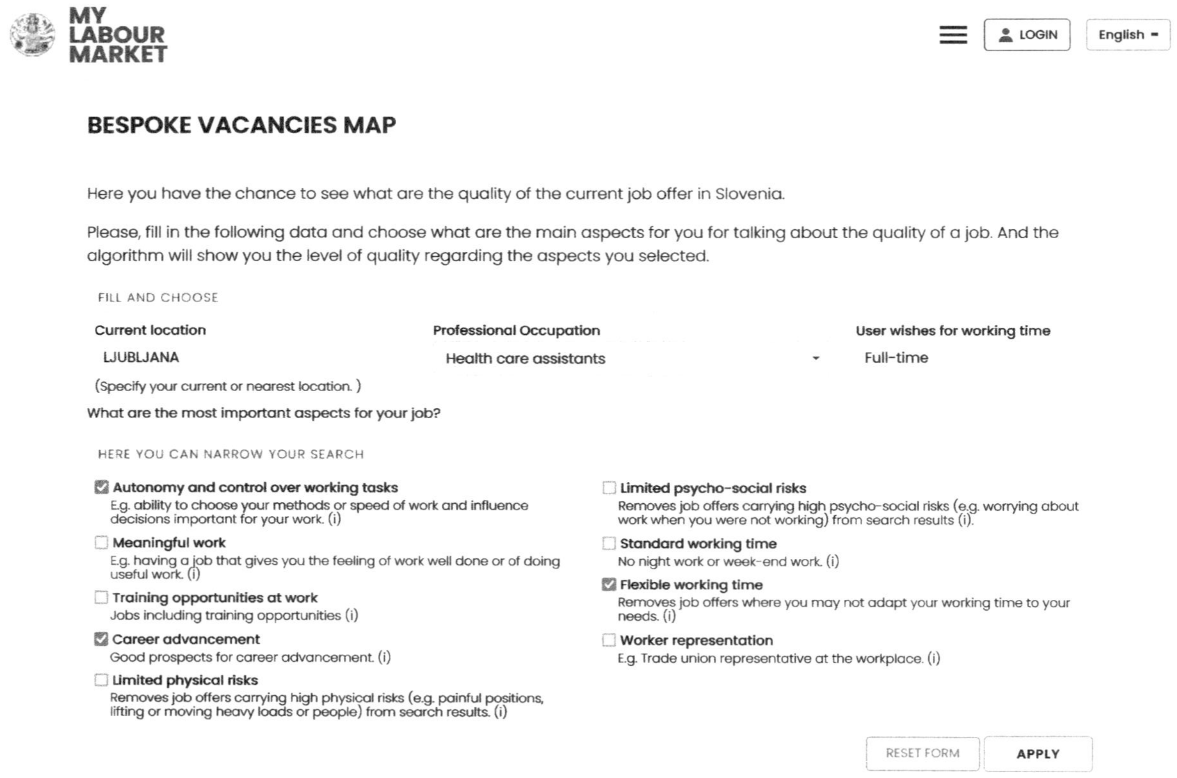

Figure 7A.2: Results of the search

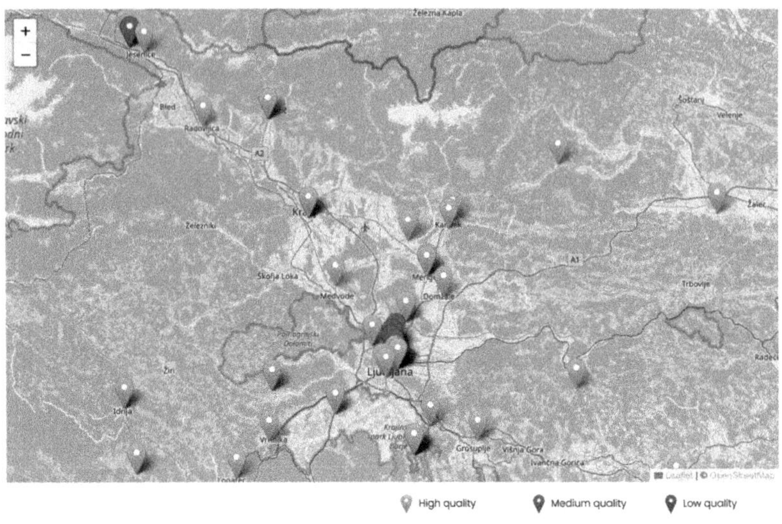

Health care assistants

	POSITIONTITLE	LOCATION	HOURS PER WEEK	PAYAND OTHER REWARDS	JOB WORKING TIME	DISTANCETO WORK	AVERAGE EARNINGS
	BOLNICARV URGENTNI IN OPERATIVNI DEJAVNOSTI TER INTENZIVNI TERAPIJI (E034004) ZA POTREBE UKC LJUBLJANA, PEDIATRICNA KLINIKA, KO INTENZIVNE TERAPIJE OTROK-M/Z	LJUBLJANA	40	similar	Full-time	near location	879.0€
	OSKRBOVALKA - M/Z	LJUBLJANA	40	similar	Full-time	near location	879.0€
	OSKRBOVALKA - M/Z	LJUBLJANA	40	similar	Full-time	near location	879.0€
	OSKRBOVALKA - M/Z	LJUBLJANA	40	similar	Full-time	near location	879.0€
	BOLNICAR - NEGOVALEC - M/z	LJUBLJANA	40	similar	Full-time	near location	879.0€
	OSKRBOVALKA - M/Z	LJUBLJANA	40	similar	Full-time	near location	879.0€
	OSKRBOVALKA - M/Z	LJUBLJANA	40	similar	Full-time	near location	879.0€
	BOLNICAR V URGENTNI IN OPERATIVNI DEJAVNOSTI TER INTENZIVNI TERAPIJI (SIFRA DM: 34004) ZA POTREBE UKC LJUBLJANA, KIRURSKA KLINIKA, OPERACIJSKI BLOK -M/Z	LJUBLJANA	40	similar	Full-time	near location	879.0€
	BOLNICAR - NEGOVALEC - M/Z	LJUBLJANA	40	similar	Full-time	near location	879.0€

Figure 7A.2: Results of the search (continued)

Home-based personal care workers

POSITION TITLE	LOCATION	HOURS PER WEEK	PAY AND OTHER REWARDS	JOB WORKING TIME	DISTANCE TO WORK	AVERAGE EARNINGS
VARUHINJA VODENJE, VARSTVO IN ZAPOSLITEV POD POSEBNIMI POGOJI – M/Ž	LJUBLJANA	40	similar	Full-time	near location	807.0€
VARUHINJA II – M/Ž	LJUBLJANA	40	similar	Full-time	near location	807.0€
VARUH – M/Ž	LJUBLJANA	40	similar	Full-time	near location	807.0€
OSEBNI ASISTENT – M/Ž	LJUBLJANA	40	similar	Full-time	near location	807.0€
VARUHINJA VODENJE, VARSTVO IN ZAPOSLITEV POD POSEBNIMI POGOJI – M/Ž	LJUBLJANA	40	similar	Full-time	near location	807.0€
OSEBNI/A ASISTENT/KA – M/Ž	LJUBLJANA	40	similar	Full-time	near location	807.0€
SPREMLJEVALEC SKUPINE V ZAVODU ZA GIBALNO OVIRANE OTROKE IN MLADOSTNIKE – M/Ž	LJUBLJANA	40	similar	Full-time	near location	807.0€
OSEBNI ASISTENT INVALIDNI OSEBI – M/Ž	LJUBLJANA	40	similar	Full-time	near location	807.0€
VARUHINJA INSTITUCIONALNO VARSTVO (TER	LJUBLJANA	40	similar	Full-time	near location	807.0€
OSEBNI ASISTENT – M/Ž	LJUBLJANA	20	similar	Part-time	near location	807.0€
OSEBNI ASISTENT – M/Ž	LJUBLJANA	20	similar	Part-time	near location	807.0€
OSEBNI ASISTENT INVALIDNI OSEBI – M/Ž	LJUBLJANA	30	similar	Part-time	near location	807.0€
OSEBNI/A ASISTENT/KA – M/Ž	LJUBLJANA	20	similar	Part-time	near location	807.0€
OSEBNI/A ASISTENT/KA – M/Ž	LENART	20	similar	Part-time	far location	807.0€
OSEBNI ASISTENT – M/Ž	ŠKOFJA LOKA	30	similar	Part-time	far location	807.0€
OSEBNI ASISTENT GIBALNO OVIRANI OSEBI – M/Ž	TOLMIN	20	similar	Part-time	far location	807.0€
VARUH NEGOVALEC – M/Ž	NOVA GORICA	32	similar	Part-time	far location	807.0€
OSEBNI ASISTENT – M/Ž	CERKNICA	10	similar	Part-time	far location	807.0€

Figure 7A.3: Details when clicking on a vacancy

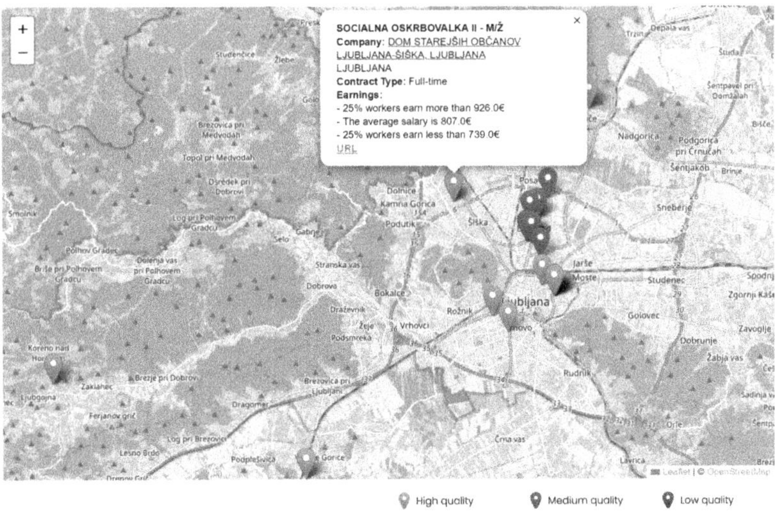

8

Looking for a job: what types of information matter to jobseekers?

Didier Demazière

Introduction

The digitalisation of public employment services is resulting in major changes in the way jobseekers are supported. Traditionally, public employment services (PES) advisers have been on the front line, guiding and directing jobseekers in their search for work. With digitalisation, the human and relational dimension is weakening; jobseekers are receiving targeted information that is supposedly appropriate to their situation, which will have been analysed by artificial intelligence algorithms. But this smooth and fluid pattern could be seriously disrupted: what guarantee is there that the information relevant to the machine will be perceived as such by the unemployed? Fieldwork carried out in PES in Germany (Clouet, 2022), France (Lavitry, 2015), Belgium (Demazière and Zune, 2021), Poland and Sweden (Garsten et al, 2016), as well as more widely across Europe and the United States (Eichhorst et al, 2008), show recurring disagreements and differences of viewpoints between advisers and unemployed people. Because they involve human actors, these tensions can only be eased or resolved through debate and negotiation – that is, through the very social interaction that digitalisation tends to eliminate.

The importance of this relational dimension suggests that the relevance of advice or information is not a quality intrinsic to it: rather, it depends on the social context in which the advice is given (or the information transmitted). In other words, the information that unemployed people receive during their job search is more than just external data. It is inextricably linked to the judgements, evaluations and interpretations produced by unemployed people in interaction with others, in order to guide themselves and conduct their job search. We will explore this avenue by looking at a type of information rarely considered in job search analyses: targets, that is, the jobs that unemployed people are looking for, the opportunities that make sense to them, or those that they overlook. Our hypothesis is that the value and the relevance of information depends less on its quantity, which can be amplified by the use of digital tools, than on the social conditions in which it is produced and delivered.

Our research relies on in-depth interview fieldwork, conducted in France with around 60 jobseekers to study how they identify the occupational targets relevant to them. Rather than addressing job search methods, as most of the literature on job search does (Bachmann and Baumgarten, 2013; Manroop and Richardson, 2016; Van Hoye, 2018), our analysis focuses on *what* unemployed people look for, as opposed to *how* they look for a job. Unlike the quality of job vacancies advertised on the labour market or the quality of jobs obtained by the unemployed (Bethmann, 2013; Brand, 2015), the qualities of jobs targeted or sought after by unemployed people is under-researched. Little is known about the ways in which the unemployed define their targets nor how they revise them in order to increase their chances of leaving unemployment, for example, by widening their targets, lowering their expectations, anticipating a deterioration in their future job, preparing a career turning point, and so on. Yet these questions are crucial, especially in contexts – such as contemporary France and most European countries in general – where forms of employment are diversifying (employment contracts, self-employment, subsidised jobs), non-standard employment is on the rise (Lind and Møller, 2018) and employment status is becoming more precarious (Rodgers and Rodgers, 1989; Kalleberg and Vallas, 2017; Lewchuk, 2017).

The central issue is to explore the mechanisms used to value (and devalue) the information jobseekers receive: what is important to them, and for what reasons, and what do they neglect or disregard? At a time when support for jobseekers is increasingly based on digital tools, these questions are crucial. Even more, digital search tools' information increasingly is based on the profile of the unemployed. The tools collect a great deal of information on both jobseekers and labour markets with a view to passing it on to those seeking employment. But the significance of the data and information disseminated depends how unemployed people interpret and value it. This is why we need to better understand how unemployed people reason, and how, in their job search, they value certain information – and only that information.

Job search is traditionally conceptualised as a set of behaviours aimed at acquiring information about job opportunities and offers. The economic theory of job search sees it as a rational investment in information (Stigler, 1962). To make their job search 'profitable' (Cahuc et al, 2014), jobseekers gather information in order to identify the jobs closest to their preferences. They analyse the information and discard those that fall short of their preferences – or more precisely, their 'reservation wage' (Kiefer and Neumann, 1979) – that is, the minimum wage at which rationality dictates acceptance of a job offer. It is a mechanism that leads to a revision of initial preferences. The longer the time spent unemployed, the worse the benefit and the lower the employability, so that getting a job gradually becomes a more pressing objective. The jobseeker is then led to revise the expected gains from future employment downwards and accept a lower-paid job. Unemployed people must therefore interpret the information they gather about available jobs. However, since their evaluation is modelled according to a rule of rational optimisation, it is not the subject of empirical studies. From this perspective, the digitalisation of services for unemployed people, and the development of artificial intelligence tools, would be an exercise in efficiency: they make it possible to deliver information to jobseekers that is both more reliable and more relevant, and this will trigger rational adjustments to their job search.

However, the postulate of rational optimisation has the flaw of being only a postulate. Information about job opportunities doesn't just fall from the sky; it circulates in relational networks that also help shape its meaning. Sociologists have made this point repeatedly. Some stress the importance of developing contacts, investing in relational networks, building up 'social capital' (Lin et al, 2001), making the 'extraordinary effort' (Lin, 2001: 53) that promotes access to better jobs (Van Hoye et al, 2009). Others indicate that information circulates through a wide variety of social relationships, such as 'weak ties' (Granovetter, 1973), which are not necessarily activated with the goal of finding a job (McDonald and Elder, 2006). In this way, any social interaction, any exchange with others, or indeed any space for sociability is relevant. And classic fieldwork has clearly shown that information flows are also part of belonging to groups and communities which are not the product of networking strategies, but rather inherited from the paths taken by unemployed people (their family, local acquaintances, former colleagues, and so on). As such, they are characterised by the social proximity of their members, and are located within restricted territories (Bakke, 1933).

Moreover, information acquires meaning as it circulates: the accumulation of information cannot be thought of independently of the attribution of meaning. Little research has been done on the interpretation of information collected or received during the job search: how do unemployed people reason, how do they assign (or disallow) value to it? In our view, this process of evaluation is a diffuse phenomenon, dependent on the many events that punctuate the job search (Gabriel et al, 2013; Sharone, 2013), as well as on exchanges and encounters with various other people (Demazière, forthcoming). Receiving no reply to an application, observing former colleagues finding new jobs more quickly than you, feeling humiliated at a recruitment interview, being offered a much lower salary than you had, being encouraged by a career adviser to consider part-time work, being questioned by friends and family about the achievability of your objectives – all of these are ordinary episodes in the course of the job search. They fuel the unemployed person's reflection – on where they fit in the labour market, on the relevance of their occupational targets, and on their chances of success. Job seeking necessarily involves a wide variety of interactions, with employers, recruiters, advisers, trainers, family and friends, and other unemployed people. Each interaction is a vehicle for the circulation of information, which is to say, in accordance with our perspective, for evaluation of the information circulating.

Our study of these processes is based on in-depth interviews with 57 jobseekers and eight advisers from a local PES agency. The fieldwork was carried out at the end of the last decade in an area of northern France marked since the 1980s by deindustrialisation and persistently high unemployment (+3 points in comparison to the national average). The fieldwork with jobseekers was carried out in 2017 and 2018. As Table 8.1 shows, the interviewees varied in terms of sex, age, duration of unemployment,

Table 8.1: Characteristics of the unemployed interview

Sex	Men	28
	Women	29
Age	Under 30	11
	Between 30 and 39	19
	Between 40 and 49	18
	50 and over	9
Duration of unemployment	Between 8 and 11 months	15
	Between 12 and 18 months	23
	Between 19 and 24 months	14
	Over 24 months	5
Level of training	No qualifications	14
	Vocational secondary school qualification	11
	Baccalaureate (8 of which were 'vocational')	15
	Qualification representing 2 years of higher education	8
	Qualification representing at least 3 years of higher education	9
Family situation	Alone	20
	Alone with dependent children	10
	With a partner without children	9
	With a partner and dependent children	18
Employment prior to unemployment	Identified themselves as managers (in banking and insurance,	6
	chemicals, retail trade, logistics)	9
	In intermediate occupations (technician, salesman, site manager,	21
	accountant, social worker)	20
	Employees (in business services such as cleaning, security, transport,	1
	or in personal services such as home help, or in retail trade)	
	Industrial workers (in more or less qualified positions in	
	the plastics, automobile, logistics, food-processing and	
	mechanical industries)	
	Shopkeeper who went bankrupt	
Unemployment benefit	Unemployment insurance benefit (550 to 2200 euros)	32
	'Active solidarity income' (530 to 910 euros)	14
	No benefit	11

education levels, family situation, previous job and unemployment benefit status.

The interview guide was designed to foster a conversational exchange, encourage and support a reflective posture, and help interviewees to formulate their stories as personal histories (Forster, 2012). To this end, few specific questions were included, although a number of major themes were addressed: career path, job-seeking activities and how they evolved over time, key experiences during unemployment, hopes and disappointments, and visions of the future. We have paid particular attention here to the informational aspect of the job search, with the aim of understanding what information marks out the job search of an unemployed person: how they categorise and evaluate the information with which they are confronted and by which processes certain information comes to both matter, and gain credibility, in the job search.

Interviews with advisers were carried out in 2019. The aim was to understand how they advised the unemployed in their job search, especially in defining targets and expectations, prioritising opportunities and preferences. This made it possible to gather their perceptions of the reasoning and of jobseekers. To do this, we fed part of the interview grid with the results of the fieldwork with unemployed people. Eight of the 11 advisors working at the local PES agency agreed to be interviewed. Their profiles are varied (five women, three men, one in her 30s, four in their 40s, three in their 50s), and they have been working for the PES for quite some time (over 16 years for seven of them).

Our analysis shows that unemployed people attach particular significance to information about the job targets they are aiming for, in terms of occupation, sector of activity, contract, location, and so on. In the course of their job search, they define and redesign their own job market. Our aim here is to identify the main mechanisms for adjusting or consolidating the labour markets, rather than to analyse their properties. We have identified three processes in which a value is assigned to information during the job search, which are differentiated by the status that particular information acquires through social interactions, and consequently by the value or relevance accorded to it. In the first case, it becomes indisputable matter of course to which the unemployed person submits; in the second, it becomes credible knowledge which is embraced by the unemployed person; in the third, it becomes a shared belief to which the unemployed person adheres.

The imposition of indisputable matter of course

Some of the information mentioned by the unemployed people we interviewed about their place in the job market and their career aspirations is expressed as indisputable matter of course, a truism that can't be ignored: 'That was the moment I realised my craft was dead', 'I was knocked back mercilessly', 'In that job interview, I hit a wall', 'What I heard called everything into question', 'The guy put an end to my ambition'. Since this is information that cannot be questioned, it has a direct and powerful impact on the unemployed person's job search – particularly when it suddenly closes off avenues hitherto pursued. This is information imposed without discussion, or that ends up shutting down any discussion because it is delivered within the framework of a relationship of authority. Unemployed people interact with those who have power over them – in particular, the power to hire or fire them, but also to validate or invalidate their aspirations. Relational asymmetry is the mainspring of the imposition of the obvious.

In describing their job search, some unemployed people talk about turning points that correspond to the specific episodes that led them to see their job market, and their position within it, differently. Often, it was a meeting with an employer or recruiter, or sometimes a career adviser, that 'took the wind out of their sails', as one of the interviewees put it. The most explicit cases correspond to the formulation of sentences or convictions that both disqualify the prospects envisaged up to that point and result in the unemployed person being expelled from the labour market. While the process of imposition can take the form of a brutal shock, it can also be the result of receiving the same information over and over again, the meaning of which gradually becomes clear. In this case, relentless reiteration serves to reinforce the weightiness of the information, transforming it into unshakeable certainty. The two stories outlined next illustrate these two scenarios.

Odile, 54, spent more than 20 years working as a mechanical engineer, until she was made redundant and went through a 'bad period' during which she divorced and 'lost the plot'. Then she found another job, this time as a floor manager at a department store. She remains somewhat ambivalent about this change of direction, which she describes as one 'that I chose, well no, it's not quite that. Basically, yes, all the same'. A year ago, she lost her job again. Determined to 'fight to get back on her feet', she is looking for the same type of job. Though she was initially both enthusiastic and optimistic, she later began to express increasingly intrusive doubts. She recounts having been 'destroyed' by a recruiter who told her that it was 'really respectable to still believe in yourself at your age'. This had aroused an impotent revolt in her: 'At the time, I could have ripped his tongue out. That's right. What else could I do? I can't fight it. I don't have the means.' She came to see her age as a disabling factor that marginalises and blocks her, an insurmountable obstacle on the road to employment: 'Age, you can't change it, can you? It's like a handicap, that's how I see it. Whatever you try, it's something that's there and you can't hide it. It's like the nose on your face.' Ever since, she has defined her situation in terms of her age, seeing it as something there is just no way around. In so doing, she has internalised the brutal sentence handed down to her in the course of a single job application.

Elodie is a 35-year-old professional make-up artist who has worked in the cultural and fashion sectors and has gradually internalised the oft-repeated idea that there were no more jobs in her field. After around ten years, she took maternity leave twice – a three-year break. She points out while that her family responsibilities make it difficult to hold down a job with irregular hours, she is proud of her ability to 'manage everything at the same time, I know how. I don't see that as a problem. It's a question of organisation, where there's a need, there's a need, I can manage'. She is however concerned about the feedback she has received on an application: not that there's any problem with her profile, but she is told time and again that jobs are becoming scarce: 'It gave me a strange impression of, how can I put it? I kept hearing the same story about the sector being in crisis, there being no more work … two, three times, twenty times, it was getting worrying.' As a result, she refocused her job search on members of her network, with whom she could have more open and frank exchanges. This provided her with both confirmation of the difficulties in the sector, and more precise information: 'I do know some people. But still, nothing came of it. There's no more money. It's all about cutting costs, so they don't hire make-up artists anymore. I hadn't understood. And then I realised, well, savings, they'd rather pay overtime than, well, that's a shock.' In Elodie's case, the shock results from repetition of the same information over and over again, rather than being crystallised in a single interaction, eventually leading to the realisation that there is no longer a place for her: 'It's a crazy thing, it's as if I no longer fit in. I leave, I come back, it's over. You have to come to terms with it, but it's not that easy.' Elodie finds it hard to accept the information she has received, yet she has internalised it, and accepts that there is no possibility of contesting it; it has imposed itself on her.

Certain information can be described as *indisputable* matter of course precisely because it is imposed on jobseekers, without them being able to avoid it. They are subjected to it and submitted to it because it is an expression of market forces, mediated by actors in positions of authority. These last have the power to redefine the unemployed person's position on the labour market, to objectify it via reformulation – either abruptly, or in a more courteous (but no less definitive) way. In the event that certain information becomes indisputable matter of course, it is because it provides answers to (or explanations for) the growing uncertainties encountered by unemployed people in their job search. The emergence and affirmation of these uncertainties are probably more pronounced in areas of high unemployment, such as the one where the fieldwork was carried out. This matter of course legitimises a pessimistic view of the chances of getting a job, and, at least where they are seeking to stay in a role similar to their previous one, underlines the need among unemployed people to find explanations for their situation – a need that becomes exacerbated, the harder the person struggles to find work.

Negotiating credible knowledge

Some information is procured in situations that are explicitly dedicated to managing the job search: during interviews with advisers, for example, or with others who have expertise in a trade or sector. Information thus received can acquire the status of substantiated, well-argued knowledge with strong credibility. It can give rise to both agreement and disagreement, and is generally the subject of deliberation, either with others or as part of a reflective process, as illustrated by the following expressions: 'I kept it in the back of my mind, and little by little it made its way into my head', 'by listening to all this I started to think differently', 'for me it was just an old diploma, but in the end, why not give it a try', or 'at the time I thought it was just a bunch of stupid statistics'. These short extracts show that the unemployed play an active role in assigning value to the information that comes their way: they receive it, weigh it up and think about it. They may take it on board immediately, reject it temporarily or gradually re-evaluate it. The assignment of value to this information is the product of debate and deliberation and needs time.

Some unemployed people talk about these negotiations. They are initiated by others, who pass on new information relating to the unemployed person's occupational targets, and the boundaries of the labour market they are searching in. Often, these 'others' are professionals responsible for advising unemployed people, though they can also be members of their entourage. In all cases, they position themselves as experts, connoisseurs of the sector, trade, area, holders of knowledge they mobilise in order to provide information to unemployed people. Expertise in the source of information – and therefore the cognitive component of it – does not automatically lead to the assignment of value. But it does encourage argumentation designed to convince, and this in turn provokes debate and fuels interpretations that are more or less convergent. The assignment of a value to this information produces credibility – achieved to a certain extent jointly, or as the result of a conscious effort.

Maurice, a 44-year-old law graduate, held a number of security positions before becoming Security Director at his last company. Discussions with his career adviser have now provided him with important information about his speciality, prompting him to consider adapting his approach. Tradition dictates that he would begin by looking for jobs equivalent to the one he had lost, but he was unable to do so – even though, as his adviser confirms, he had 'very good references'. Based on a shared observation that he is highly employable, they discuss what is standing in the way of his return to work. His adviser highlights two developments in the security field: a trend towards companies outsourcing security, and an increase in the number of companies specialising in the field. Maurice says: 'He showed me statistics that said security was booming. And that reassured me, but it also worried me, because it meant that there was work out there – so why couldn't I find any? That's when he showed me the job offers. It was a bit of a surprise … because if you want to be a security manager, well, there's nothing, no offers. And that's normal, he told me, because now it's the security companies that are hiring. And yes, I've seen the offers, it's huge, security guards yes, managers less so, but still.' This information does help Maurice to understand his difficulties, but he tells his adviser he isn't ready to broaden his search to include companies in the security sector. In return, he receives further information and advice: 'He told me that fixed-term contracts and assignments are standard in the sector. But, well, I'm looking for stability. The other thing is that there's high demand out there, so if you get in at a lower level, you can work your way up quickly enough, to get a permanent contract and a better job. He gave me a good explanation of how these companies work. And it makes you think, maybe you shouldn't miss out.' Guided by this detailed information from his adviser, Maurice is gradually adjusting his analysis of the situation, though he is not, for the time being, adjusting his career targets.

Hélène tells another tale of negotiation, involving both her Pôle Emploi adviser (with whom the disagreement remains unresolved) and a volunteer who opens up new horizons for her. At the age of 53, she had for many years been a French teacher in private schools. She had 'taken advantage' of difficulties at her school to get redundancy and leave a job that had become 'unbearable'. Her targets are fairly vague; she is looking to use her 'people skills'. When her search is unsuccessful, her adviser steers her back to her original profession, or to other activities with children, for which he produces job offers. This is precisely what Hélène can no longer stand: 'Neither of us was listening to the other, really. I said I wanted to do something else, but he kept bringing me back to that. He kept showing me offers, but he didn't understand. I'm not saying that I'll have a nervous breakdown if I work with children … I don't want to be seen as fragile or whatever.' As we have already seen with Maurice, receiving solid information (in this case, job offers) does not automatically lead to adjustments being made to the job search. Feeling that she has reached an impasse, Hélène contacts a voluntary sector organisation that helps and supports unemployed people. A volunteer there puts her in touch with a cousin working in migrant literacy, and after discussions with this person, Hélène retains several items of information: that the work is different from that of a teacher; that she has the necessary skills; that vacancies come up regularly. She then goes back to her Pôle Emploi advisor to look into the matter further and assess the value of this information: 'He gave me a whole file on the field, and we decided I would go and see three different organisations, to understand the work involved. Then I came back, and we validated the choice together.' At the time of our meeting, Hélène was undergoing a short training course that would give her 'a better chance' of being recruited.

The information provided in these cases is based on knowledge (statistical data, job offers, sector documentation, precise knowledge of a given field, and so on). Yet this is no guarantee that jobseekers will take it on board. They interpret and assign value to it (or not) via different processes: convergence and immediate agreement, disagreement and rupture, gradual adjustment, and so on. The information does paint a new picture of the labour market and open up new perspectives, but jobseekers need to be convinced – and those they talk to need to be convincing. Deliberation and negotiation are therefore essential stages in the process of assigning value, because it is through discussion and argumentation that knowledge acquires credibility in the eyes of the unemployed. This is also how experts can earn the trust of unemployed people. And the relationship of trust – so different from the relationship of authority identified earlier – seems to be a source of credibility for the information, a mechanism for recognising knowledge. Here again, the conditions in which information is delivered and received play a key role in the process.

Sign-up to shared beliefs

Some of the information capable of having a practical impact on job seeking circulates on the fringes of the labour market, in the circles of friends and family, and potentially through any everyday interaction in the lives of unemployed people. The basis of the value attributed to this information is specific. Indeed, as shown in the following short expressions, it is shared with familiar others who endorse it: 'we said to ourselves, well yes, that's the plan', 'we hadn't thought about it but as we talked it gradually came to us', 'yes, it seemed obvious to us to go down that road'. The use of collective pronouns (we, us) indicates that unemployed people included themselves in groups in which they shared information and thoughts about their situation. The 'others' in this case are groups of close friends or relations, rather than people they have met more formally in the course of their job search. The relevance of the information is fuelled by this complicity, which produces shared beliefs. Here, the assignment of value to information is a process of 'signing up' to it that is distinct from the imposition or negotiation of meaning.

In order for information to circulate, acquire value and be invested with relevance, it must be carried by groups of people close to the unemployed person. The members of these groups share a number of salient characteristics: they are not defined by institutional positions, they are part of the unemployed person's life, they belong to networks that often predate the episode of unemployment, and they are involved in relationships usually referred to as strong ties. It is not that the unemployed person has asked these people for information about the labour market, but rather that, in the course of everyday relationships they have shared confidences and doubts – and this has encouraged these others to express their opinions and offer advice. And it is in the often-disorderly circulation of points of view that common perspectives emerge, attracting support and becoming shared beliefs.

Labiba, aged 43, used to work in the administrative roles her secretarial qualification had prepared her for. After taking a long break to bring up her three children, she took on several blue-collar jobs. She had difficulty getting a job in the tertiary sector, because her experience was not recent enough, and she would have had to undergo training, which she does not wish to do. But she hates the physical exertion demanded by blue-collar work, and in any case, offers are few and far between. Labiba thus found herself at an impasse, feeling 'abandoned' by Pôle Emploi because her adviser seemed to consider that her application was 'not really serious'. This left her indignant: 'just because I'm bringing up my three children on my own doesn't mean I can't work'. She describes her job search as active – but also unfocused. She has identified a job market she could invest in, thanks to two former colleagues who have left the industrial world – one to be a supermarket cashier, the other a market trader. They were meeting up regularly to 'discuss everything and anything'. In the course of these meetups, it was noted that Labiba had always looked after children, and that she liked doing it. From then on, her friends encouraged her to focus her research in this direction: crèches, childminding, etc. This realisation was a relief to Labiba, and she is re-motivated: 'It's a bit of a catalyst, really. We laughed when we said that. Well yes, children are my thing. I believe in them, I've started looking.' The convergence of these three friends' views (the emergence of a common perspective) was all about Labiba's tastes, aptitudes and preferences. And it has opened up new perspectives for her.

After getting his baccalaureate in management, Rachid, aged 26, spent several years working as a sales assistant. After an 18-month period of unemployment, he is now desperate to find a job in line with his qualification, and thus avoid the sales jobs he sees himself as overqualified for. But despite his efforts, he is getting nowhere. He tells us that his morale 'started to drop' and that he went through a difficult period, withdrawing into himself. Fortunately, he has a strong friendship group, most of whom have similar educational backgrounds to him. After much discussion, he says that 'thanks to them he got back on track', taking a different view of his situation and integrating two different sets of information. The first was that his friends with management qualifications were actually doing various jobs in other fields: web designer, registrar, security guard, etc. Once this information had been shared with him, Rachid took a different view of his own situation, relativising his attachment to a job that 'matched' his qualification. The second set of information further reinforced this trend by redefining his situation in relation to sales roles: 'They see me as the chatterbox in the gang, the guy with the gift of the gab. You just can't stop me. And that's how it came about, with them saying: "That's your strong point, you're a born salesman." It became a thing, like a joke at first. To cheer me up. And then it became serious: "But it's also true, you have to do something with it." At the end of the day, I thought maybe that was it. And then it was like a spiral.' Rachid came to look on his job as a sales assistant in a different light and believe that he could be satisfied with it – perhaps even 'fulfil himself in it'. Here again, the decisive information concerned the unemployed person rather than the job market – but still significantly altered the outlook.

Circles of sociability can be places in which useful or decisive information is circulated when looking for a job. These circles are welded together by relationships of familiarity – even complicity. And thanks to these relationships, the processes of identifying and interpreting information are both collective and spread across these networks. Those close to the unemployed person produce beliefs that are reinterpretations of individual situations, which point to positive properties or qualities and outline potential outcomes to unemployment that sit in contrast to obstacles encountered in the past. The strength of this information lies in the fact that it attracts support, and is shared within groups bound together by relationships of familiarity: it becomes a belief. Familiarity does mean a relationship of trust, but this is more than that because it implies a deeper inter-knowledge, a closeness of backgrounds or experiences, and mutual understanding beyond words.

Conclusion

In the course of their job search, unemployed people glean and are given information about their occupational targets, personal labour market and position within it. In the job search, this information counts only when it is identified as relevant and meaningful. What we have analysed here is the qualification of this information, distinguishing three processes for the assignment of value. Each is characterised by a combination of distinctive features, summarised in Table 8.2.

Although these processes have been explained one by one, using different cases each time, they are not mutually exclusive and can combine in the experiences of the unemployed person. Unemployed people rely on information arising out of all three sources: indisputable matter of course, credible knowledge and shared beliefs. The first is information imposed by those in power (who exercise authority over the unemployed). The second is information negotiated with professionals (who have expertise and enjoy a degree of trust from the unemployed person). The third is information circulated in circles of friends and acquaintances (marked by a complicity that sustains the unemployed person's sign-up). These results indicate that the value attached by unemployed people to a given item of information appears to have more to do with the characteristics of the relationship established between the unemployed person and other people (who help to produce and disseminate this information) than with the nature or content of the information per se.

A number of lessons can be drawn from this, with a view to considering the use of digital tools to support unemployed in their job search. First,

Table 8.2: Process of assigning value to information gained in the job search

Others involved	Social relationship concerned	How meaning is produced	Status of relevant information
Holders of power	Based on authority	Imposition	Indisputable matter of course
Expert professionals	Based on trust	Negotiation	Credible knowledge
Circles of close contacts	Based on complicity	Sign-up	Shared beliefs

established or rational knowledge, in the form of statistical data or solid empirical observations on the labour markets, is not automatically superior. This is because the relevant information, according to the unemployed person, can have another, (non-inferior) status, such as matter of course or beliefs. Simply processing more data is therefore not enough to add credibility to the information unemployed people are provided with. Moreover, unemployed people are not alone in considering and assigning value to information varying in status; they do so as a result of their interaction with a multiplicity of 'partners' in situations in which information is produced and circulated. Consequently, the dissemination of established knowledge through digital tools is always in competition with other sources of information coming from a variety of others and having different status. Lastly, if the value assigned to information depends less on its intrinsic properties than on the conditions in which it is produced and disseminated, it becomes essential to take these conditions of delivery and reception into account. In this respect, it can be argued that the dissemination of information derived from artificial intelligence tools does not fall within the register of complicity that is characteristic of circles of close contacts, and must distance itself from the register of authoritarian imposition that annihilates the unemployed person's reflexive capacities. We have shown that discussion and argumentation are key mechanisms by which documented knowledge can become credible, and therefore effective. Consequently, this dissemination of information must leave room for negotiation.

References

Bachmann, R. and Baumgarten, D. (2013) How do the unemployed search for a job? Evidence from the EU Labour Force Survey. *IZA Journal of European Labour Studies*, 22(2): 1–25.

Bakke, E.W. (1933) *The Unemployed Man: A Social Study*. London: Nisbet.

Bethmann, A. (2013) Occupational change and status mobility. *Journal for Labor Market Research*, 46: 307–319.

Brand, J.E. (2015) The far-reaching impact of job loss and unemployment. *Annual Review of Sociology*, 41: 359–375.

Cahuc, P., Carcillo, S. and Zylberberg, A. (2014) *Labor Economics*. Cambridge, MA: MIT Press.

Clouet, H. (2022) *Rationner l'emploi: La promotion du temps partiel par les services publics d'emploi allemand et français*. Paris: Éditions de la Maison des sciences de l'homme.

Demazière, D. (forthcoming) Job expectations theorised as feasible work. In V. Chen, S. Pultz and O. Sharone (eds) *Handbook on Unemployment and Society*. Edward Elgar.

Demazière, D. and Zune, M. (2021) When job search is deemed insufficient: Experiences of unemployed people disbarred following compliancy monitoring. *Social Policy and Society*: 1–15.

Eichhorst, W., Kaufmann, O., Konle-Seidl, R. and Reinhard, H.J. (2008) Bringing the jobless into work? An introduction to activation policies. In W. Eichhorst (ed) *Bringing the Jobless into Work? Experiences with Activation Schemes in Europe and the US* (pp 1–16). Berlin and Heidelberg: Springer Berlin Heidelberg.

Forster, K. (2012) Work, narrative identity and social affiliation. *Work, Employment and Society*, 26(6): 935–950.

Gabriel, Y., Gray, D.E. and Goregaokar, H. (2013) Job loss and its aftermath among managers and professionals: Wounded, fragmented and flexible. *Work Employment and Society*, 27(1): 56–72.

Garsten, C., Jacobsson, K. and Sztandar-Sztanderska, K. (2016) Negotiating social citizenship at the street-level: Local activation policies and individualization in Sweden and Poland. In M. Heidenreich and D. Rice (eds) *Integrating Social and Employment Policies in Europe: Active Inclusion and Challenges for Local Welfare Governance* (pp 265–293). Cheltenham: Edward Elgar Publishing.

Granovetter, M.S. (1973) The strength of weak ties. *American Journal of Sociology*, 78(6): 1360–1380.

Kalleberg, A.L. and Vallas, S.P. (eds) (2017) *Precarious Work*. Leeds: Emerald Group Publishing.

Kiefer, N.M. and Neumann, G.R. (1979) An empirical job-search model, with a test of the constant reservation–wage hypothesis. *Journal of Political Economy*, 87(1): 89–107.

Lavitry, L. (2015) *Flexibilité des chômeurs, mode d'emploi. Les conseillers à l'emploi à l'épreuve de l'activation*. Paris: Puf.

Lewchuk, W. (2017) Precarious jobs: Where are they, and how do they affect well-being? *The Economic and Labour Relations Review*, 28(3): 402–419.

Lin, N. (2001) *Social Capital: A Theory of Social Structure and Action*. Cambridge: Cambridge University Press.

Lin, N., Fu, Y.C. and Hsung, R.M. (2001) Measurement techniques for investigations of social capital. *Social Capital: Theory and Research*, 4: 57–81.

Lind, J. and Møller, I.H. (eds) (2018) *Inclusion and Exclusion: Unemployment and Non-standard Employment in Europe*. New York: Routledge.

Manroop, L. and Richardson, J. (2016) Job search: A multidisciplinary review and research agenda. *International Journal of Management Reviews*, 18: 206–227.

McDonald, S. and Elder Jr, G.H. (2006) When does social capital matter? Non-searching for jobs across the life course. *Social Forces*, 85(1): 521–549.

Rodgers, G. and Rodgers, J. (eds) (1989) *Precarious Jobs in Labour Market Regulation: The Growth of Atypical Employment in Western Europe*. Genève: International Labour Organization.

Sharone, O. (2013) *Flawed System/Flawed Self: Job Searching and Unemployment Experiences*. Chicago: University of Chicago Press.

Stigler, G.J. (1962) Information in the labor market. *Journal of Political Economy*, 70(5, Part 2): 94–105.

Van Hoye, G. (2018) Job-search behavior as construct: A review of different job-search behaviors and sources. In U.C. Klehe and E. Van Hooft (eds) *The Oxford Handbook of Job Loss and Job Search* (pp 259–274). Oxford: Oxford University Press.

Van Hoye, G., Van Hooft, E. and Lievens, F. (2009) Networking as a job search behaviour: A social network perspective. *Journal of Occupational and Organizational Psychology*, 82: 661–682.

9

Digitising exclusion: the challenges of modern unemployment and public employment service delivery

Antoinette Kelly and Zach Roche

Introduction

Protecting the socially and economically vulnerable is a priority of contemporary welfare policy, with the long-term (12+ months) unemployed (LTU) emerging as a key group that social policy often struggles to reach.

This chapter focuses on the Department of Social Protection's (DSP) service delivery to LTU people, who often face contextual limitations including but not limited to numeracy, literacy and digital barriers. This chapter will establish how evolving social protection policy can better perform in recognising the barriers of the LTU as they interact with the increasingly digitised welfare system. We draw upon original qualitative data to show how the LTU are increasingly marginalised and excluded from the very reforms that are supposed to help them.

From a policy perspective, and after Ireland's European Union/International Monetary Fund bailout in 2010, the system of social protection transitioned from what was ostensibly a 'passive' model towards an 'activation' model (Boland and Griffin, 2015). Many countries at the time, Ireland included, were faced with the dual challenges of high unemployment and growing state deficits, choosing to reorient the welfare system towards a 'workfare' model characterised by active labour market policies.

This evolution led to intensified precarity in the context of low-paid employment growth precipitated by the workfare policy reforms implemented in 2010, whereby various vulnerable cohorts are overlooked (Brodkin, 2021). According to the National Adult Literacy Agency (2020), one in six Irish adults struggle with reading and understanding everyday text; one in four has difficulties using maths in everyday life; and one in five struggles with basic digital tasks. These people are often left behind by higher level government economic and social policy, leaving agencies and street-level organisations (SLOs) that implement policy at street level to engage and resolve their unique challenges (Brodkin, 2021).

Contracting, privatisation and digitisation have fundamentally altered the public employment services (PES) welfare landscape, creating alternative and blended forms of service provision with difficult delivery arrangements. The role and impacts of digitisation in welfare service provision are explored in this chapter.

Pathways to Work (PTW) 2021–2025 recognises the scale challenges faced in delivering PES. It refers to the need for more efficient use of resources and the necessity to embrace automated tools to process large volumes. It also refers to the:

> need to adapt its model of service delivery to take advantage of digital capability and to respond to client's preferences. This will require innovation in the development of a digital model of service delivery to complement and augment the traditional 'face-to-face' model of service delivery. This approach will also help maximise the capacity of the service to respond to the scale challenge. (Irish Government, 2021)

In the Irish policy context, PTW 2021–2025 has a specific aim to go digital through 'taking advantage' of remote and online service capabilities. Here, the DSP's intention is to extend its reach and achieve efficiencies in service delivery. In this regard, the DSP states that it recognises the requirement to modify its model of service delivery to gain the benefit of going digital and to act in response to citizen preferences. PTW 2021–2025 states it will innovate and use digital solutions to *complement and augment* its traditional 'face-to-face' model of service delivery (Irish Government, 2021).

However, our findings indicate that this has gone a step further, with digital delivery rapidly becoming the norm, replacing rather than augmenting street-level service provision. While the COVID-19 pandemic provided a sudden impetus in this regard, unemployed applicants are still directed to screen-level rather than street-level resources (especially mywelfare.ie). Meetings with case officers take place remotely by default unless the applicant makes a specific request, but even this must be done online. This pushes Ireland towards similar frameworks in other countries such as the UK, which Alston (2019) has argued is fading into obscurity behind webpages and algorithms, or Australia where the administration of welfare has become wholly remote and privatised (O'Sullivan et al, 2021). As we demonstrate in this chapter, this policy transformation has significant impacts not only for the unemployed, but also for the case officers who seek to help them.

Methodology

This qualitative research study was exploratory and inductive in nature, developing a narratological analysis based upon the views of the participants themselves, from their own social milieu. This was useful to gain rich personal and group data, including participants' attitudes, perceptions and beliefs. Our data comes from two sources, six semi-structured interviews with unemployment street-level case officers (SLCOs) and a follow-up focus group with five other SLCOs.

All findings were anonymised, transcribed and thematically coded during the research to identify common topics arising across the data. All participants had a minimum of five years' experience and gave their informed consent to participate in this research. In addition to this, a pilot interview was first conducted to ensure that questions were relevant and had validity. While this sample is small, two factors should be noted. First, Irish SLCOs within the welfare system have been characterised as a difficult to access group, and do not usually give interviews (Boland and Griffin, 2015). Second, the research was carried out during the COVID-19 pandemic, meaning that the ordinary challenges that go with an interview (matching schedules, finding time) were amplified. This latter factor did, however, give our participants more to discuss, as the COVID-19 pandemic accelerated processes of digitisation in Irish welfare, as face-to-face meetings with unemployed clients were not permitted.

Our aims were:

- To assess how the 'digital by default' PES model impacts SLCOs.
- To understand how policy is implemented in practice at 'street level'.
- To explore the lived experience and impacts of a 'digital' service delivery model on SLCOs.
- To understand how processes align across the DSP ecosystem.
- To identify potential solutions that may improve performance of policy delivery.

The focus group was facilitated and centred on a discussion based on three stylised *vignettes*. Finch (1987) discusses how vignettes can be utilised to explore people's attitudes, beliefs and experiences about given situations or scenarios. According to Hughes (1998), using the vignette approach is considered a particularly useful research method for exploring issues that may otherwise be potentially difficult for people to discuss. He asserts that vignettes allow people to discuss issues from a 'non-personal and therefore less threatening perspective'. These vignettes presented the focus group with three scenarios SLCOs are likely to encounter in the regular course of their work. The first focused on a single mother trapped in a cycle of low-paid work with frequent bouts of unemployment; she also evidences cultural capital struggles, finding it difficult to fill out forms and engage with the correspondence and bureaucracy of the modern welfare system. The second highlighted the difficulties of a migrant living in Ireland, who lacks

English language skills, a permanent fixed address and bank account. The third focused on an older person who has little or no work history and who likely left school early and therefore also lacks qualifications. All participants responded positively to the vignettes, emphasising that they encounter such people on a daily basis and are frustrated by the additional barriers created by digital-first welfare systems.

Following each *vignette*, the participants were asked several open-ended questions to facilitate discussion, and this allowed an exploration of participants' perceptions and understandings of the welfare ecosystem, their own experiences operating within that system, and the impacts of policy delivery and digitised PES at street level.

Meeting unemployment through street-level bureaucracy

Lipsky's (1971) theory of street-level bureaucracy (SLB) assesses the workplace in terms of practical 'dilemmas' that front-line workers must overcome. While undertaking their work, SLBs are frequently faced with structural constraints, that is, inadequate resources, increasing demands, ambiguous policy goals and complex evaluations of users' claims. To perform their job while managing these work constraints, SLBs may adopt various discretionary approaches, which indirectly but substantially shape policy on the ground.

According to Lipsky (1980), front-line workers are best positioned to assess individual client needs and effective assistance requires that they hold 'considerable autonomy and discretion'. Several studies have analysed elements of street-level discretion and how it is exercised in practice and the consequences for the implementation of policy on the ground. According to Perna (2021), elements that may affect discretion include workers' policy predilections, their gender, race and degree of professionalisation.

Brodkin (2015) describes SLOs as 'form(ing) the operational core of the welfare state' and situated at the centre of the 'missing middle' where organisational practices and politics are mediated. Here Brodkin refers to the organisational practices through which policy ideas are converted into day-to-day practice as the 'missing middle – the opaque spaces between formal policy provisions and social outcomes in which the essential work of the welfare state and its policies takes place' (Doster, 2014). Brodkin (2021) refers to public, private, for-profit, non-profit and hybrid SLOs who, through a series of outsourced government arrangements, strive to deliver public services on behalf of the welfare state. For example, in the Irish context, it includes outsourced partnerships, including SEETEC (a private company that delivers marketised welfare in contract with DSP) and Local Development Companies. We refer to this collective of employment SLOs as the DSP ecosystem.

Brodkin (2021), drawing on Barbier (2007), recognises that although formal policy matters, it is not definitive. In certain circumstances, law (policy) is described as a 'political *référentiel*' or 'cognitive framework' that 'deploys vague 'fuzzy generalities' to 'mask divergent realities'. The construction of these divergent realities at street level, and how they are subsequently resolved, is crucial. Their construction and resolution represent the political aspect of SLB theory and determine how government policy is applied in action.

Brodkin (2021) points out that SLOs are where most people routinely encounter the state. She emphasises the importance of SLOs in the delivery of services to vulnerable and marginalised people and those with limitations/barriers. People with limitations/barriers are viewed as 'dilemmas'. SLOs are required to resolve these individual and sometimes complex needs at the point of consumption.

Brodkin (2021) also refers to SLOs being useful in resolving 'sticky problems', that is, claims that are 'politically contested and difficult to resolve through formal or visible means'. These 'sticky problems' are, according to Brodkin, left behind in vague 'fuzzy' generalities. They may be subject to ambiguous legal provisions or possibly left to street-level delegated discretionary frameworks to resolve. In effect, the 'sticky problems' are delegated to SLOs to resolve while implementing policy, typically by using their discretion.

New technologies are intended to facilitate and enable new processes and new management practices. The digitisation of welfare and employment services is transforming SLB. A 'screen-level' bureaucratic approach has emerged, thereby diminishing previously held SLB discretion. In the current welfare 'digital by default' model, it is important to distinguish between *street* and *screen*-level bureaucracy.

Bovens and Zouridis (2002) explore how digital welfare systems impact SLB administrative discretion. They found that digital welfare solutions were rapidly changing the landscape whereby SLO administrative discretion in dealing with individual clients or 'sticky problems' was being undermined by screen-level bureaucracy. This raises important questions, including: What degree of discretionary power does screen-level bureaucracy have? How is this power governed? And how is due process and fairness guaranteed in difficult cases, 'dilemmas'? (Bovens and Zouridis, 2002).

Boven and Zouridis (2002) found the removal of 'street-level' discretion in digital solutions had potentially negative impacts for relevant programmes. Larsson (2021) describes digitisation as further distancing citizens from policy makers, with a reliance on digital systems and different technology platforms to facilitate *access* and *engagement*. Larsson (2021) also referred to 'screen-level' bureaucracy replacing 'street-level' bureaucracy but without the local discretion that can sometimes apply in the latter. Larsson (2021) also found that people may be excluded in digitised system entry criteria, and therefore being unable to access public services.

Madsen and Kræmmergaard (2016) also identify the deficiency in digital skills as a barrier to being able to *access* and/or *engage* with services, therefore making it more burdensome for such people to avail of services. O'Sullivan and Walker (2018; in Considine et al, 2022) also refer to these barriers, stating, 'machine bureaucracies may become inaccessible to those with low digital literacy, people living in areas with poor internet connectivity [broadband] infrastructure, and those who simply cannot afford the devices and broadband capacity needed to self-service'.

Overall, the research showed that when *access or engagement* is digitised, governments burden citizens by requiring them to fill in forms online, navigate webpages via devices or provide back-up documentation online (Scholta et al, 2019). Online solutions were found to be less adequate depending upon the complexities or complications of users (Hetling and Postmus, 2014). Breit et al (2020) found that citizens experienced a complex relationship between themselves (citizens), front-line workers and digital systems. The term 'digital divide' emerges and refers to a gap between those who have access to technology and those who do not.

In the Irish context, we note that in PTW 2021–2025, the DSP recognises the requirement to modify its model of service delivery to the extent that it states that it has committed to innovate and use digital solutions to 'complement and augment' its traditional 'face-to-face' model of service delivery (Irish Government, 2021).

What policy says versus what is done

According to Brodkin (2015), 'decades of implementation and organizational research make clear that what you see in terms of formal or written policy may not be what you get'. The actions and behaviours of SLOs represent policy on the ground and not the *verbatim* of policy. SLOs not only implement policy but also perform an important role as mediators in the delivery of state employment policy and politics. This research will focus on *what is done* in practice in front-line delivery of services to the LTU rather than *what the policy says*.

Policy making: 'bottom-up' perspective

Cooper et al (2015), albeit referring to a medical setting, refer to the importance of SLBs having a voice when policy is being formulated, asserting that 'ways forward include even greater consideration in policy making of the perspectives of patients and front-line [clinicians]'.

Furthermore, Aviram et al (2021) found that scholars studying SLBs such as nurses, teachers and social workers have called for a broadening of their role in policy making from formulation to implementation, evaluation and review.

Mass processing

According to Lipsky (1971; 2010), demand by service users may always be likely to outstrip supply due to finite resources (cost, time or service access) and because service users have no alternative. This research seeks to gain insight into whether SLOs adopt what Lipsky (1980) refers to as 'mass processing' relating to excessive case officer workloads when they have no other option.

Management of 'sticky problems'

SLOs are responsible for resolving social needs and 'dilemmas'. This includes what Brodkin (2021) describes as 'sticky problems' for people who are challenged in engaging with such services. The researcher is interested in assessing how SLOs manage in what Brodkin (2021) calls the 'fuzzy space', and who according to Lipsky (1980) 'can develop frustrations with the institutional framework inhibiting them from doing their jobs professionally'.

Personal discretion

Both Lipsky and Brodkin refer to the role of discretion SLOs have when managing workloads, particularly those who undertake face-to-face interaction with service users. Moore (1987) describes the need for case officers to use personal discretion to become 'inventive strategists' to formulate solutions to resolve excessive caseload, but also complex cases, that is, 'dilemmas', and unclear work performance metrics.

Digital impacts on individual discretion

SLB theory offers the prospect of understanding the effect of reduced case officer autonomy and discretion on DSP front-line performance. The inability to assist a person requires further consideration in an emerging 'digital by default' sphere and whereby the DSP are requiring service users to engage with a 'one size fits all' digital welfare processes. The research assesses the impacts of these emerging digital solutions for the LTU and ascertain whether the DSP's use of digital solutions is to 'complement and augment' or replace its traditional 'face-to-face' model of service delivery.

We draw on SLB theory to understand street-level attitudes, beliefs and practices regarding the digitised delivery of welfare and employment services to the LTU. Drawing on SLB/SLO theory with a view to providing more insight into otherwise potentially invisible processes, and the effectiveness of such processes, Brodkin (2021) states that from a democratic (and a social justice) perspective, it is not possible to challenge what one cannot see.

Findings

This chapter unpacks how our expert participants inform how social protection policy can better perform in recognising the contextual limitations of the LTU. Our expert participants recognised the people represented in the vignette style scenarios and stated that they would interact with similar people day-to-day. Participants firmly identified with the contextual limitations experienced by the people presented, alongside the prevalence of these limitations, in particular, literacy, language and digital barriers. While the focus group participants considered that the LTU were not adequately supported by DSP during activation, some interviewees believed they *were* adequately supported. In general, all research participants were supportive of some form of screening prior to activation, to identify potential areas of support for the unemployed.

One of the most significant issues which arose, and one referenced by all research participants, was the government's strategic drive towards digitisation. It emerged that, while necessary and efficient during the COVID-19 pandemic, and not without merit, ultra-modern digitisation was not a *panacea*, particularly when dealing with people with contextual limitations. Overall, the research participants identified that many process challenges exist, and which prevent the LTU from accessing and/or engaging with digital solutions. There was agreement across all research participants that it is commonplace for LTU to be impeded when attempting to access and/or engage with digital solutions by virtue of their barriers – a known issue within the DSP for some time, according to our interviewees.

According to focus group participants, the LTU are subject to high levels of stress and anxiety when attempting to access and/or engage with the system digitally. It also emerged that 'one size fits all' ultra-modern digitisation has virtually eliminated SLCO discretion. The street-level 'safety net', that is, the human element, which previously existed in the form of 'discretion', has been removed. This impedes the ability of the SLCO to help the most vulnerable people and prohibits them from applying a person-centred approach to implement policy at street level.

The focus group identified organisational attributes that contribute to confusion for, and impede service delivery to, the LTU. Participants highlighted the lack of consistency in policy interpretation, a lack of 'joined up' thinking and communication within the DSP ecosystem, and disconnects between the DSP and front-line agencies. The focus group participants claimed that the random nature of the referral process, alongside the simultaneous referral of jobseekers to multiple employment service providers, was a cause of confusion as jobseekers tried to navigate the web of PES. The focus group participants placed this confusion on the way policy is implemented at organisational level.

Participants advocated a client-centred approach for the LTU. While the focus group participants claimed they were already working to this approach, some interviewees expressed frustration with the adherence within the DSP to 'process' over 'person', stating that the personal interaction and the ability to help a vulnerable unemployed person was impeded, rather than aided, by digitisation. As such, we identify a double exclusion whereby not only is the jobseeker excluded at the organisational level but the SLCOs, whose role it is to help jobseekers, are also excluded.

Overall, the research group discussion was useful in that research participants offered possible solutions to overcome the issues they raised. Solutions offered included: a policy to address barriers; on-site assistance for digital engagement; and a policy for discretionary pathways for LTU. While our full findings are broad and wide-ranging, we will focus on how the process of double exclusion emerged in our analysis.

Exclusions at 'street and screen (digital) level'

Street level

It was apparent that the SLCOs frequently encountered 'dilemmas' in the shape of 'sticky problems' (LTU). When presented with the people represented in the vignettes, all of whom had 'sticky problems', all research participants said such people were commonplace. Notwithstanding this, all research participants saw their primary role as assisting the LTU.

This emerged in the focus group:

> [O]ur job is to sit down with them [LTU] and to register them [with digital welfare solutions] … it is quite cumbersome to say the least.

> We are trying to deal with them … we have to work and see what capabilities they have.

Although all research participants said they would do what they could to help LTU who were having trouble engaging with the system, all stated emphatically that they had no discretion. Our interviewees concurred with this: 'The personal interaction is gone and the ability to help a person with poor skills is gone in general.' Our participants were agreed that policy would be better implemented if the DSP more effectively utilised its trained, competent and, in the main, empathetic staff, rather than excluding staff from fully interacting with vulnerable clients in the first place. These staff can engage compassionately with LTU but are excluded from doing so by the diminishing discretion at street level. When asked if there should be discretion for certain people (LTU), the SLCOs responded: 'In an ideal world, yes, absolutely.'

Screen (digital) level

As in other similar countries (Brodkin, 2021), people with poor digital literacy are commonplace in the Irish social welfare system: 'Yes, yeah, especially in ours. They [LTU] would be the majority of our new stuff [*sic*].' We found that there are substantial negative impacts of digital solutions on the LTU. Issues mentioned included no access to digital devices and an inability to use digital devices where they were available. These issues collectively exclude the LTU at screen level from independently engaging with DSP online services. One interviewee also stated that it is common for people to have difficulties navigating the DSP digital system and indicated that the DSP was aware of this problem for two years.

Examples of the negative impacts are captured by these quotes:

They [people with digital barriers] would be the least well served.

Primarily because of the drive for digitisation, Michael [vignette three], and people like him probably suffered the most because of this [drive for digitisation].

That particular older, unemployed man with poor literacy, are [*sic*] out of the loop completely.

I had a guy who came on only recently, and he had his smartphone ... maybe in his late 40s, early 50s, and he told me ... I have one of these fancy phones, that's what he called it, and he said, my niece gave it to me. And the reason he took that phone from her he said, I don't do ... I can take a call on it. My digital Covid cert is on it ... to say he was vaccinated ... so that's why that was important to him. But what the phone does? Absolutely, he has no idea.

As we can see, basic digital media literacy skills are a major obstacle for many LTU, who may not even own a smartphone – or if they do may not possess the knowledge to use it to its fullest potential. Digital-first welfare strategy has therefore amplified existing exclusions by adding (rather than subtracting) a barrier to welfare entry. The reflections of our interviewees regarding a 'digital by default' approach also referenced that it was known within the DSP that people had difficulties navigating the digital system, however, now there is no discretion: 'the personal interaction is given and the ability to help a person with poor skills is gone in general – it's a disgrace'.

The focus group discussion provided the following recent example of how the move to a digital process negatively impacted the LTU, demonstrating a mismatch between policy as formulated, and policy in action. During the COVID-19 pandemic, the DSP changed the process relating to benefit claims. Any new or existing claimant attempting to apply for, reinstate or adjust a benefit claim was now required by the DSP to apply online through the MyGov.ie and/or MyWelfare.ie portals. This resulted in stress and anxiety for many of their programme participants exiting employment programmes such as Tús and Community Employment and looking to re-establish their claims.

The Focus Group elaborated on how these exclusions manifest in practice:

> So, what used to happen was when you did your 12 months you were able to go into an office and make an appointment to make your claim back. Now, this is all done online. So, you have to make your application and load up any necessary documents online before you actually … [*sic*] then are entitled to get back on your Jobseeker's Allowance payments.

> Now, it is sold as a fast-track system. … But the system now is all digitised. Okay, so you need to go online and set up an email account, set up/register with MyGov.ie, there's a whole process … then you need to get back into payments. … There is a whole, quite actually cumbersome process of actually [*sic*]. … I'm [caseworker] trying to wrap my head around how to add all the steps that are involved in it. So, it is much more difficult now than when they entered into it … they wouldn't have known. The process changed during the pandemic.

> [W]e [the implementing body] were given a formal notice, but I am not aware of any of the actual clients being actually formally notified … it is huge … you can now no longer go into the office and just have someone to help you with the forms, that it is all done online … there is a number of issues, one is access … 20 per cent of the clients, possibly 30 per cent of the clients I work with, do not have smartphones, they just do not have them. And then you are on to actually having the skills and knowledge … 40 per cent to 50 per cent of the people that I work with would not have the skills or knowledge to set up their own email, to upload documents onto websites, and things like that.

Notwithstanding those people who may have a language barrier, even the LTU and LTU who claim English as their first language may not possess the relevant 'digital language' to describe their difficulties when they are seeking to access or engage with DSP digital processes (what's a webchat or a chatbot?).

As one focus group participant stated: '[I]t is difficult for people who are not digitally aware to talk over the phone with somebody and explain what the problem is. [Other Speakers: Yeah. Yeah]. So, it is a different language.'

The LTU are found to be excluded at screen level from digital solutions. Multiple negative impacts of the 'digital by default' ultra-modern model on the level and quality of service to the LTU were identified. It emerged that yet again SLCOs themselves are excluded, this time at screen level, by digital solutions.

An interviewee echoed these concerns: 'If I meet someone that I can't help, I refer [them] to the Citizens Advice Centre who would … help with engaging with the Department digitally … the personal interaction is gone and the ability to help a person with poor skills is gone in general – it's a disgrace.' The LTU are effectively thwarted by the mismatch between the 'one size fits all' ultra-modern digital process, their contextual limitations, and the removal of SLCO discretion.

This research offers a useful perspective for better understanding the impacts of the removal of discretion by the shift towards digitisation on both the LTU and the SLCOs themselves. Considine et al (2022) suggest that digitising processes can result in some bias being integrated into the digital process, shifting from SLBs to system-designers and programmers responsible for programming the algorithms. However, according to Jorna and Wagenaar (2007; in Considine et al, 2022), SLB decisions have been scrutinised for decades, but the level of political control over IT programmers' 'hidden discretion' is considerably more limited. The decision of which data to include, and the implementation of systemised outcomes, may all contain errors, inconsistencies and biases, just like work done by front-line staff, and the basis for decision-making becomes increasingly opaque. Elements of SLCO discretion are steadily being undermined by the DSP's shift to digitisation and this has been detrimental to the LTU.

While the government have, to date, embraced a 'one size fits all' digitised self-service framework, they have *not* employed digital solutions to 'complement and augment' the traditional 'face-to-face' model of service delivery, they are in fact replacing it. The DSP digital model has inadvertently created a mismatch between welfare process engagement requirements and the contextual limitations of the LTU, while simultaneously removing SLCO discretion. Brussig and Knuth (in Brodkin and Marston, 2013) refer to this as 'institutional blindness', which is policy's failure to formally, or informally, respond to the contextual limitations of the LTU.

Both the LTU *and* SLCOs are excluded at the strategic level and the street and screen levels. The LTU are also excluded at the organisational level and there is no longer scope for SLCOs to be 'inventive strategists', and therefore there is no scope for complex cases to be resolved effectively at street level. The DSP framework has replaced personal discretion with the introduction of digital welfare solutions. Essentially, street-level work has been made redundant by the screen level which now stands between the SLCO and LTU.

The DSP framework and digitisation have inadvertently introduced a new 'dilemma' of 'double exclusion' where both LTU *and* SLCOs are excluded, albeit in different ways, by the DSP digitised framework. There is convincing evidence that certain unemployed people, including the LTU, are excluded by the very system that allegedly exists to provide support for them. Skilled and experienced SLCOs are excluded by the same digitised system, prevented from utilising their experience and skills to help the very people that they were employed to assist and support. Their professional role and skills have been all but relegated to helping people navigate the 'machine bureaucracy'.

Conclusion

The adverse effects of unemployment are substantial, especially for long-term unemployed people. This research study focused on the DSP's service delivery to LTU people with contextual limitations with a view to establishing how evolving social protection policy and digitisation can better perform in recognising the barriers of the LTU as they interact with PES and the wider welfare system. SLB theory and SLO research were drawn on, in conjunction with international research studies relating to the drive towards the digitisation of public services. This offered a useful framework to contextualise the subject matter.

This research has uncovered a 'double exclusion' whereby the LTU are excluded in the first instance by language issues, innumeracy, lack of skills, length of time spent unemployed, and so on, however we have also shown that even the SLCOs who aim to help them are also excluded. We found that the LTU *and* SLCOs are excluded at the street and screen levels. Notwithstanding the DSP's recognition of the requirement, and their stated commitment to innovate and use digital solutions to 'complement and augment' their traditional 'face-to-face' model of service delivery, the DSP's digital first approach has inadvertently introduced this new 'dilemma' of 'double exclusion'. Both the LTU *and* SLCOs are excluded by the DSP's very own framework whose *raison d'être* purports to provide a safety net for the most vulnerable citizens. There is no longer scope for complex cases to be resolved effectively at street and screen levels because the framework has replaced personal discretion with digital welfare solutions. This will compound and exacerbate existing inequalities because the LTU cannot reach the professionals who are trained to help them.

The DSP's mission is 'to promote active participation and inclusion in society'. Their stated overall objective for 2020–2023 is 'to continue to put their clients at the centre of all their operations, providing an efficient and effective service, and to continue developing staff, structures, and processes' (Irish Government, 2020). The research acknowledges the DSP has a stabilising and equalising effect on Irish society. However, in the case of the push for more digital services, and the privatisation of local providers, the effect has been that some of the most vulnerable people are being excluded.

This research study advocates the need for the DSP to adopt a multifaceted approach to improve service delivery to the LTU through understanding and managing the interconnections that exist between the micro-level of SLBs' work practices, the meso-level of the organisation, and the macro-level of strategic policy formulation and delivery through the DSP ecosystem.

While digitisation is useful and can provide efficiency and consistency, it is not the *panacea* for delivering public services, especially to people with contextual limitations. Enabling more caseworkers, those people with advanced skills who can meet the unemployed face-to-face and recognise their special circumstances, is the way to mitigate the tensions between efficiency and exclusion, consistency and compassion. A revised approach would be advised whereby SLBs are granted more discretion. SLBs need to be trusted to tailor their judgement and exercise their discretion so that they can recognise the barriers and assist those with 'sticky problems'. We advance the view that continued person-to-person interactions are an essential element of DSP service delivery. Adopting this approach will ensure that social protection policy *can* better perform not only for the LTU as they interact with the welfare system, but also for those of the trained SLCOs working within the landscape of welfare.

References

Alston, P. (2019) *Visit to the United Kingdom of Great Britain and Northern Ireland – Human Rights Council Forty-first session 24 June–12 July 2019 Agenda Item 3.* https://documents-dds-ny.un.org/doc/UNDOC/GEN/G19/112/13/PDF/G1911213.pdf

Aviram, N.F., Beeri, I. and Cohen, N. (2021) From the bottom-up: Probing the gap between street-level bureaucrats' intentions of engaging in policy entrepreneurship and their behaviour. *The American Review of Public Administration*, 51(8): 636–649.

Barbier, J.C. (2007) From political strategy to analytical research and back to politics, a sociological approach of 'flexicurity.' in: Jørgensen H and Madsen PK (eds) Flexicurity and Beyond. Copenhagen: DJØF Publishing, 155–188. https://halshs.archives-ouvertes.fr/halshs-00157430/document

Boland, T. and Griffin, R. (2015) *The Sociology of Unemployment.* Manchester: Manchester University Press.

Bovens, M. and Zouridis, S. (2002) From street-level to system-level bureaucracies: How information and communication technology is transforming administrative discretion and constitutional control. *Public Administration Review*, 62(2): 174–184.

Breit, E., Egeland, C., Loberg, I. and Rohnebaek, M. (2020) Digital coping: How frontline workers cope with digital service encounters. *Social Policy Administration*, 55(5).

Brodkin, E. (2013) *Work and the Welfare State: Street-Level Organizations and Workfare Politics*. Washington, DC: Georgetown University Press.

Brodkin, E. (2015) Street-level organizations and the 'real world' of workfare: Lessons from the US. *Social Work and Society International Online Journal*, 13(1).

Brodkin, E. (2021) 'Street-level welfare politics': A video recording of Evelyn Brodkin presenting at Economy & Society 2021: Afterthoughts. Economy & Society Research Centre, Waterford Institute of Technology & University of Cork, 20 April. https://hecat.eu/2021/04/20/street-level-welfare/

Brodkin, E. and Marston, G. (2013) *Work and the Welfare State: Street-Level Organizations and Workfare Politics*. Washington, DC: Georgetown University Press.

Considine, M., McGann, M., Ball, S. and Nguyen, P. (2022) Can robots understand welfare? Exploring machine bureaucracies in welfare-to-work. *Journal of Social Policy*, 51(3): 1–16.

Cooper, M.J., Sornalingam, S. and O'Donnell, C. (2015) Street-level bureaucracy: an underused theoretical model for general practice? *British Journal of General Practice*, 65(636): 376–377.

Doster, A. (2014) The University of Chicago School of Social Service. *Administration Magazine*, 21(2).

Finch, J. (1987) The *vignette* technique in survey research. *Sociology*, 21(2): 105–114.

Hetling, A. and Postmus, J. (2014) Financial literacy and economic empowerment of survivors of intimate partner violence: Examining the differences between public assistance recipients and nonrecipients. *Journal of Poverty*, 18: 130–149. doi: 10.1080/10875549.2014.896308.

Hughes, R. (1998) Considering the *vignette* techniques and its application to a study of drug injecting and HIV risk and safer behaviour. *Sociology of Health & Illness*, 20(3): 381–400.

Irish Government (2020) *Department for Social Protection Statement of Strategy 2020–2023*. Dublin.

Irish Government (2021) *Intreo: the Public Employment Services*. https://www.gov.ie/en/organisation-information/3c095-intreo-the-public-employment-services/

Larsson, K. (2021) Digitisation or equality: When government automation covers some, but not all citizens. *Government Information Quarterly*, 38(101547).

Lipsky, M. (1971) Street-level bureaucracy and the analysis of urban reform. *Urban Affairs Quarterly*, 6(4): 391–409.

Lipsky, M. (1980) *Street-Level Bureaucracy: Dilemmas of the Individual in Public Services*. New York: Russell Sage Foundation.

Lipsky, M. (2010) Street-level bureaucracy: Dilemmas of the individual in public services. *American Political Science Review*, 76: 1–275.

Madsen, C. and Kræmmergaard, P. (2016) Warm experts in the age of mandatory e-government: Interaction among Danish single parents regarding online application for public benefits. *Electronic Journal of E-government*, 14(1).

Moore, S. (1987) The theory of street-level bureaucracy: A positive critique. *Administration & Society*, 19(1): 74–94.

National Adult Literacy Agency (2020) *10-Year Adult Literacy, Numeracy and Digital Literacy Strategy for Ireland: A Whole of Government Approach 2020–2030*. https://www.nala.ie/wp-content/uploads/2020/12/NALA-submission-to-10-year-ALNDL-strategy-December2020.pdf

O'Sullivan, S., McGann, M. and Considine, M. (2021) *Buying and Selling the Poor: Inside Australia's Privatised Welfare-to-Work Market*. Sydney: Sydney University Press.

Perna, R. (2021) Street-level workers, managers, and institutional tensions: A comparative ethnography of healthcare practices of in/exclusion in three Italian public organisations. *CMS*, 9(16).

Scholta, H., Mertens, W., Kowalkiewicz, M. and Becker, J. (2019) From one-stop shop to no-stop shop: An e-government stage model. *Government Information Quarterly*, 36(1): 11–26.

Schoua, J. and Pors, A.S. (2018) Digital by default? A qualitative study of exclusion in digitalised welfare. *Social Policy Administration*. https://doi.org/10.1111/spol.12470

10

Co-designing digital services with service users, caseworkers and senior policy makers: the affordance and limitations of expert panels

Ray Griffin, Magnus Paulsen Hansen, Sabina Pultz, Maggie Müller, Didier Demazière and Martina Rameša

The political and ethical challenges of co-design

Policy makers, researchers and research funding bodies that service users, intermediaries and the public should be 'involved' in research. Interdisciplinary research has become popular, particularly among research funders and where cross-country collaborations set out to investigate and advance social, economic and technological challenges (Sonetti et al, 2020). The most recent European Commission strategy document that guides the funding calls for the 2025–2027 Horizon Europe framework programme calls for research that is based on co-creation and 'a co-design approach engaging a broad number of stakeholders' (European Commission, 2024: p 3), that establishes co-benefits through participative methods such as living labs and lighthouses focused on the social economy and grassroots stakeholders. The aim is to ensure research, particularly where digitalisation is central to economic progress and stability (European Commission, 2024).

Co-design is considered a new participatory configuration for policy development, variously a method, mindset, process and set of tools (Blomkamp, 2017), that brings a more active involvement from a diverse range of participants to explore, develop and test responses to complex, shared challenges. The abbreviated 'co' of co-design is loosely defined, but hints at cooperative or collaborative creation and designing, drawing on the Nordic tradition of participatory design (Steen et al, 2011), common in technology development (Sanders and Stappers, 2014), aligned to the growing interest in design-thinking (Mintrom and Luetjens, 2016). Indeed the methods of co-design are similarly unresolved, encompassing everything from ethnographic fieldwork, brainstorming and ideation activities, to using generative co-design tools that focus on user involvement and engagement, to more downstream design testing with users (Steen, 2013; Patrick, 2020).

Co-design is considered to have particular practical and values-based benefits in achieving more effective, democratic or innovative public policies, an alternative to conventional consultation or engagement (Andersen et al, 2017). Yet, like its definition, there is little settled between the various perspectives on how to co-design, and little formal evidence (Blomkamp, 2018) to guide an approach.

Given this, it is worth exploring what co-design particularly strives to accomplish. Bringing administration, end-users and the public into policy development addresses criticisms of expertocracies, through the co-production of knowledge, that explicitly allow individuals and groups to articulate their own issues and have a say in decisions that impact them. So, control of the production of knowledge (Foucault, 1977) about citizens is opened up to a broader network of relations from which knowledge and meaning are produced. In this way co-design symbolically assembles a technical democracy (Callon et al, 2011) to stand in the stead of the demos (Brown, 2015) and explicitly opens up expertocracies by allowing others in.

The aspiration is to ensure that voices from below and from the field – particularly service users and administrators – contribute to policy development. Often such groups are mistakenly thought of as lacking initiative (Garcia-Lorenzo et al, 2018). It is an aspiration to partially mitigate the power differential of top-down policy development. Beyond a principled stance, co-design is also advanced as a way of enhancing the relevance, efficacy and implementability of policy, by bringing in a better real-world understanding of contextual and practical constraints to policy goals. How this happens is by producing boundary objects (Bergman et al, 2007), a thing that intervenes, translate and negotiates to bridge intersecting practices. For example, we learned that caseworkers often have just 10 to 15 minutes with a client, and so any assistive technology needs to be immediately useful to stand a chance of being used in a meeting – this data produces the boundary object of the ten-minute case meeting that greatly influences the development of a digital tool.

So, co-design is also, in part, a recognition that wicked problems (Rittel and Webber, 1973) and globally pressing issues (Blomkamp, 2018) require open innovation (Chesbrough, 2003) as not one person, or type of person, has the knowledge, skill or legitimacy to understand and solve them.

Public employment service digitisation and co-design

Public service digitalisation projects are heavily contingent on existing structures and resources (Veale et al, 2018). Within public emplyoment service (PES) profiling algorithms, work to date follows 25 or more years of implementation of both formal and informal methods of identifying those at risk of long-term unemployment (Desiere and Struyven, 2021).

However, the predominant working model sees such models developed using individualised approaches which rarely rely on the currently recognised 'best practices' globally. Adopting a case-by-case approach to the development and deployment of new systems, failure to integrate across governmental factions and, more concerningly, failure to scope initially, have massive detriment to the success of these projects. Adding to this, the slow adoption of IT updates in governmental factions presents additional 'locked in systems' that fail to be transformative in the manner expected (Wenzelburger et al, 2024). This leads to what can often be described as a closed-loop innovation and is a keen factor in the failure of many such systems of this kind. Growing work looks at the role that humans play in algorithm development and deployment in response to development. However, while theoretical sense is made in the desire to build algorithms with their data subjects in mind, the stark reality reveals an almost oppositional case.

Algorithm imaginary, for instance, is an idea used to explore the spaces where people and algorithms meet (Bucher, 2018). This considers not just where and when algorithms are deployed or, indeed, their functionality, but rather delves into the role individual subjects should play in advancing the very tools under consideration (Büchi et al, 2023).

For all those reasons, co-design is particularly relevant considering unemployment policy and services, particularly activation policies and digital services as delivered by PES. Active labour market policies are long considered to be somewhat anti-democratic, where the state actively intervenes in citizens' lives, sometimes with behavioural interventions that nudge, sometimes with harsher disciplinary techniques (Watts and Fitzpatrick, 2018; Dwyer, 2019) to shepherd individuals back to the labour market. Similarly, researchers have criticised the use of datafication (Sztandar-Sztanderska and Zielenska, 2020) for replicating the inequalities experienced in the labour market in welfare systems (Gallagher and Griffin, 2023). Beyond these principled stances, both digital systems and activation policies are frequently abandoned (Allhutter et al, 2020), fall short of expectations or do not work as imagined.

So, to address practical shortcomings and the power differential, particularly the difficult trade-offs and muddled aspirations, it would appear that co-design should be used when conceiving new digital and activation services. In particular, both activation and digitisation policies are top-down in nature, imposed on various front-line actors, caseworkers and jobseekers, and there is considerable uncertainty over the effectiveness and relevance of these policy movements, particularly when these actors' views and constraints on action are not considered. As a result, this chapter reports on the experience and reflection of bringing unemployed people, caseworkers and senior policy makers and actors into the process using a co-design scenario vignette methodology in the development of disruptive technology for use in public employment services. The purpose and contribution of this chapter is to surface the impact of such design practices on the outcome of developing and deploying a digital platform that is usable, useful and of value.

Method

This chapter draws on data that was collected as part of an EU-funded research project to design, develop and deploy a digital-first tool for use by European PES to support job-search and career decision planning. The project aspired to embed co-design principles and practices for both philosophical and practical reasons. As an interdisciplinary project that aspired to develop working practices that encompassed open innovation and agile working arrangements between social scientists, data scientists and practice-based researchers, a key part of the design phase was to bring stakeholders' voices together to address the project goals. To achieve this, a series of expert panels – where a variety of individuals with highly specialised, close to practice experiences and opinions engage in focused debate and discussions – were convened.

These panels deployed vignettes that presented three concrete and realistic situations around the use of algorithmic tools to support the counselling of unemployed people in PES. As part of the scoping and benchmarking phase of the project, we wished to enhance our understanding of the needs, concerns and potential challenges of designing and deploying digital systems in PES beyond our single pilot site. The expert panels aspired to acquire a wide range of stakeholder views on the introduction of a digital decision support platform across four European countries – Denmark (DK), France (FR), Ireland (IE) and Slovenia (SL) – using a largely standardised format to collect data from the three separate panels of unemployed people, PES caseworkers (a blanket term that includes counsellors and advisors) and policy makers. Each group brings a specific perspective and experience to the digitisation of PES.

The data was collected by experienced social science researchers, who were part of the research team in each of the four countries (see Table 10.1), including the authors. Each focus group was conducted in their native language and translated into English by each of the three non-native-English-speaking teams. Following each focus group, a standardised report was completed by each of the four national research teams, findings were presented to the whole project consortium and then the reports and raw data were stored on the project repository for open analysis by consortium members. Each focus group, across all countries, drew on three scripted case scenario vignettes about the interaction between unemployed people and digital tools, seeking to solicit the views and responses from the three expert cohorts (Bloor, 2001).

Table 10.1: Schedule of data

Country	Policy makers	PES caseworkers	Unemployed people	Total
Denmark	3	5	4	12
France	5	9	9	23
Ireland	5	6	5	16
Slovenia (direct interviews replaced group discussions)	4	4	4	12
Total	17	24	22	63

Participants were recruited based on a purposive sampling technique to maximise representation from diverse backgrounds. Each focus group session commenced with an overview of the study's objectives and an assurance of participant confidentiality and anonymity; pseudonyms are used in this chapter. After repeated efforts to establish panels in Slovenia, we undertook direct interviews with participants instead of collective discussions, breaking the rubric, which has natural implications for the comparability of this data. The case vignettes were then presented to the participants, who were given sufficient time to review and comprehend the scenarios. A pilot version of the digital tool was shown to each group, including a demonstration of its key features. Each research team facilitated the discussions, encouraging participants to share their responses, opinions, ideas and concerns.

The three vignettes were carefully designed to present various realistic challenges and opportunities for discussion, each scenario developed based on interviews with Slovenian caseworkers and unemployed people. By way of analysis, each team of researchers summarised the discussions in each focus group for each vignette while including exemplary quotes in a report of around 50 pages. This formed the basis for a second-order analysis, using qualitative latent content analysis (Bengtsson, 2016) to understand and interpret the data. Latent analysis explores, at the interpretive level, what is the text talking about, and what is the underlying meaning of the text (Krippendorff, 2018). It was at this stage we incorporated the Slovenian interview vignette data into our interpretations, carefully annotating its origin to consider the implications of the difference in method. So, the transcripts were carefully read several times to gain familiarity with the information, and from this immersion in the visible text, gradually a deeper, overall meaning of the text became clear.

Reflecting on the aspirations for co-design, in both practice and principle, the analysis allows for a consideration of the affordance and limitations of expert panels as an approach to accomplishing co-designed policy. Beyond this, the exercise surfaces the complex views and trade-offs around trust in data, job quality and discrimination. When key stakeholders and users address concrete dilemmas they often and variously discuss issues through pre-existing frames, in this case around unemployed people's motivation, replicate systematic paternalism in ways that flattened citizen's autonomy.

Considering scenarios

The first vignette presented a scenario where a digital tool provided an unemployed person with a graph predicting the estimated time frame for finding a job and returning to the labour market. The discussion sought to surface what focus group participants thought about such algorithmic predictions, how trustworthy they are compared to the judgement of a PES caseworker, and whether it was helpful for PES to share such data with unemployed people. While statistical tools can offer valuable insights and guidance for decision-making, several key considerations must be taken into account to ensure their ethical and effective use. Discussions highlighted concerns regarding the limitations of statistical predictions in accounting for unexpected events and individual differences, emphasising the importance of considering individual circumstances and avoiding unrealistic expectations. Furthermore, while there was general agreement on the potential value of statistical predictions as an assessment tool for counsellors, participants stressed the crucial role of transparency, explainability and personalised support in communication. Stakeholder perspectives also emphasised the need for effective communication and sensitivity in utilising statistical data to avoid demoralisation or lack of confidence among unemployed individuals. Overall, the findings underscore the importance of approaching the use of statistical data for predicting periods of unemployment with caution, transparency and respect for individual circumstances to enhance decision-making processes and support provided to unemployed individuals. Here, communication of information has decisive consequences, with broad concern for the impact on individuals of self-discovery that might lead to self-stigmatisation and demoralisation. The role of caseworkers is understood to be vital to ensure supportive communication of sensitive data.

The second vignette highlighted the importance of job quality, expectations and stability of employment, and the complex personal trade-offs and compromises an unemployed individual might make in choosing high-quality sustainable employment that meets personal career goals. With minor differences between and across the various cohorts, the panels were very interested in the idea of using quality data to support unemployed people's decisions. This data appeared novel to all cohorts, and they appreciated the ability to parse job stability using factual data rather than anecdotal evidence. Policy makers and caseworkers were less enthusiastic than the unemployed cohorts about how job stability data should be presented, concerned that it would make unemployed people less flexible if they were to hold out for more stable work. Many panels felt that the intrinsic discrepancy between aggregated statistical data and personal situations, between a complex, real person and their stereotype, requires some mediation or translation through high quality casework and mentoring. All panels liked the idea of being able to play with the system, to try out different scenarios for changing careers, with counsellors particularly enthusiastic about having a tool that would provoke robust conversations about changes unemployed people might consider making. There was mixed reaction to the inclusion of training and skills data, information that impacts job quality, as caseworkers and policy makers wondered if it would divert attention from direct job search and promote unrealistic employment goals. The role of employers in training and skills engagement was a point of contention, with differing opinions on responsibility. In this way, in this revealing vignette, panels alluded to the political dimension of such a data infrastructure, with caseworkers steering the design towards something that would align with their goals for casework. As a result, these discussions surfaced the complex politics between job-first approaches against unemployment policies that favour slower human-capital-orientated approaches to job search that might yield more stable, sustainable or satisfying work.

The final vignette involved a scenario where a digital system revealed, very explicitly, an instance of clear ethnic discrimination in the labour market. This case aimed to invoke a discussion on the sensitivities of working with highly marginalised individuals. All panels indicated an abhorrence and intolerance for discrimination, lamenting its presence in the labour market, and broadened discussions about discrimination beyond race to include age, gender and ethnicity. Unemployed panels highlighted the role of the government and PES in overcoming discrimination, often in strong terms, but also saw the worth in having discrimination established as a fact for those who are subject to it. Caseworkers and policy makers considered the issue more strategically, accepting that the labour market is a site of discrimination, they wondered what could be gained from surfacing it so clearly and putting it in front of unemployed people, wary of how they would respond and what kind of conversations it might provoke.

Analysis: the imagined unemployed in digital services

As a pathway into exploring digital PES systems our exploration of the data began with ways in which caseworkers and counsellors draw on their cognitive schema – the inner organisation of their vast personal knowledge of clients and context into manageable categories. Not unlike the persona scenario method used in the development of technology to overcome the gap experienced between ideal-functional modelling of a system and the behaviours or needs of real-time users (LeRouge et al, 2013). When making sense of the vignettes presented in the focus groups with the caseworkers, it is clear that they build and articulate an imagined client pieced together from their codex of memories and vast experience of interactions with unemployed people; from those who will easily find employment to those who will always find it most difficult to gain sustainable employment due to issues such as health problems, addiction problems or inherent societal discrimination. We were struck by how little time they had with caseworkers, and so, how instantly useful a tool needed to be to impact on their time with a client. Interestingly, the unemployed also imagine other unemployed people, in a phenomenon we termed 'passing stigma', which we encountered interviewing unemployed people (Boland et al, 2022).

Our early, latent content analysis suggested two key dilemmas that surrounded all three vignettes.

First, all stakeholders were sensitive, in various ways, to the presentation and communication of information in a caring, empathetic, responsive way, a concern to mitigate any potential harm from a digital system being too honest, too forthright and harsh. Conversations oscillated and rolled around these mutually incompatible ambitions of being forthright, objective and clear with unemployed people, while also being sensitive to the impact on their motivation and perception of self-worth.

The second dilemma circled around data realism and personalisation. While all panellists accepted that data offered facts and the objective truth of a situation, they also felt that people are much more than their data, and needed to be treated in the round as complex, nuanced, irreducible humans. In ways, this discussion was nucleated in conversations around bias, that were much richer and broader than incomplete or inaccurate data, by speaking more to the potential for any person to be captured meaningfully in data.

Overall, the thematic analysis highlights the multifaceted considerations involved in using statistical information and data to advise unemployed individuals, underscoring the importance of tailored, empathetic and transparent approaches to supporting individuals in their journey towards re-employment and upskilling. These two dilemmas shape the terrain of the challenge when designing digital systems – they are put out into the world for use in ways that the designer and manager of the system are not fully aware of, and so lack feedback. They also capture the complex social challenge of delivering high-quality, empathic and meaningful services to unemployed people.

Reflections on co-designing

Our study aspired to surface the concerns and insight of administration, end-users and the public into the use of digital and algorithmic tools to support the counselling of unemployed people in PES. In our work, expert panels play a crucial role in co-designing our project's solution. Our deep commitment to co-design was perhaps elemental to our project being funded, supported and gaining legitimacy, and genuinely created a space for us to listen, in a deep and meditative way, to voices from across the world that we aspire to impact. It is perhaps too much to aspire to overcome the embedded top-down policy, technology and process orientation that drives existing welfare provision, after all, participants have been fully accultured in the world of unemployment, a pre-existing frame for the encounter. Yet, conversations were rich, reflective and meditative, echoing and amplifying established debated on digital welfare, activation, motivation, trust, paternalism and autonomy in and around the contemporary experience of unemployment. In total, 67 people generously gave between one and three hours of their time to consider the issues we raised, engage with the dilemmas and share their insight and experience.

The form of expert panels we used certainly broadened and clarified our understanding of the dilemmas that arise when using digital systems to deliver complex social services. While the vignettes relay the challenges, they did not directly offer a way through them, they did not immediately make our solutions any more efficacious or implementable. Rather, they established the challenges as intractable paradoxes, trade-offs, that may well be generic to all digital welfare systems. And yet, they had a significant effect by becoming somewhat immutable boundary objects that simply had to be negotiated and worked through, over and around in our research. Bringing in a wide range of stakeholders and caseworkers, from four different national contexts, and accessing all that real-world understanding of contextual and practical constraints did not make the digital services any more practical. Rather, we got the sense that these trade-offs are well-known and understood and that practitioners, particularly caseworkers and policy makers, accept their limited agency in shaping the role of digital solutions. Indeed, our primary reflection on the data is that all participants, to a greater or lesser extent, refused to fully engage with the idea of digital welfare services delivered without the input of front-line service providers, fortified by considerable discretion in how they interpret and apply policies and their critical role in orientating PES towards work-first policies even if they are not in the best long-term interest of their unemployed service users.

As a result, in our particular execution of expert panels, focus groups that use scenario vignettes worked in principle, in that they brought in important and often neglected voices – particularly those of unemployed users. We found when advocating and showcasing our project, as well as the ideas and contributions arising from the project, in policy forums, this offered us an important form of legitimacy. It is surprising how little research and knowledge production on and around unemployment includes the voice of unemployed people in the scope of the study. Indeed, a key feature of the panels with policy makers was how remote and aloof they are from unemployed people, compared to caseworkers. In this sense, unemployment research often works *on* people, rather than *with* them.

Our particular execution of expert panels worked more subtly in practice. In the first instance, the careful execution of the expert panels, and the act of paying attention gave the data a potency and worth within the research project. Once uttered in the expert panels, a thought or idea had currency across the project, particularly with technology, infrastructure and piloting partners. In such a troubled landscape of technological innovation, with many projects abandoned or criticised, sometimes with political implications, the voice from the field created space for more careful development. As a result, the vignettes became a boundary object for collaborating stakeholders in the project – a data artefact that acts to bridge intersecting practices. In our project, the unresolved anxiety over how digital systems can present information in an uncaring and harsh way, a fear expressed in almost all panels, drove an acute sensitivity to how we used language and framed data within our project's solution. The expert panels generated the authoritative boundary object through the specifically collaborative, democratic and creative mode of engagement with the field. In their absence, many of the more sociologically attuned researchers would have expressed a similar ethos, but such a view would have arisen from a paternalistic epistocracy of social science researchers knowing better. Within the project, this acute sensitivity to language and presentation led to specific taskforces that bridged the sociological and technological teams in designing the system in as sensitive a way as possible. Considerable effort went on making the system speak the users' language with words, phrases and concepts familiar to the user rather than system-orientated terms.

Data from the expert panels that problematised data realism and personalisation, and the shared concern that people are much more than their data, led to a boundary object of our research consortium conceiving of a minimalist and modest tool rather than a solution. This harks back to a key distinction made at the foundation of the internet between tools and solutions (Moore, 1998) – a tool is a simple single-function object, cheap, practical and used when useful; whereas solutions are large complex bespoke multifunctional problem-solvers. Based on that insight from the expert panels, we concluded a solutions approach would encourage us to solve the unemployment of a person; whereas a tool might be useful to someone autonomously figuring out their labour market situation. This subtle difference encouraged us to pull back from over-specifying the capacity of a digital system to help a person.

As a result, the two outcomes of our thematic analysis generated strong boundary objects that shaped the development of our project's tool. The data, translated into knowledge that our entire consortium had to come to understand, and then was negotiated with in specialist domains as we sought to produce something co-designed. Here, co-design did not solve problems for us, rather they translated them into boundary objects that were the hidden-in-plain-sight design constraints. These boundary objects allowed us as a consortium to unite and form a working relationship, particularly overcoming the two cultures (Snow, 1998) – sciences and humanities – an enduring challenge of interdisciplinary, problem-based research.

Conclusion

This short chapter sought to relay our experience of using co-design scenario vignettes to involve stakeholders – users, intermediaries and the public – as co-designers of a digital data-driven tool to support unemployed people. We reflected upon the affordance and limitations of expert panels in co-designing, assistive to anyone seeking to use expert panels to co-design, highlighting how important this involvement is in principle to symbolically assemble a technical democracy to stand in the stead of the demos. In our project, attending to co-design was vital to secure funding support and patronage. The expert panel approach helped to surface and clarify the dilemmas and trade-offs inherent in moving to more digitised welfare. In particular, they highlight that digitalisation is not just a matter of tool production, data robustness and dissemination within PES organisations, but rather it is an intervention into concrete situations, the lives of unemployed people and the work of caseworkers and front-line officers, all with distinctive constraints, situations and ambitions.

Beyond this, they relay significant practical wisdom, phronesis, from the field, from the world of practice, implementation and impact of social policy actions. In advancing co-design through the use of scenario vignette panels, a focus group of a sort, there was little by way of immediately relevant input that would improve the efficacy and implementation of our solution. Rather these panels were useful in clarifying the dilemmas and trade-offs inherent in the development of digital social policy. This wisdom, earnest but often unhelpful, becomes a boundary object within the research community, a site of interpretation, understanding, translation and negotiation between the various professional disciplines that work on digital welfare. Finding a way through or around such boundary objects is vital to attending to the practical issues of implementation, it comes from listening carefully, paying attention, and deep reflection on mobilising a response through research engagement.

References

Allhutter, D., Cech, F., Fischer, F., Grill, G. and Mager, A. (2020) Algorithmic profiling of job seekers in Austria: How austerity politics are made effective. *Frontiers in Big Data*, 3: 502780.

Andersen, N.A., Caswell, D. and Larsen, F. (2017) A new approach to helping the hard-to-place unemployed: The promise of developing new knowledge in an interactive and collaborative process. *European Journal of Social Security*, 19(4): 335–352.

Bengtsson, M. (2016) How to plan and perform a qualitative study using content analysis. *NursingPlus Open*, 2: 8–14.

Bergman, M., Lyytinen, K. and Mark, G. (2007) Boundary objects in design: An ecological view of design artifacts. *Journal of the Association for Information System*, 8(11): 546–568.

Blomkamp, E. (2018) The promise of co-design for public policy 1. In *Routledge Handbook of Policy Design* (pp 59–73). Routledge.

Bloor, M. (ed) (2001) *Focus Groups in Social Research*. London: SAGE.

Boland, T., Doyle, K. and Griffin, R. (2022) Passing stigma: Negotiations of welfare categories as street level governmentality. *Social Policy and Society*, 21(4): 657–667.

Brown, W. (2015) *Undoing the Demos: Neoliberalism's Stealth Revolution*. Cambridge, MA: MIT Press.

Bucher, T. (2018) *If … Then: Algorithmic Power and Politics*. Oxford: Oxford University Press.

Büchi, M., Fosch-Villaronga, E., Lutz, C., Tamò-Larrieux, A. and Velidi, S. (2023) Making sense of algorithmic profiling: User perceptions on Facebook. *Information, Communication & Society*, 26(4): 809–825.

Callon, M., Lascoumes, P. and Barthe, Y. (2011) *Acting in an Uncertain World: An Essay on Technical Democracy*. Cambridge, MA: MIT Press.

Chesbrough, H.W. (2003) *Open Innovation: The New Imperative for Creating and Profiting from Technology*. Cambridge, MA: Harvard Business Press.

Desiere, S. and Struyven, L. (2021) Using artificial intelligence to classify jobseekers: The accuracy-equity trade-off. *Journal of Social Policy*, 50(2): 367–385.

Dwyer, P. (ed) (2019) *Dealing with Welfare Conditionality: Implementation and Effects*. Bristol: Policy Press.

European Commission (2024) *2025–2027 Horizon Europe Framework Programme*.

Foucault, M. (1977) *Discipline and Punish: The Birth of the Prison*. London: Allen Lane.

Gallagher, P. and Griffin, R. (2023 accuracy in algorithmic profiling of the unemployed: An exploratory review of reporting standards. *Social Policy and Society*: 1–14.

Garcia-Lorenzo, L., Donnelly, P., Sell-Trujillo, L. and Imas, J.M. (2018) Liminal entrepreneuring: The creative practices of nascent necessity entrepreneurs. *Organization Studies*, 39(2–3): 373–395.

Krippendorf, K. (2018). *Content Analysis: An Introduction to Its Methodology*, 4th edition. Los Angeles: SAGE.

Lerouge, C., Ma, J., Sneha, S. and Tolle, K.M. (2013). User profiles and personas in the design and development of consumer health technologies. *International Journal of Medical Informatics*, 82(11): 251–268.

Mintrom, M. and Luetjens, J. (2016) Design thinking in policymaking processes: Opportunities and challenges. *Australian Journal of Public Administration*, 75(3): 391–402.

Moore, G.A. (1998) *Crossing the Chasm*. Capstone.

Patrick, R. (2020) Unsettling the anti-welfare commonsense: The potential in participatory research with people living in poverty. *Journal of Social Policy*, 49(2): 251–270.

Rittel, H.W. and Webber, M.M. (1973) Dilemmas in a general theory of planning. *Policy Sciences*, 4(2): 155–169.

Sanders, E.B.N. and Stappers, P.J. (2014) Probes, toolkits and prototypes: Three approaches to making in codesigning. *CoDesign*, 10(1): 5–14.

Snow, C.P. (1998) *The Two Cultures*. Cambridge: Cambridge University Press.

Sonetti, G., Arrobbio, O., Lombardi, P., Lami, I.M. and Monaci, S. (2020) 'Only social scientists laughed': Reflections on social sciences and humanities integration in European energy projects. *Energy Research & Social Science*, 61: 101342.

Steen, M. (2013) Co-design as a process of joint inquiry and imagination. *Design Issues*, 29(2): 16–28.

Steen, M., Manschot, M. and De Koning, N. (2011) Benefits of co-design in service design projects. *International Journal of Design*, 5(2): 53–60.

Sztandar-Sztanderska, K. and Zielenska, M. (2020) What makes an ideal unemployed person? Values and norms encapsulated in a computerized profiling tool. *Social Work & Society*, 18(1): 1–16.

Veale, M., Van Kleek, M. and Binns, R. (2018) Fairness and accountability design needs for algorithmic support in high-stakes public sector decision-making. *Proceedings of the 2018 Chi Conference on Human Factors in Computing Systems*. ACM Conference on Human Factors in Computing Systems, 21–26 April, Montreal.

Watts, B. and Fitzpatrick, S. (2018) *Welfare Conditionality*. London: Routledge.

Wenzelburger, G., König, P.D., Felfeli, J. and Achtziger, A. (2024) Algorithms in the public sector: Why context matters. *Public Administration*, 102(1): 40–60.

11

Digital or human support for the unemployed? Profiling tools and advisers at work in the French public employment services

Alizée Delpierre, Didier Demazière and Aurélie Gonnet

Introduction

Tools designed to profile unemployed people are basically a means of calculating the individual risk of experiencing long-term unemployment (Grundy, 2015). The proliferation of algorithmic technologies in public employment services (PES) in many Organisation for Economic Co-operation and Development countries (Loxha and Morgandi, 2014; Desiere et al, 2019; Haug, 2022) has had a significant impact on profiling. Traditionally, profiling was carried out by advisers, who relied on their professional expertise to characterise the situation of each unemployed person and deduce the appropriate support. With profiling tools, the risk of remaining unemployed instead becomes a statistical calculation, and the relationship of this calculation to the adviser's estimation of the same risk raises questions. Do the two methods coexist, or does the new replace the old? Are they experienced as complementary? And do they cause tensions in advisers' work?

We address these questions from the perspective of the French case, which has certain distinctive features: statistical profiling was implemented within the public employment agency (Pôle Emploi) very late (towards the end of the 2010s), but has become inescapable. So much so that it structures the script for registration interviews, and has technical features designed to make it more acceptable to advisers. To study how advisers use statistical profiling, we conducted fieldwork at Pôle Emploi between 2020 and 2023. We brought together various materials: interviews with people involved in the implementation of statistical profiling, numerous written documents on the debate underlying profiling policies, interviews with 20 advisers working at several local Pôle Emploi agencies, and observations of jobseeker registration interviews, in the course of which profiling is carried out. We develop our analysis around three questions:

1. How statistical profiling was set up to assist advisers.
2. How this technical tool fits into adviser workplace environments.
3. How advisers use it in various ways.

Statistical profiling in France: a helpful tool for advisers?

The spread of statistical profiling tools within the PES is part of a broader trend towards the digitisation of PES (and public services in general). User contacts with welfare state services are 'increasingly digitalized' (Pors and Schou, 2021), and widespread use of IT and computers has been interpreted in terms of the transformation of street-level bureaucracy into 'system-level bureaucracy' (Bovens and Zouridis, 2002) or 'screen-level bureaucracy' (Hansen et al, 2018). In some cases, 'digitized welfare' (Coles-Kemp et al, 2020) goes beyond the delivery of certain services via online applications; indeed, as shown by the Australian experiment with a 'fully automated PES', it can mean remote monitoring of most users via algorithms (Casey, 2022). In a fairly similar configuration, the role of front-line agents is limited to assisting users or customers in their use of digital tools (Bullock, 2019).

In the French PES (as well as in most others), the information system is less invasive and hegemonic, and the service relationship only partially digitised. This is the case for the instrument we are studying here, namely statistical profiling, which is part of a 'double activation' policy (Considine et al, 2015): it is not only a matter of disciplining the unemployed, but also of influencing the practices of front-line advisers. Consequently, examination of both how this framing is produced, and how it is received by advisers, contributes to analyses of street-level bureaucracy (Maynard-Moody and Portillo, 2010). This in turn fuels questions about the future of the discretionary component, which is deemed inherent (or even necessary) (Brodkin, 2011) to advisers' work under the influence of digitisation. Despite the variety of technologies considered and situations studied, most studies diagnose a malaise among professionals: a downgrading of expertise, a reinforcement of remote hierarchical control, and reduced autonomy in supporting the unemployed (Jansson and Erlingsson, 2014; Nordesjö et al, 2022). This yielding of the discretionary aspect of work (Busch and Henriksen, 2017) to rising levels of automation (Jorna and Wagenaar, 2007) or disciplinarisation (Zouridis et al, 2020) has also been diagnosed in other public services.

As one of the PES's many digitalisation tools, statistical profiling is an interesting example, because it goes to the heart of the work of front-line advisers. When they meet unemployed people for individual interviews, they gather information about the person and qualify their situation in terms of employability and exposure to the risk of long-term unemployment, then deduce prescriptions and an appropriate form of follow-up. In the French case at least, the heuristic value of profiling lies in the place assigned to the technical tool in production of the service. This is because profiling does not produce any imperative recommendation that would impose itself on both unemployed person and adviser; rather, it is designed to assist the adviser in his or her activity. Of the various existing PES services digitalisation models (Considine et al, 2022), it falls into the 'technology-assisted' category, that is, technology that is targeted at the adviser and designed to influence his or her work with the unemployed.

The challenge is to understand precisely what 'assisted' means here, that is, how profiling algorithms modify the work of advisers. These algorithms also produce a breakdown of jobseekers into categories, but according to an alternative – supposedly more efficient and rational – method, based on a calculation of statistical risk. As a result, the purpose of these algorithms is not simply to assist advisers, but also to take over part of their work. And since these conditions make it difficult for an adviser to 'say no to a computer' (Sztandar-Sztanderska and Zielenska, 2022), the question arises as to whether this instrument replaces, complements or weakens the profiling traditionally based on adviser expertise. The first step towards answering this question is to analyse the characteristics of the profiling tool and the conditions under which it is implemented at adviser workstations.

Between 2005 and 2008, an initial profiling algorithm was introduced within the public employment agency. It was designed to save money by identifying the most employable unemployed people and encouraging them to take up work more quickly. This first attempt was a failure. This can largely be explained by the algorithm's shortcomings in terms of precision and accuracy (Desiere and Struyven, 2021). Advisers shunned it, because their own profiling often produced different results, and external evaluations showed that it was based on incomplete information. This undermined its effectiveness, and the management of ANPE, the national public employment agency (which had no control over how it was set up), publicly challenged its validity. This failure had a direct impact on the reintroduction of statistical profiling from the mid-2010s. Three main points emerge from this second experiment: the development of profiling was late in coming, but became an imperative necessity; it was introduced into the organisation by stealth, as part of a wider digitalisation plan; the tool incorporated a large amount of data and was designed to be a decision-making aid for advisers (Delpierre et al, 2024).

After statistical profiling was abandoned in 2007–2008, this question disappeared from the Pôle Emploi agenda, as well as from its management's communication. There were, however, oblique indications that major investments were underway. The information systems department was recruiting regularly, and expanding its team of data scientists. As part of the national plan to digitise public services, Pôle Emploi was developing its web portal, grafting onto it multiple applications destined to be accessible to jobseekers. Specific funding had been obtained for the initiation of large-scale data collection projects such as Intelligence Emploi. For the management, this digitisation was a major step forward, because it offered a means of responding to the pressure of jobseeker flows that were experienced internally as unbearable, and were interpreted by advisers as detrimental to their work. Officially, the average adviser portfolio was set to 350 – a figure that assumed many jobseekers were being followed up exclusively by e-mail or telephone. But actual portfolio size varied widely and could reach 700. Against this backdrop of scarce resources, profiling tools were seen by management as a response to the bottlenecks that had built up in many local agencies. Statistical ('good') profiling can be a way of modulating the service provided by offering 'individually tailored follow-up' and devoting 'more time to those who need it most', as some management representatives put it.

The strategic priority was therefore clear. Yet, the Pôle Emploi managers we met during our fieldwork were unanimous in their astonishment when we asked them about profiling: for them, there is neither a tool, nor a policy, of statistical profiling. According to our fieldwork, over the past decade, statistical profiling seems to have completely disappeared. The term is never mentioned by Pôle Emploi managers. This disappearance is however no more than a façade: it is the word 'profiling', above all, that has been banished from internal and external communication. According to a member of the management team, this was because 'it created a lot of tension ... more problems than solutions'. Bruised by the failure of the first experiment, management was now cautious, highlighting the 'personalised jobseeker diagnostics' tools aimed at ensuring each jobseeker would be 'directed to the right service, the one that is a good match for his or her situation'. This is precisely what profiling does – but the word was left lurking in the shadows. Only the data scientists responsible for developing the algorithms were willing to say that the 'personalised diagnostics' were based on profiling tools, which had in fact been discreetly implemented as part of the information system update. The IT interfaces were now installed on adviser workstations, and henceforth the application used for registration interviews incorporated a profiling and recommendation algorithm that has found its way into the heart of the workplace environment by stealth.

The jobseeker's 'personalised diagnostics' application is now the mainstay of the mandatory interview at registration, at the end of which jobseekers are assigned to different types of support. Those considered to be 'most in difficulty' are directed towards 'reinforced' support, while those who are 'most autonomous' get simple 'follow-up'. Those placed in an intermediate category are directed towards 'guided' support. The three types of service differ in terms of frequency of meetings with advisers, contact methods used (face-to-face or remote), and range of services on offer. This personalised diagnosis differs from the initial profiling tool in several respects. The information base is very different: the data included is both more numerous and updated during the interview by the adviser, who supplements it with qualitative variables that serve to open up space for the exercise of his or her expertise. This additional data includes information on living conditions, job-seeking behaviours, deviations from occupational targets (being qualified for a job for which demand is low, not having the qualification corresponding to the target), and so on. The algorithm assesses the jobseeker's position in relation to employment, breaking it down into different dimensions: occupational project, job search, labour market situation and 'peripheral obstacles'. It is, then, much more than just a score for distance to work or the risk of long-term unemployment. Rather, the classic measure of employability is supplemented by, for example, an assessment of the jobseeker's behaviour and social situation. Profiling does not boil down to a single score, and even less to an automated system for decision-making or suggestions. The profiling tool uses its technical characteristics to enable (or even encourage) the adviser to work in an interpretative way. As one member of Pôle Emploi's management team put it: 'One of the difficulties is to ensure that the adviser uses the algorithm correctly. … That's why we enrich what the algorithm says, by adding the reasons why it thinks this or that. It's a real plus for advisers, and we hope they'll embrace it more easily too.' The fact that profiling aggregates more, and more varied, information may build its acceptability in the eyes of advisers, possibly underpinning the decision support provided to them, and thus weigh on the relationship between statistical-based profiling and caseworker-based profiling. For this reason, we must now examine how this technical tool fits into advisers' workplace environment.

Profiling tools within advisers' workplace environments

The discreet, though effective, embedding of profiling (through personalised diagnostics in particular) does impact advisers' day-to-day work – first and foremost via the computer interface that frames their interaction with jobseekers. Like any technical tool (Akrich, 2010), it helps codify the exchange by predefining not only roles and modes of interaction, but also the expectations and intentions of the parties involved. The room for manoeuvre available in carrying out the registration interview is therefore constrained by the current socio-technical system, which at the same time puts the relationship in tension. Indeed, the script imposed by the diagnostics tool immediately positions the jobseeker not so much as a benefits claimant or someone seeking support towards finding employment, but as someone required to answer a series of questions concerning the verification of administrative data, the definition of a 'reasonable job offer' and the identification of potential obstacles. He or she is then presented with details of the services on offer at Pôle Emploi – with an emphasis on digital tools and online platforms. Given the sheer number of these – according to one adviser, there are 'almost 270 applications dedicated to job search, training and guidance' – only a few are generally mentioned, often on-the-fly. This does nonetheless enable advisers to point to their knowledge and skills in terms of support. In this way, they distance themselves from the image of a simple 'data entry operator' that the personalised diagnosis tends to convey.

Lasting between 30 and 45 minutes on average, these interviews are particularly dense in terms of the amount of data entered, information delivered, tools mentioned, services suggested, and so on, despite the advisers' efforts to render intelligible the workings of an institution stuffed with acronyms and tools. Observation of these interactions reveals a tension between the relative passivity of the unemployed person (imposed from the outset by the diagnosis) and the desire to make them 'self-responsible', capable of taking charge of their own job search by leveraging the tools made available. In fact, it is as if the newly registered unemployed person is seen as a jobseeker who, while perhaps not deficient, at least needs a 'diagnosis' so that they can be 'prescribed' the means to rapidly gain autonomy in navigating the PES service offer, meet the institution's expectations and, ultimately, find a job.

Yet another tension also regularly arises out of the fact that this last perspective (like matters of compensation), is ultimately scarcely touched upon in the course of this interview. It is largely devoted to profiling, despite the fact that many unemployed people expect that this first (and sometimes only) face-to-face meeting will result in the identification of concrete job leads. Because of this tension, advisers end up frequently repeating the principle that 'Pôle Emploi is not here to find you a job, but to help you find one on your own' – and profiling is intended to help target this assistance.

The diagnosis, followed by assignment to the various support modes, may well be confusing to unemployed people. But within the advisers' practice, it is all perfectly routine – in some respects forming the common bedrock of their work. These registration interviews are an integral part of their weekly schedule and everyone, regardless of status (fixed-term or open-ended contract), seniority or expertise, conducts them. Far from being a cause for criticism, the fact that these procedures are both amply equipped and institutionally framed seems, if anything, to contribute to their acceptance. They enable advisers to get by even without having a thorough grasp of all the systems and information required for the work of offering jobseekers guidance and support (the multiplicity of which is described by all), while still leaving a certain amount of room for interpersonal skills to come into play.

In fact, besides smoothing out the terminology used in the first profiling experiments, the 'personalised diagnosis' has another advantage that makes it easier to accept. With a few (not insignificant) exceptions (such as contact information, reasonable job offer), the tool allows you to leave certain items unprocessed, or indeed to switch to another interface (online applications, various websites and so on) during the compulsory post-registration interview. The diagnostics tool also includes free text spaces for adviser comments – limited, of course (we'll come back to this), but nonetheless praised by many and used by all. Lastly, the results produced by the algorithm do not automatically assign the case in question to a given portfolio: this is decided by the adviser, and may even be discussed with the jobseeker.

These technical configurations contribute to rendering statistical profiling discreet (or even stealthy) – even in the eyes of the researchers, who have observed advisers juggling screens or gathering accounts from professionals who indicate (in hushed tones) that they do not complete all or part of the diagnostics, at risk of being called to order. The possibility of bypassing the tool, while very limited and rarely used, might suggest a failure of the tool, but seems more likely to be read as a condition of its appropriation – an appropriation which, in the case of technical innovation, can be seen as proof of success (Akrich et al, 1988). This 'human/machine', or 'human/non-human' combination (Latour, 1992), saves a space for the adviser's relational work. Indeed, while most advisers scarcely question the usefulness of the personalised diagnostics tool, or even understand its value, all insist that it is no more than a technical support. Advisers tend to stress that it cannot (and should not) replace the 'human', signalling – as others, including doctors, have done (Méadel and Akrich, 2010) – both their expertise and the relational dimension of their work. For these professionals, the proper functioning of the profiling algorithm requires them to identify the needs, resources and individual difficulties of the unemployed person. They argue that some of these difficulties can only be solved within a dialogue that happens in a climate of trust (health problems, phobias, experiences of professional harassment, housing problems, addictions, and so on) and/or cannot easily be resolved within the categories offered by the interface – partly for legal reasons.

> Someone who has recently experienced harassment at work, when she was only 21 and it was her first job, she develops a work phobia and it's not registered in the file. Oh yes, it does say that there's a barrier to employment. Yeah, but what kind of barrier? And the person can't fill out the file with this. To talk about this, they need to trust you. Otherwise they will simply avoid applying for a job, because they're scared. (Interview with Mrs K., adviser, 7 December 2022)

If the files are correctly filled out, which is no simple matter – and all the more so, given the dematerialisation of support – these tools can be used to 'personalise' support by means of filters that enable advisers to target parts of their portfolios to promote offers of training, employment or support – but also to identify those unemployed people in difficulty: '[I]t's really tools that enable us to do what we call portfolio segmentation, so to really work in-depth on candidates in a general way, to do the famous "stock take" for very long-term jobseekers' (interview with Mrs M., adviser, 6 December 2022). Indeed, while the majority believe that profiling tools are likely to facilitate certain aspects of advisers' work, they do, like any innovation (Alter, 2010; Gaglio, 2011), also carry a risk of disappointment which is all the greater because of high expectations – particularly under the influence of public discourse on the revolution to be brought about by the digitisation of public service in general, and the increased use of algorithms in particular (Baudot et al, 2015).

Thus, while few advisers dispute the principle of assigning jobseekers to categories on the basis of their degree of autonomy, all acknowledge the presence of internal discrepancies in their portfolios that are at odds with the profile-to-service offer match. This is the case, for example, for some jobseekers in the 'follow-up' category, who are supposed to be highly autonomous and have thus been prescribed a direct return-to-employment without need of any lengthy training – but who nonetheless express the need for it. This is also, and above all, the case with the 'guided' category, which is meant to apply to jobseekers seeking retraining or training. But through a series of communicating vessels, those who have no such project but are not sufficiently autonomous (especially in terms of digital confidence) to be assigned to the (now entirely dematerialised) simple 'follow-up' category, get lumped together with others who would ordinarily be covered by 'reinforced' support, whose portfolios regularly prove to be oversubscribed.

While the principle of digital tools (including the personalised diagnostics tool) is rarely questioned, their use is frequently criticised as being cumbersome, sometimes random, and requiring a plethora of actions and clicks:

> What I find a bit difficult is that we still have a lot of clicks, pages and things to check. … So with all that, there's a kind of data entry, there's a real data entry job to be done. If only for the interviews we have – every interview involves a few lines of writing. Well, sometimes we have a lot to say … unfortunately, the database doesn't allow me to put it all in the same place. So, I have to cut them out. This job involves a lot of processing. (Interview with Ms P., adviser, 6 December 2022)

Lastly, even though personalised diagnostics are now fully integrated into the adviser's day-to-day professional practices, both its perceived limitations and potential criticisms of it are less likely to be voiced because of the tool's success than because of the lack of space in which to express difficulties or suggest avenues for improvement – a *sine qua non* for the long-term success of any innovation (Akrich, 2006). Moreover, this absence of a concerted approach (one that is attentive to the concrete practice of advisers) is likely to fuel their fears about the risk of the human being replaced by the machine – or at least of their skills, and the way in which they see their profession, as being called into question. This can be seen clearly in the different ways in which these tools are used.

Two ways advisers use profiling in their day-to-day work

The fact that algorithmic profiling has become an inescapable part of the daily work of Pôle Emploi advisers does not however mean that they rely on the statistical results produced by profiling. It is true that there has been no collective mobilisation aimed at removing profiling from the digital tools at their disposal. Individually, however, advisers are voicing criticisms, the main one being that profiling threatens their professionalism by replacing their own assessment of individual situations. It is not so much that they are questioning the ethical issues involved in the systematic use of profiling, more that they fear the consequences for their professional skills and identity. In interviews, advisers emphasised their expertise, based on 'face-to-face' assessment of the unemployed person's situation and career path. Here, we find a rhetoric that has classic status within professional worlds vulnerable to automation and digitalisation, namely that of the threat of the human being replaced by a tool, as in the case of cashiers faced with automated checkouts (Bernard, 2012).

> On the second day of our fieldwork in the local agency B. branch, the manager called us together to pass on some feedback from the advisers we'd met the day before. 'They were worried, because they're afraid everything will be handed over to Artificial Intelligence' she reports, 'they feel devalued if it's the machine that decides everything.' (Agency B., notes dated 7 December 2022)

Some advisers expressed fears that our academic research could be used to establish new algorithmic profiling tools. Such fears crystallise the opposition advisers have established between themselves and the tool. In practice, however, these fears underlie their more nuanced day-to-day negotiations with the tool. While all the advisers agree that the tool should not be totally relied upon, they also all express the complementarity between their expertise and the tool's calculations. Their practices reveal a compromise between suspicion (or even rejection) of the tool's categorisation, and the injunction to obey the institution (Pôle Emploi) responsible for promoting reliance on the tool. In other words, no adviser completely disregards the profiling tool, and neither does any adviser intend to subjugate their own expertise to the tool's categorisation. There are, however, several variations to be found within this common approach to professional assessment and profiling. At Pôle Emploi, there is a polarisation of practices and uses. While one adviser might stick to a 'procedural' approach characterised by a concern to fill in the form items almost exhaustively during an initial registration; another might be described as more 'selective', leaving some boxes blank and more room for personal assessment.

> At Agency B., we attend a first individualised follow-up interview with Mr C. He is interviewing a young woman holding a French 'business' baccalaureate, who has 7 months' work experience in a bakery. She has filled in the online application prior to attending the appointment. The adviser scrupulously goes through all the items, and asks her about her career plans. The young woman is sure of herself: she wants to train to work in eyelash extensions, and her goal is to work in a beauty salon, or for herself. The adviser explains that training opportunities in this field are rare, and moves on to the next items, which ask her to say what she would consider a 'reasonable job offer'. Although she assures him there is only this one plan that is close to her heart, the adviser insists that she must fill in all the boxes. He quotes a list of jobs along the lines of 'receptionist, secretary', and despite the young woman's objections, concludes with a satisfied look. 'OK? Shall we confirm?' He then criticises her for 'going off in all directions' and reminds her that she needs to 'secure the plan' by going through the steps dictated by the form. Once the form is fully completed, the algorithm informs her that she will be in the 'guided' category. The young woman has already uploaded two CVs to her personal digital space, but the adviser says he'll book her in for the 8-week 'skills prep'. The young woman tells him that she can't afford to wait 8 weeks to look for a job, and he replies: 'but you have to go step by step, that's the protocol'. (Observation in Agency B, 6 December 2022)

This particular adviser's assiduous approach to completing the form is part of a more all-encompassing approach to support that entails adherence to every detail of the roadmap set out by Pôle Emploi – in this case, the injunction to send unemployed people on training (or refresher) courses in certain skills that are supposedly required. He is not alone in using the profiling in this way, and in so doing he reveals the way in which he embodies his role – in this case, using a strongly procedural-based method, which scarcely goes beyond institutional directives.

This procedural-based use of profiling differs from the more selective approach, which entails distancing oneself, during the initial registration interview, from the items on the forms. Mrs D. is a counsellor specialising in supporting young people who face multiple barriers to employment. She, unlike Mr C., feels she can't just settle for following the tool's instructions, because she wants to be sincere and credible in the support she offers to the young people she works with. For her, the tool, and the items to be filled in, are symbolised by the computer screen that separates her from the young person sitting opposite her at her desk, hindering the human relationships that are at the heart of her work as a counsellor.

> We ask her how she combines listening to young people and filling in the form in the allotted timeslot (30 minutes). 'And so, the questionnaire, of course, comes back to something we've already grasped. But we still spend a certain amount of time in … we left some screens … aside for a while. It punctuates things. The screens are there to punctuate stages of the interview. And that's how it was before I started working with young people. We go into the questionnaire, we discuss it again, and if they agree to join, we sign them up. And when we are signing the contract, at that point, right in front of them, I enter the conclusions of the interview and we give … we decide together on the next appointment, since we're lucky enough to be able to postpone the appointment.' (Interview with Mrs D., adviser, 30 November 2022)

The young people Mrs D. is in charge of have already been categorised during an initial registration interview with another adviser. When she meets a young unemployed person referred to her for the first time, Mrs D. assesses whether they correspond to the specific follow-up category into which they have been classified. In short, what Mrs D. uses above all is her own assessment of the young person's background, characteristics and aspirations.

> So, the prescription doesn't mean we're going to monitor them, it means that we meet them for an initial interview, which is a bit like a meeting where we get to know each other, and confirm the diagnosis – or not. The person must also agree to receive the support on offer. (Interview with Mrs D., adviser, 30 November 2022)

The case of Mrs D. points us towards the variables that explain these differences in use of the algorithmic profiling tool: adviser specialisation being one such difference. Advisers in charge of supporting the most vulnerable unemployed people, who are far from employment – as Mrs D. does – insist on the artificiality of certain items, which fail to consider the multiple barriers to employment that will only come to light in the course of a discussion with the adviser. Two other variables also emerge from our fieldwork: the adviser's length of service with Pôle Emploi, and the training they have received. Because Mrs D. has been with Pôle Emploi for 17 years, her employment there pre-dates the merger. As the daughter of high school teachers, she did a degree in art history before sitting the competitive examination to become a Pôle Emploi civil servant. She says she is attached, by virtue of her family socialisation, to the notion of 'public service', which for her, takes precedence over the managerial and digital logics likely to hamper this 'service'. Along with other public service advisers recruited to Pôle Emploi more than 15 years ago, her use of the profiling tool is more occasional, and she insists that it represents a threat to the strong identity of advisers shared by these 'old hands'. This identity is characterised by the fact that they hold university degrees or work psychology qualifications, equipping them with special skills in supporting the unemployed. Whereas the 'younger' advisers come from a wide variety of backgrounds – especially digital technology, engineering and business. They have been recruited on private contracts, and share neither the professional ethos of the older staff nor their nostalgia for a PES in which digital (and even IT) tools played only a marginal role. These 'youngsters' therefore rely more readily on the institution and the profiling tool – like Mr C., who has been at Pôle Emploi for four years and was previously a retail manager.

The most divisive variables in behaviours observed around the profiling tool are: the category of public the advisers serve; their length of service with Pôle Emploi; and their training. This finding is in line with observations made by Céleste Watkins-Hayes in two social services departments in Massachusetts, United States (Watkins-Hayes, 2009). She realises, as we do, that seniority in the profession explains social workers' greater or lesser distance from prescribed work, as do other variables such as the sex, class and race of the agents and users they encounter – which opens other analytical perspectives.

Conclusion

Our fieldwork at Pôle Emploi reveals that statistical profiling is now firmly established, and without any major collective protest. This does not mean, however, that advisers fully embrace the tool, nor that they use it in the same way. Their backgrounds and modes of entry to the institution are extremely heterogeneous, and reflect different conceptions of the adviser role. Because it reinforces the weight of the institution in their work, statistical profiling reveals diverse conceptions of the profession. In this respect, the statistical profiling tool – and more broadly, the digitalisation of the work of advisers – has a paradoxical, even counterintuitive, effect: by limiting the discretionary power of advisers, it is meant to reduce inequality of treatment and variability of practice, even as room for flexibility remains, but it allows room for flexibility and does not erase the diversity of professional practices. As a result, a new source of unpredictability arises in the workplace: one that is indexed to the use of tools and the conception of the work and the profession.

References

Akrich, M. (2006) Les utilisateurs, acteurs de l'innovation. In M. Akrich, M. Callon and B. Latour (eds) *Sociologie de la traduction* (pp 253–265). Paris: Presses des Mines.

Akrich, M. (2010) Comment décrire les objets techniques? *Techniques & Culture. Revue semestrielle d'anthropologie des techniques*: 54–55: 205–219.

Akrich, M., Callon, M. and Latour, B. (1988) A quoi tient le succès des innovations? 1: L'art de l'intéressement; 2: Le choix des porte-parole. *Gérer et Comprendre. Annales des Mines, 11-12*: 4-17.

Alter, N. (2010) *L'innovation ordinaire*. Paris: Presses Universitaires de France.

Baudot, P.-Y., Marrel, G. and Nonjon, M. (2015) Encore une révolution informatique? Open et big data dans les organisations administratives. *Informations sociales*, 191(5): 8–18.

Bernard, S. (2012) *Travail et automatisation des services. La fin des caissières?* Toulouse: Octarès.

Bovens, M., Zouridis, S. (2002) From street-level to system-level bureaucracies: How information and communication technology is transforming administrative discretion and constitutional control. *Public Administration Review*, 62(2): 174–184.

Brodkin, E.Z. (2011) Policy work: Street-level organizations under new managerialism. *Journal of Public Administration Research and Theory*, 21: i253–i277.

Bullock, J.B. (2019) Artificial intelligence, discretion, and bureaucracy. *The American Review of Public Administration*, 49(7): 751–761.

Busch, P.A. and Henriksen, H.Z. (2017) Digital discretion: A systematic literature review of ICT and street-level discretion. *Information Polity*, 23(1): 3–28.

Casey, S.J. (2022) Towards digital dole parole: A review of digital self-service initiatives in Australian employment services. *Australian Journal of Social Issues*, 57(1): 111–124.

Coles-Kemp, L., Ashenden, D., Morris, A. and Yuille, J. (2020) Digital welfare: Designing for more nuanced forms of access. *Policy Design and Practice*, 3(2): 177–188.

Considine, M., Lewis, J.M., O'Sullivan, S. and Sol, E. (2015) *Getting Welfare to Work: Street-Level Governance in Australia, the UK, and the Netherlands*. Oxford: Oxford University Press.

Considine, M., Mcgann, M., Ball, S. and Nguyen, P. (2022) Can robots understand welfare? Exploring machine bureaucracies in welfare-to-work. *Journal of Social Policy*, 51(3): 519–534.

Delpierre, A., Demazière, D. and El Fatihi, H. (2024) The stealth legitimization of a controvefrsial policy tool: Statistical profiling in French PES. *Regulation & Governance*, 18(2): 499–512.

Desiere, S. and Struyven, L. (2021) Using artificial intelligence to classify jobseekers: The accuracy-equity trade-off. *Journal of Social Policy*, 50(2): 367–385.

Desiere, S., Langenbucher, K. and Struyven, L. (2019) *Statistical Profiling in Public Employment Services: An International Comparison*. OECD Social, Employment and Migration Working Papers.

Gaglio, G. (2011) *Sociologie de l'innovation*. Paris: Presses Universitaires de France.

Grundy, J. (2015) Statistical profiling of the unemployed. *Studies in Political Economy*, 96(1): 47–68.

Hansen, H.T., Lundberg, K. and Syltevik, L.J. (2018) Digitalization, street-level bureaucracy and welfare users' experiences. *Social Policy & Administration*, 52(1): 67–90.

Haug, K.B. (2022) Structuring the scattered literature on algorithmic profiling in the case of unemployment through a systematic literature review. *International Journal of Sociology and Social Policy*, 43(5–6): 454–472.

Jansson, G. and Erlingsson, G.Ó. (2014) More e-government, less street-level bureaucracy? On legitimacy and the human side of public administration. *Journal of Information Technology & Politics*, 11(3): 291–308

Jorna, F. and Wagenaar, P. (2007) The 'iron cage' strengthened? Discretion and digital discipline. *Public Administration*, 85(1): 189–221.

Latour, B. (1992) *Aramis ou l'amour des techniques*. Paris: La Découverte.

Loxha, A. and Morgandi, M. (2014) *Profiling the Unemployed: A Review of OECD Experiences and Implications for Emerging Economies*. Washington, DC: World Bank Group.

Maynard-Moody, S. and Portillo, S. (2010) Street-level bureaucracy theory. In R.F. Durant (ed) *The Oxford Handbook of American Bureaucracy* (ch 11). Oxford Academic. https://doi.org/10.1093/oxfordhb/9780199238 958.003.0011

Méadel, C. and Akrich, M. (2010) Internet, tiers nébuleux de la relation patient-médecin. *Les Tribunes de la santé*, 29(4): 41–48.

Nordesjö, K., Scaramuzzino, G. and Ulmestig, R. (2022) The social worker-client relationship in the digital era: A configurative literature review. *European Journal of Social Work*, 25(2): 303–315.

Pors, A.S. and Schou, J. (2021) Street-level morality at the digital frontlines: An ethnographic study of moral mediation in welfare work. *Administrative Theory & Praxis*, 43(2): 154–171.

Sztandar-Sztanderska, K. and Zieleńska, M. (2022) When a human says 'no' to a computer: Frontline oversight of the profiling algorithm in public employment services in Poland. *Sozialer Fortschritt*, 6–7: 465–487.

Watkins-Hayes, C. (2009) *The New Welfare Bureaucrats: Entanglements of Race, Class, and Policy Reform*. Chicago: University of Chicago Press.

Zouridis, S., Van Eck, M. and Bovens, M. (2020) Automated discretion. In T. Evans and P. Hupe (eds) *Discretion and the Quest for Controlled Freedom* (pp 313–329). London: Palgrave Macmillan.

12

Cyborg futures of care and welfare: acceptance and resistance of digital public employment services technologies as competent caregiver

Aisling Tuite

Introduction

In teasing out the nexus between the material practices and the technological imagination of social welfare provision, this chapter reflects upon the possibility for digital public employment services (PES) to achieve a cyborg future that blends human and digital in seamless acts of caring. I draw on Haraway's (1991: 150) notion of a cyborg as 'a condensed image of both imagination and material reality, the two joined centres structuring any possibility of historical transformation'. Practices of care, the material social reality of caregiving, are largely relational, having been parsed in many ways as naturally occurring concern for others, consciously planned or provided through market actors. Technology has long been part of care practices, from medical interventions to organising who gets care, where and when it is delivered. Organising of resources through markets, organisations and state bureaucracies, which include care, has been noted as a means for equity if done right, or discrimination if misguided (Ferguson, 1984; Liedtka, 1996; Du Gay, 2000; Tronto, 2013). In a similar vein, I explore the role of technology in PES, an often-overlooked site of caregiving.

Although often designated as a site of care, explorations and analysis of PES rarely start from a baseline of it being a mission to care organisation, unlike healthcare, child and family services, or pastoral supports. Increasingly the delivery of social welfare supports are being meshed with technologies designed to help make service delivery more efficient and effective for both PES staff and the unemployed service users. Beyond technologies that support general administration, which have been part of the landscape of PES for many years, the emerging technologies explored in this chapter are primarily based on statistical categorising and algorithmic logics, which are increasingly moving towards artificial intelligence (AI). At the most basic level these systems are designed to categorise unemployed people to determine their eligibility to access and receive PES supports, and at the advanced level they aim to profile and predict how long a person will remain unemployed, based on a rationale that those furthest from the labour market should receive more intense supports. Advances in digitalisation of PES makes probable a future social reality of lived experiences concomitant with the organising and decision-making power of 'black-box' technologies that form a coupling of human and machine (Haraway, 1991).

The development and implementation of digital technologies used by PES advisers to support employment outcomes for unemployed people has been patchy to date. Discussed later in this chapter, and forming part of the theoretical analysis, these systems have experienced a number of difficulties and failures, but progress continues towards further advancement of digitalisation. While the business case of increased efficiencies and effectiveness of service delivery is often cited as the driving force behind use of digital PES systems, the policy dimensions currently sit within the goal of the European Union Digital Compass and Digital Decade policy that aims to have all key public services fully digitised by 2030 (European Commission, 2023). Advancement toward this goal increased in momentum during the COVID-19 pandemic (OECD, 2022). In finding ways of delivering in-person services during the pandemic, digitally mediated PES services became increasingly pervasive and normalised.

Vallor (2011), recognising the increasing presence of robots in care settings, calls for ethical consideration of 'carebots' and their implication for caregivers, especially their development of 'moral goods' that are central to practices of relational care. Paying heed to this, the chapter aims to surface the imagined and material role of technology as a competent caregiver inserted into a traditionally human–to–human and relational care assemblage. This makes necessary an analysis that goes beyond thinking of technology as being a tool to be used by humans (Beyes et al, 2022), and to consider it as potential actor with equal status as a caregiver. In doing this, the chapter begins by contextualising the development of digitalisation in PES and how theories of care are represented in practice across the PES landscape. This brief introduction is followed by setting the scene at the point of care delivery, considering it as a Deleuzian assemblage and analysing the relations of human and non–human interactions, inspired by actor-network theory (ANT) and science and technology studies (STS) (Callon, 1986; Deleuze and Guattari, 1987; Law, 2004; Latour, 2005). Using these perspectives, data in the form of detailed literature and case reviews tracing the rise (and fall) of PES digital technologies is combined with focus group responses to a pilot assessment of a new digital technology. Following principles of ANT, the chapter seeks to explore and explain the assemblage as a way to determine if it can be considered as a true cyborg practice of care, along with reflecting on what is missing from the technological imagination to develop good care for a digital infused future.

Care and public employment services

The study focuses on a very particular site of care that is traditionally delivered as a human-to-human practice, and, therefore, relational by nature. From this position Fisher and Tronto's (1990: 40) definition encompasses both this practice and the purpose of social welfare; that it is 'a species activity that includes everything we do to maintain, contain, and repair our "world" so that we can live in it as well as possible. That world includes our bodies, ourselves, and our environment, all of which we seek to interweave in a complex, life-sustaining web'. While this definition complements the complex and ever-changing nature of care and its understanding based on individual experience and perspective, when viewed as a 'species activity' care relations are largely perceived as belonging to the living world. Care as relational is regarded as being laced with emotions and meaning, which may limit the inclusion of technology, but Fisher and Tronto additionally note that it can also be applied to 'things and other living beings' (1990: 40). I take up the challenge here to explore an assemblage of care between human and non-human actors, to determine the role of digital technologies as caring agents in PES and consider the challenges and potentiality of a cyborg future where the boundary between human and machine is blurred (Haraway, 1991).

In public institutions, as well as the market, caregivers work within the boundaries of policy, rules, best practice, as well as national, and sometimes international, regulations. The relational nature of PES work lends itself to analysis through the application of feminist theories, that view care as relational, emotional and an ethic with the purpose of reacting to and addressing individual needs as they arise (Gilligan, 1982; Fisher and Tronto, 1990; Kittay, 1999; Lynch, 2022). In the institutional setting of PES care practices are often bounded by procedure. While it is not the intention to discuss the finer details here, it is noted that rules of operation influence and legitimise practice, discretion and decisions made by the caregivers (caseworkers, advisers or counsellors) and control access and outcomes for the care recipients (unemployed people). Epistemologically this division is discernible in tensions between relational care ethics as theorised by feminist philosophers and the liberal philosophies of universal justice. Liberal philosophers, basing their ideas on public concerns, espouse ideals of universal justice, impartiality and rationality as being the primary concern, while relational care is subordinate as a private concern (Gilligan, 1982; Noddings, 1984; Liedtka, 1996; Moore, 1999). From this perspective, equality in society is imagined as achievable only if individuals are treated as one among many with individual needs being inconsequential to the needs of the masses (Nagle, 1970; Rawls, 1971; Moore, 1999). Where this tension becomes relevant is at the juncture of rules, discretion, power and autonomy within the assemblage.

Similarly, having concern for interactions of structure, practice and meaning pays attention to care as both 'a mental disposition' and the 'actual practices that we engage in as a result of these concerns' (Tronto, 1998: 16) while also indicating that there are greater forces at play outside of the assemblage analysed here. These governmental and institutional forces complement the first two of Joan Tronto's four stages of care, that of *caring about* where the need for care is acknowledged but at a distance such that it recognises 'unspoken needs'; and *caring for* where responsibility for care is passed on to the institutions of care, such as PES, to 'meet identified needs' (Fisher and Tronto, 1990; Tronto, 1993; 1998). More pertinent to this exploration of digital PES are the practices, emotions and actions that fall into the final two levels of *caregiving* and *care receiving* (Fisher and Tronto, 1990) and their entanglement across relationships between humans and technology. Caregiving encompasses those practical acts supported by knowledge and competence, while care receiving elicits a response based on individual (or group) assessment of the acts of care (Fisher and Tronto, 1990; Tronto, 1993; 1998). A limitation of using a structured and layered model is a danger of overlooking that the relational aspects of care are not one-directional with clearly defined boundaries. Similarly, there is a danger that digital technologies, based on rational logics and rules, are overlooked as too static and unresponsive to be an integral part of a caring relationship.

The increasing presence of digital technologies in delivering social welfare supports cannot be ignored when aiming to understand meaningful experiences of care delivery as material reality in contemporary PES. Digital PES systems, built on statistical, algorithmic and AI models, are integral agents in the caring relationship, working both alongside caseworkers as part of their decision-making process and as independent actors with potentially unlimited 'big data' knowledge. While these advancing technologies have the potential to deliver predictive, prescriptive and administrative welfare, what is poorly understood at this moment is how they may affect the human touch of traditional welfare delivery and whether this emerging network will improve or diminish outcomes for unemployed people.

Practices of care: on method and data

To explore the central theme of this chapter the association between PES officers (broadly identified as caseworkers), unemployed people and technology, I draw on a longitudinal study of the experiences of unemployment. Since 2012, the Waterford Unemployment Research Collaborative (WUERC) has been studying experiences of unemployment. The expertise gained through this work is drawn from extensive interviews with unemployed people, support workers, administrators and managers of PES, along with in-depth literature reviews of academic works, reports and policy documents. As part of this collaborative a distinct project examining the Probability of Exit algorithm introduced by the Irish government included an in-depth literature review and mapping of the global emergence of digital technologies in PES. Gathering data concerning the development and deployment of such technologies has continued and as part of an additional distinct piece of research, the Horizon 2020 HECAT project. This data was collected through attendance at workshops, seminars and focus groups. Specifically, in the analysis of the human/non-human assemblages in this chapter, I use two forms of data. First, are the human-to-human and human-to-technology discussions from focus groups that gathered feedback on the pilot-stage design of a novel PES technology. Second, these lived experiences from the 'pilot' scenario are supported by experiences reported from two cases of live PES technologies.

The first data source is drawn from focus group responses from six caseworkers (CW1–CW6) in an Irish PES and five unemployed people (U1–U5). These focus groups were held as part of the HECAT project and sought expert feedback on the presentation of a pilot PES technology designed and built along ethical principles of transparency and providing broad labour market data to both caseworkers and unemployed people. The focus groups were presented with a conceptual version of the new platform along with a series of vignettes that sought to elicit responses to certain scenarios based on the data outputs of the platform. The vignettes presented scenarios where an unemployed person was given a graph to show an estimate of the time frame for their return to employment; a scenario where trade-offs between job quality, career goals and sustainable employment were presented; and a scenario where a digital system presented data that was clearly discriminatory.

The second sources of data draw on existing literature on the use of a reported high-accuracy digital caseworker support tool in Finland, primarily analysed through the work of Riipinen (2011), and from research notes and existing literature regarding the use of a digital tool by caseworkers in Croatia presented to a TAIEX briefing event in October 2020. These secondary sources of data are used to support the findings from the pilot study as they are practice based live cases and lend more depth to understanding the interaction and strategies of control used by human PES advisers within the assemblage. Each source of data has been chosen to represent practices of caregiving (PES advisers and PES technology) and care receiving (unemployed people).

Assemblages of caring practice

The cyborg, being a hybrid of human and non-human that challenges the 'natural order' and taken-for-granted social hierarchies (Haraway, 1991), presents an opportunity to draw out and consider how digital technologies are shaping, and will continue to shape, the landscape of social welfare provision. For this exploration of digital PES, the study takes inspiration from ANT, STS (Callon, 1986; Law, 2004; Latour, 2005) and the Deleuzian tradition of assemblages (Deleuze and Guattari, 1987; Deleuze, 1994) to trace the material relationality of particular incidents and practices of care between caseworkers, unemployed people and the technologies adopted by PES. Taking this approach aims to expose the hidden and complex elements, or 'black box' (Latour, 1999), of the technology and of this particular assemblage; where each component is considered as having equal status and influence across the relationship of human and non-human actors and actants (Law, 2004; Latour, 2005).

The fundamental principle of ANT and STS, that all a priori assumptions about power and knowledge are dismissed, may seem incompatible with exploring caring relationships. Care is often conceived of as being inherently an unequal status condition (Tronto, 1993; 1998; 2013; Kittay, 1999; Mol, 2008). In the PES assemblage explored here this difference is one of power legitimised through regulation, but also knowledge of the labour market and the infrastructures of support systems. It is more appropriate, then, to disassemble power and view its effect on actions rather than conceive of it as a cause of actions (Latour, 1999). In doing this, it shifts the focus of analysis away from a single powerful entity to the many ways in which power is used, received and, as an act of translation, instigates behaviours and actions that flow within the assemblage (Latour, 1984). Despite an outward appearance of a large power differential, the PES assemblage is not one of total domination, each party is able to disassociate from the network – a necessary position for all actors in any assemblage, and a foundational position for speculating about the ability of technology to become embedded as a caregiver. The enrolment in a network and forms of translation across the relationships are often based on the multiplicity of individual actors' perceptions of the value and worth of remaining in the network (Latour, 2005; Callon, 1986; Law and Singleton, 2014).

Across these 'horizontal differences' (Mol, 2008) that surpass the broad category of 'being unemployed' to recognising individual needs, values and worth, the heterogeneous elements (Deleuze and Guattari, 1987; Deleuze, 1994) that make up this assemblage are taken apart and explored as relevant actants, or entities that can influence the actions of others. Placing these horizontal differences as a central 'matter of concern' that can influence association or disassociation with the network does not set out to fix the outcomes but to present an understanding of the reasons for acceptance and resistance to the presence of the non-human digital technology in the caring assemblage (Latour, 2004; Puig de la Bellacasa, 2011). The following paragraphs briefly outline the role of each element of the assemblage, before detailed cases are explored in the next section.

Street-level bureaucrats as competent caregivers

In many contemporary models of PES, social welfare supports to the unemployed require caseworkers to manage administrative tasks with career-focused duties of assessing their clients' situation and guiding them towards work or gaining skills through training and education. Knowing the landscape of the labour market, sources of education and training and deep local knowledge are often relayed as being requisite to the role. The site of PES caregiving explored for this inquiry is where caseworkers engage in administrative practices that align with those of street-level bureaucrats (SLB) (Lipsky, 2010; Brodkin, 2012). As practitioners in the relational practices of caregiving they are placed between the universal rules, regulations and policies that govern social welfare supports and those who need care; the unemployed. A role, according to Lipsky (2010), that requires practices of discretion around decision-making to meet the needs of their clients. The core work of SLBs is the face-to-face interactions where calculative judgements based on knowledge and experience assist with interpreting the scope of policy and rules to meet the needs of their unemployed clients (Brodkin, 2012). Brodkin (2012) extends the purpose of discretion to include assurance of personal career success for SLBs, with decisions often embedded in institutional structures that judge SLBs' performance, in this case moving the unemployed person into the labour market or on to a training programme. This discretionary power gives SLBs a significant influence over the outcomes of public services, shaping the lived experiences of individuals and communities.

Artificial intelligence, algorithms and profiling tools as competent caregiver

As a form of care, PES supports move between government policy and rules to sites of care practice mediated by a range of actors, increasingly both human and digital. Being a public service, it responds to large populations making complex administrative practices and processes inevitable and necessary. PES have been embracing technological advancement for a number of decades, albeit in a piecemeal fashion. Early adoption of algorithmic driven systems for categorising and sorting unemployed people from the mid-1990s set in motion continuous development cycles of seeking better digital solutions to support PES caseworkers and administrators. Australia, the United Kingdom and the United States developed the first generation of algorithms in the 1990s, but with mixed success. The United Kingdom and the United States abandoned early attempts to implement algorithmic tools (O'Connell et al, 2009), while Australia continued to embrace this form of technology, with various uses and designs (Considine et al, 2022).

These first-generation algorithm-based technologies have driven a turn towards digitalisation of PES as a method of making service delivery more efficient and effective, especially in times of crisis where sudden increases in demand for the service is experienced. This was particularly noticeable after the 2008 global financial crisis where PES were forced to reduce their staffing levels, but the number of clients increased. In response, PES looked for ways to increase efficiency of their services with less resources by focusing on digital technologies for profiling clients as a way to determine efficient resource allocation based on individual needs (European Commission, 2017). Over the next 20 or so years digital systems have been introduced and dropped for a number of reasons, including being too administratively heavy, concerns about data (design robustness, lack of trust, the General Data Protection Regulation, bias) and caseworkers failing to use systems (Rosholm and Hammer, 2004; O'Connell et al, 2009; Larsen and Jonsson, 2011; Riipinen, 2011; Loxha and Morgandi, 2014; Wijnhoven and Havinga, 2014; Madsen, 2015; Niklas et al, 2015; Griffin et al, 2020; Kaun et al, 2023).

The digital systems analysed as part of the assemblage are primarily used to categorise unemployed people and determine the probability of returning to employment within a set time period. Increasingly these technologies are becoming part of the network of support provision between the state (through PES) and unemployed people. They are placed in the caring relationship as having data and mathematical led knowledge that aim to provide better outcomes for unemployed people. In doing this they are part of the cycle of caregiving and the quality of their outputs impact their use and whether they are trusted as competent caregivers.

Care receivers

Those who receive care often do so based on decisions to accept or refuse types of care (Mol, 2008; Pols, 2015), and they are also those who will judge if the forms of care they receive are good or bad (Mol, 2008; Tronto, 2013; Pols, 2015). It is becoming increasingly normalised to be given choice between forms of care, especially in healthcare (Mol, 2008). Unemployed people participate in the PES assemblage through an assessment of entitlement based on rules of access. Ideally, enrolment in a network should be voluntary and include options to disassociate. In this case, there is no obligation for the unemployed to seek or continue to accept care. Although this is not a straightforward association, the care receiver enrols in the network to access social welfare payments and supports, which, in the absence of suitable alternatives, makes unemployed clients of PES 'non-voluntary' (Lipsky, 2010). The ability of an unemployed person to survive without income from paid work in the contemporary world instigates behaviours that, more often than not, result in their continued association with PES. The persistent vulnerability to poverty often compels people to stay within the system, acting in ways influenced by SLBs and shaped by power legitmised through established rules and practices. Of benefit to this analysis is that without being able to withdraw the unemployed participants of this study surface experiences of both good and poor care, indicating which practices are of value to their individual needs.

Assemblages of humans and technology

To understand how digital PES technologies are received and evaluated two recent cases of deployment are analysed. In 2007 Finland introduced a statistical profiling tool. Using logit mathematical modelling to estimate a new entrant's risk of becoming long-term unemployed the tool has been assessed to be highly efficient with close to 89 per cent accuracy (Riipinen, 2011). According to Riipinen (2011), despite the caseworkers having control over final decisions and recommendations to the unemployed, the tool failed to become integrated into casework, with 53 per cent of caseworkers stating that they did not find it useful and 20 per cent not trusting that the predictions were accurate. Eighty-four per cent of caseworkers felt that the tool did not have a positive outcome for the client and only one in four caseworkers discussed the prediction with their clients. The use of the tool was largely left at the behest of the caseworkers and was not programmed into their work routine or made mandatory for use with clients (Riipinen, 2011). This is in contrast to the Croatian Statistically Assisted Profiling (StAP) tool which was piloted in 2016 and 2017 (European Commission, 2018).

StAP, similar to the Finnish system, was designed to work with caseworker interaction and not as a fully automated system. The difference lies in the integration of the profiling tool into the normal routine work of caseworkers. The primary data output from StAP was the probability of returning to work within the following 12 months. Once this calculation was made the client began a series of meetings with caseworkers, which resulted in an individual action plan, compulsory actions such as CV development and evidence of job search combined with follow-up face-to-face meetings every 12 weeks (Griffin et al, 2020). The tool has a reported prediction accuracy for long-term unemployment of 69 per cent while caseworkers have a large amount of override capability, being able to reclassify a client into another category if they fail to show for meetings or, under certain conditions, de-registering them for six months. This tool is currently operational, however the deregistration element was criticised and has been removed and replaced with client activation towards motivational activities.

The discretionary powers of SLBs are surfaced in these two cases and are the backbone of how the digital technology is used in their own caregiving practices, its acceptance or rejection within the network, and when choosing to pass on the data outputs to their clients. A number of the reasons for disassociating with the Finnish tool are mirrored in the caseworker focus group from Ireland. The caseworkers rarely show enthusiasm towards the showcased platform or other digital tools that they use in their work, seeing them as providing information but not being powerful enough to overwrite their discretionary powers to assist their clients, as noted by CW3:

> We've had tools that we've trained on and clients aren't really interested in tools as a whole. We've tried out tools with clients and they're very much dependent on our experience. I think the councillor would need to be able to explain to the client where this data is coming from and our knowledge and our perception of things rather than the tools.

Instead, they see them 'as a tool in my armoury' (CW6), something that they can call upon when necessary but not as having equal status in the practice of care. These actions reduce the role and power of the technology, and somewhat disassociate it as a competent caregiver. This is additionally echoed when the caseworkers again demonstrate their power in deciding whether the data would be useful and trusted by their clients and which information to pass on, especially when the news is negative, as noted by CW2:

> They wouldn't trust the process at all. The other thing then from our perspective is that we're trying to build up their confidence. ... As I said, we're full of trying to encourage them to ... as in telling them 'this won't happen' and helping them to get a job much quicker ... we'd be looking at training anyway. That would come into it. Even if, in our own minds we're thinking 'this is going to be difficult because of age or because of lack of work experience of whatever it might be'. But we never say that obviously.

The ability of caseworkers to limit and shape the type of data given to their clients appears central when using their discretion to shape the experience of unemployment. In resisting the digital platform that would provide realistic labour market data to both caseworker and client they indicate its potential to interfere with discretion and their ability to direct preferred forms of translatory actions onto their clients. These actions limit choice and autonomy for their clients that could be gained through equal access to data-led knowledge. This response from the caseworkers mirrors analysis of both the Finnish and Croatian cases where the data outputs from the technology are largely ignored or only provided at the discretion of the caseworkers.

In response, the unemployed cohort, when presented with the pilot platform and having all the functionalities and potential data outcomes explained, embraced the idea that the platform would allow independence from the caseworkers, as noted by U2: 'I personally think the tool that you are planning on bringing … I would rather trust that and make my own mind.' When being given a choice of having access to the same data as the caseworkers and having autonomy over using the platform, the participants were accepting of the technology. There was a levelling effect, with participants noting that they could bring this data to their meetings with the caseworkers and discuss options from an objective stance, with the technology having knowledge equal to the caseworker.

However, when the participants were asked to comment on a data result that indicated a longer than expected time frame for returning to the labour market, their opinion on being given realistic and potentially negative data changed their outlook and caseworker experience takes precedence over knowledge, as noted by U1:

> It's good it that she has the … counsellor to kind of help her through that. To like, help her to make a plan for those months and to consider different areas. Yeah, just like using the statistics and the evidence to kind of make it a positive situation. … But it would be daunting to hear that you know it's 12 months. But if you have someone to … help you through that it would be better.

The technology then becomes less trusted when it does not give out positive news and is sidelined in favour of caseworker intervention, thereby returning to the traditional mode of human-to-human care relations with caseworkers being assigned with an ability to react quickly and interpret data given by the digital platform, as noted by U1: 'I think, to do with the algorithm where it's kind of myself but then it's led by a caseworker that if I had questions. If it was that kind of dual approach … but I would trust that data and the algorithm to throw up suggestions.'

The unemployed cohort are largely familiar with using digital tools for their job search, and one even makes the point that despite being unsure of the digital platform and its data, this does not mean that they are 'anti-technology'. Overall, there is a sense that this cohort, in making sense of the new platform, were excited by their ability to use it autonomously, having new forms of data and even making suggestions for improvements. At the same time, however, they were cautious of replacing caseworkers and surfaced a sense that a hybrid situation would be preferable to allow for both knowledge and experience to merge in the caregiving arrangement.

On cyborg futures

Two fundamental concerns arise when considering the future of digital technology as a seamless and equal partner in the assemblage of caregiving through social welfare services; one is whether or not the conditions exist for the boundaries between human and technology to become blurred enough for its acceptance as a caring agent; the other is whether or not digital technologies can be designed and deployed as systems that understand the principle that 'to care well requires the recognition that care is *relational*' (Tronto, 2013: 140). There is no doubt that the digital technologies deployed in PES for profiling and categorising citizens have the potential to organise care by directing suitable interventions and supports to those most in need. Similar to Tronto's (2013) analysis of the capacity for markets to care, technology is at the mercy of those that conceptualise its use, design and functions, particularly if their logics take little heed of individual experiences and societal discrimination that may inhibit access to sustainable labour market outcomes. Emerging from the data is that PES technologies, as a standalone caregiver, are limited by flexibility, a gap between knowledge and experience, and problems with addressing the intimate and emotional nature of caring relations.

The arbitrary use of the PES technologies by caseworkers, based on the two cases where the technology was both accepted and rejected and supported by the sentiments expressed in the focus groups, surface a barrier to digital technologies being accepted as a competent caregiver. Where a technology may give data that was unexpected or negative both caseworkers and the unemployed cohort expressed a need, and a desire, for a personal response that would limit any harmful effects of the news. A significant tension in the assemblage is that while the unemployed respondents, as part of their decision-making process, approved of having access to the same data as the caseworkers, the caseworkers' reaction was to limit access to the data and only use it at their discretion. The caseworkers, as SLBs, in this study, possess a high level of discretionary power that limits the translation effects of the data on all actors in the assemblage, and therefore limits the integration of digital PES technologies into the caring assemblage. In leaning on legacy modes of casework the 'imprinted roles' (Schou and Nesheim, 2024: 15–16) of relational caring that are traditionally at the core of this work are maintained.

Recognising the need for personal interactions in PES, the unemployed cohort were in favour of a hybrid structure with impartial data and a caseworker to respond to directed questions. While it is less obvious in the caseworkers' responses, a preference for mediated passing over of data outputs was expressed. There is some hope that a cyborg future can exist that is equitable and levels the power differential between PES actors, particularly if the technology is designed based on assessments of value and worth in addressing human needs through relational care and if concern is given to the knowledge/experience gap.

References

Beyes, T., Chun, W.H.K., Clarke, J., Flyverbom, M. and Holt, R. (2022) Ten theses on technology and organization: Introduction to the special issue. *Organization Studies*, 43(7): 1001–1018.

Brodkin, E. (2012) Reflections on street-level bureaucracy: Past, present, and future. *Public Administration Review*, 72(6): 940–949.

Callon, M. (1984) Some elements of a sociology of translation: Domestication of the scallops and the fishermen of St Brieuc Bay. *The Sociological Review*, 32(1_suppl): 196–233.

Considine, M., McGann, M., Ball, S. and Nguyen, P. (2022) Can robots understand welfare? Exploring machine bureaucracies in welfare-to-work. *Journal of Social Policy*, 51(3): 519–534.

Deleuze, G. (1994) *Difference and Repetition*. New York: Colombia University Press.

Deleuze, G. and Guattari, F. (1987) *A Thousand Plateaus*. Minneapolis: University of Minnesota Press.

Du Gay, P. (2000) *In Praise of Bureaucracy*. London: SAGE.

European Commission (2017) *European Semester Thematic Factsheet: Public Employment Services (PES)*. np: European Commission.

European Commission (2018) *Promising PES Practice*. file:///C:/Users/aisli/Downloads/FichePES_HR_PromisingPractice_StAP-HD.pdf

European Commission (2023) *Shaping Europe's Digital Future: Europe's Digital Decade*. https://digital-strategy.ec.europa.eu/en/policies/europes-digital-decade

Ferguson, K.E. (1984) *The Feminist Case Against Bureaucracy*. Philadelphia: Temple University Press.

Fisher, B. and Tronto, J. (1990) Toward a feminist theory of caring. In E.K. Abel and M. Nelson (eds) *Circles of Care* (pp 35–62). Albany: SUNY Press.

Gilligan, C. (1982) *In a Different Voice: Psychological Theory and Women's Development*. Cambridge, MA: Harvard University Press.

Griffin, R., Tuite, A., Roche, Z. and Gallagher, P. (2020) *D1.3 Report Ethical, Social, Theological, Technical Review of 1st Generation PES Algorithms and Data Use*. Waterford: Hecat: Disruptive Technologies Supporting Labour Market Decision Making. https://zenodo.org/records/7913459

Haraway, D. (1991) *Simians, Cyborgs and Women: The Reinvention of Nature*. New York: Routledge.

Kaun, A., Männiste, M. and Liminga, A. (2023) *Mapping the Automated Decision-Making Landscape in Swedish and Estonian Welfare State*. Working Paper #02 of the CHANSE-funded research consortium 'Automating Welfare – Algorithmic Infrastructures for Human Flourishing in Europe' (AUTO-WELF).

Kittay, E. (1999) *Love's Labour: Essays on Women, Equality and Dependency*. New York: Routledge.

Larsen, A. and Jonsson, A.B. (2011) *Employability Profiling Systems: The Danish Experience*. Brussels: European Commission.

Latour, B. (1984) The powers of association. *The Sociological Review*, 32(1_suppl): 264–280.

Latour, B. (1999) *Pandora's Hope: Essays on the Reality of Science Studies*. Cambridge, MA: Harvard University Press.

Latour, B. (2004) Why has critique run out of steam? From matters of fact to matters of concern. *Critical Inquiry*, 30(2): 225–248.

Latour, B. (2005) *Reassembling the Social: An Introduction to Actor Network Theory*. Oxford: Oxford University Press.

Law, J. (2004) *After Method: Mess in Social Science Research*. London: Routledge.

Law, J. and Singleton, V. (2014) ANT, multiplicity and policy. *Critical Policy Studies*, 8(4): 379–396.

Liedtka, J.M. (1996) Feminist morality and competitive reality: A role for an ethic of care? *Business Ethics Quarterly*, 6(2): 179–200.

Lipsky, M. (2010) *Street-Level Bureaucracy: Dilemmas of the Individual in Public Service*. np: Russell Sage Foundation.

Loxha, A. and Morgandi, M. (2014) *Profiling the Unemployed: A Review of OECD Experiences and Implications for Emerging Economies*. Social Protection and Labor Discussion Paper, No. SP 1424, Washington, DC: World Bank Group. https://www.openknowledge.worldbank.org/handle/10986

Lynch, K. (2022) *Care and Capitalism*. Cambridge: Polity Press.

Madsen, P. (2015) *Youth Unemployment and the Skills Mismatch in Denmark*. Aalborg: Centre for Labour Market Research. www.europarl.europa.eu/RegData/etudes/IDAN/2015/536322/IPOL_IDA(2015)536322_EN.pdf

Mol, A.M. (2008) *The Logic of Care*. New York: Routledge.

Moore, M. (1999) The ethics of care and justice. *Women & Politics*, 20(2): 1–16.

Nagle, T. (1970) *The Possibility of Altruism*. Oxford: Clarendon.

Niklas, J., Sztandar-Sztanderska, K. and Szymielewic, K. (2015) *Profiling the Unemployed in Poland: Social and Political Implications of Algorithmic Decision Making*. Warsaw: Creative Commons Attribution 4.0 International. https://panoptykon.o

Noddings, N. (1984) *Caring: A Feminine Approach to Ethics and Moral Education*. Berkeley: University of California Press.

O'Connell, P.J., McGuiness, S., Kelly, E. and Walsh, J. (2009) *National Profiling of the Unemployed in Ireland*. Dublin: The Economic and Social Research Institute.

OECD (2022) *Harnessing Digitalisation in Public Employment Services to Connect People with Jobs*. np: OECD. https://www.oecd.org/employment/activation.htm

Pols, J. (2015) Towards an empirical ethics in care: Relations with technologies in health care. *Medicine Health Care & Philosophy*, 18(1): 81–90.

Puig de la Bellacasa, M. (2011) Matters of care in technoscience: Assembling neglected things. *Social Studies of Science*, 41(1): 85–106.

Rawls, J. (1971) *A Theory of Justice*. Oxford: Oxford University Press.

Riipinen, T. (2011) *Risk Profiling of Long-Term Unemployment in Finland*. Dialogue Conference, Brussels. ec.europa.eu/social/BlobServlet?docId=7583&langId=en

Rosholm, M. and Hammer, B. (2004) *A Danish Profiling System*. Bonn: Institute for the Study of Labour.

Schou, P.K. and Nesheim, T. (2024) What we do in the shadows: How expert workers reclaim control in digitalized and centralized organizations through 'stealth work'. *Organization Studies*, 45(5): 719–744.

Tronto, J.C. (1993) *Moral Boundaries: A Political Argument for an Ethic of Care*. New York: Routledge.

Tronto, J. (1998) An ethic of care. *Generations: Journal of the American Society on Aging*, 22(3): 15–20.

Tronto, J.C. (2013) *Caring Democracy: Markets, Equality and Justice*. New York: New York University Press.

Vallor, S. (2011) Carebots and caregivers: Sustaining the ethical ideal of care in the twenty-first century. *Philosophy and Technology*, 24: 251–268.

Wijnhoven, M.A. and Havinga, H. (2014) The work profiler: A digital instrument for selection and diagnosis of the unemployed. *Local Economy*, 29(6–7): 740–749.

13

Exploring omni-channel welfare experiences in unemployment services

Órla Hayes, Aisling Tuite and Ray Griffin

Introduction

The long-standing manifestation of public employment service (PES) provision in Ireland lies in the physical 'dole' office. Here, an often dreary governmental space has become the primary touchpoint for PES provision for decades. Functioning as the sanctum of PES activities, the dole office has long since been the single source of arbitration and the primary means of needs-meeting. Here, PES counsellors provide knowledge, explore employment optioning and deliver welfare needs, where strict criteria are met. Dole offices have become prime community hubs and central spaces for the unemployed as they seek to re-enter the labour market. Such activation in Ireland has traditionally focused on in-person, human-fronted engagement, wherein these offices play a central role in reaffirming the job-seeking experience for citizens while further providing for welfare and societal needs.

In the context of rapid digitalisation, technology plays a crucial role in transforming traditional operational models. Digital channels are now central to government communication strategies, enhancing and supplementing the traditional in-person service delivery. This shift is part of the broader concept of e-Government, which Baum and Di Maio (2000) define as "the continuous optimisation of service delivery, constituency participation, and governance through the use of technology, the Internet, and new media." E-Government has become the standard approach in most countries, shaping how public services are delivered and engaging citizens. This is especially apparent as digital-first approaches become commonplace, encouraging primary communication with government services solely via online platforms (Olsson and Viscovi, 2023). Digital tools and channels, in this context, augment service capacity, catering to the expanding needs of citizens for round-the-clock accessibility while functioning as administrative and service delivery conduits for PES (Pieterson, 2017).

While digital-first scenarios seek to bring PES from the banal into the mainstream and technologies continue to encourage citizens to engage via digitalised means, tradition has not fully become subservient. Even as many PES entities globally advocate for digitally mediated service provision (OECD, 2022), service users assert their agency in determining their preferred journey to PES – whether offline, online, or otherwise (Pieterson and Ebbers, 2020).

The isolation of the conventional dole office setting has been replaced with potential for mobile, on-the-go and anywhere delivery, aligning with advancing trends of digitalisation and evolving citizen expectation (Pieterson et al, 2022). Digital means do not replace the need for in-person provision, but rather add a supplementary service potential fitting a digital world (Rey-Morero and Medina-Molina, 2016). Herein, opportunities for approaches more omni-channel in nature arise, considering the offline, online and otherwise in PES operations. The difficulty here lies in balancing the established and accepted, tried and tested manner of PES provision, with the potential of digitally enhanced approaches. The research asks, how are current omni-channel PES expectations expressed in the realities of Irish service provision?

This chapter seeks to explore the potential for omni-channel PES provision, equating the long-since-done with future-forward, digital expectations. It will first explore the remit of PES digitalisation, analysing the emergence of omni-channel as an institutional strategy. Utilising Ireland as a case example, it will explore the expectations for PES digitalisation across channels and touchpoints, while further expanding on the gap between actual service offerings as experienced by the unemployed in Ireland. Obstacles compounding omni-channel PES are examined in this light, with key recommendations made for the future of such strategic offering.

Digitalisation of public employment services

As digitalised approaches become the service norm, over 70 per cent of Organisation for Economic Co-operation and Development (OECD) countries are today engaging in initiatives to enable entirely digital or remote PES delivery (OECD, 2022). Digital service is no longer a simple expectation, rather it is a form of active reform of PES operations, globally, and is spurred on by policy initiatives such as the European Digital Decade. This pivotal policy envisioning the entirety of key public services being accessible online by 2030, is prompting rapid reconfiguring of current PES approaches (European Commission, 2023).

New forms of PES service delivery have been emerging within the past decade, accelerating the move to digital-first. Many of these innovations align with burgeoning information and communication technology trends.

This includes greater prospects for artificial intelligence in a range of capacities, including job seeking and welfare provision, increased prevalence of technologies that foster social connections and rapid expansion of the internet and its assumption into everyday life (Davern, 2023). Web-based tools are the most common form of contemporary digitalisation, where o government websites and PES-specific interfaces are used to supplement traditional, in-person service delivery (ILO, 2022). This has been especially compounded in a post-COVID-19 world, wherein PES globally have been forced to reconfigure service provision and rapidly integrate digital means to meet unprecedented service need across national lockdown periods (OECD, 2022). As states emerge from this crisis, this time of instability has highlighted the importance of aligning PES offerings for 21st-century requirements.

Increasingly, digital-first presentations have emerged, wherein digital touchpoints become the primary means of PES engagement. A key example of this is Norway, where the preferred contact medium for government services is via online channels, a concept becoming more prevalent across an increasingly digital welfare ecosystem globally (O'Reilly et al, 2023; Schoyen, 2023). While effective in providing experiences beyond the traditional 'dole' office setting which can no longer are the totality of PES services, the digitalisation of primary services needs considerable caveats. A particular risk is digital exclusion, where the removal of human PES services can entirely marginalise whole communities and groups within society who do not have the digital skills needed to access services. As digital upskilling becomes a priority across Europe, discussion on digital inclusion seeks to advocate for PES approaches that consider the needs of all citizens, regardless of digital literacy levels. The primary challenge for PES today is not the decision to digitalise, but rather lies in finding a 'new balance between in-person and digital delivery of services' in reaching the needs of all (PESNetwork, 2022: 72).

Public service omni-channel

A key consideration emerging here is potential for omni-channel (OC) service provision models. Compounded by the COVID-19 pandemic and the need for rapid consideration of digitalisation, such strategies seek to address the rapid mainstream move towards new channel behaviours and availability (Zhuang et al, 2020; Kannan and Kulkarni, 2021), including those within PES service provision. OC approaches seek to seamlessly integrate the online and offline, using insight learned from the recent global pandemic, to recognising best practices from in-person approaches, and preparing for an evermore digital future. Unlike other strategies, OC is both channel- and citizen-focused, ensuring that consistent messages and information reach the target audiences across their preferred platforms (Verhoef et al,

2015). Employing a diverse array of channels and touchpoints, this strategic paradigm seeks to meet citizens where they are and increase both service quality and efficiency in response to changing channel behaviours (Pieterson and Ebbers, 2020). In this regard, OC approaches do not seek to negate traditional, caseworker-led experiences, but rather supplement support via addition channels and touchpoints fitting key digitalisation expectations and citizens' needs in tandem.

The concept of OC still continues to emerge across disciplines, notably within the domain of government and welfare studies. As such, it is of merit to amalgamate emerging conceptual understandings from fields with more enhanced research and debate. In aligning current thought on OC as a strategic consideration, a public-service fronted definition can, as such, be configured. Through this lens, *OC refers to a modern approach in which government agencies and departments provide a seamless and integrated experience for citizens across multiple communication channels.* Considering the key concepts of OC and the unique capacity of public service interactions and service provision, Pieterson et al (2022) discern the following early definition of OC public service management: 'OC management is the holistic management of all available service channels in which all channels are fully integrated and allow the seamless delivery of all services to all segments of the population.' OC approaches offer consistent and coordinated services and information to the public through various means such as websites, mobile apps, social media, unemployment centres and in-person interactions (Schenk et al, 2021). The overarching goal is to address citizens' needs and preferences by affording them the flexibility to interact with PES through their channel of choice while ensuring a cohesive and unified experiential continuum.

While Pieterson et al (2022) have provided one of the early formal definitions of public service OC, the conceptualisation has been taken up in strategic discourses led by the European Union, the OECD and, notably, the EU's informal PES Network. These discourses emphasise the need for diverse channels to be employed in order to 'provide a seamless and consolidated cross-channel experience' (European Commission, 2018). Furthermore, the OECD, in its guidance for service provision in PES, underscores the significance of OC approaches, specifically advocating for the maintenance of 'multiple coherent service delivery channels such as digital, in-person, and telephone' (OECD, 2021: 49). This is echoed in emerging academic research seeking to explore the potentiality of OC in PES-specific scenarios (Rey-Moreno and Medina-Molina, 2016; Schenk et al, 2021; Pieterson et al, 2022). Country-specific work, though currently not extensive in regards to case-examples, increasingly confirms interest in policy-led OC PES adoption in the wake of enhanced global digitalisation, including in Europe, Latin America, New Zealand and beyond (OECD, 2020; ILO, 2022; Pieterson et al, 2022).

In this sense, this chapter will next explore the emergence of OC approaches, using Ireland as a case example. It will first consider policy expectations, aligned with European regulations guiding consideration on approaches to digitalisation in government. Next, the reality of lived experiences of the unemployed facing this change in the Irish system is examined in considering potential gaps between service expectation and reality.

Omni-channel and the Irish case

Like most PES globally, the digitalisation of Irish welfare services is an active government priority with emerging policies displaying characteristics OC in nature. The national employment strategy, Pathways to Work 2021–2025, notes 'the Public Employment Service will need to adapt its model of service delivery to take advantage of digital capabilities and to respond to client preferences' (Government of Ireland, 2021).

Herein, three key policies have effect on digital enactment within public services (see Table 13.1).

At the heart of Ireland's welfare digital transition is Pathways to Work, a comprehensive labour market policy designed to address unemployment and reduce long-term joblessness by providing personalised support to jobseekers. This policy explores key actions and challenges that the Irish PES landscape must address in an increasingly digitalised world. Key to this is consideration for digital tools and services to facilitate increased job securement, of which 'leaving no one behind' is a major priority. Within this policy, several key OC undertones emerge, explored in the following.

The restructuring of the Irish welfare system through digitally oriented policies has been complicated by the escalating integration of online tools and

Table 13.1: Current Irish policy effecting the digitalisation of public employment services

Policy	Implications
Harnessing Digital 2030	Ireland's overwriting digital strategy which seeks to 'drive and enable the digital transition across the Irish economy and society'
Connecting Government 2030	Outlines Ireland's current Digital and ICT Strategy for Public Service including expectations for 90% of applicable service users consuming government services online by 2030
Pathways to Work 2021–2025	The Irish government's key national employment services strategy which seeks to assist people back to work as the economy and labour market recovers from COVID-19

digital channels. Ideally, both online and offline means should be broached succinctly for service provision, satisfying a key parameter of OC service delivery outlined in policy. Online, the introduction of MyGovID in 2017 facilitates single-login authentication and identification verification across the PES and government service landscape in Ireland, including revenue taxation services and welfare applications. Specific to social welfare, MyWelfare, an online welfare activation tool, allows for full digital registration for many PES services, including jobseekers' payments traditionally only obtainable via in-person means. The site allows welfare payment applications, progress tracking via online tools to encourage employment and information provision (Gov. ie, 2023). Such platforms seek not to replace traditional service but, rather, present opportunities, cost-saving advantages and round-the-clock service delivery not previously accounted for within in-person delivery (Rey-Moreno and Medina-Molina, 2016). This service provides an additional tool that can be used in tandem with caseworker engagement and is applied during in-person meetings to lead job-seeking activity.

Interestingly, Ireland's Pathways to Work policy outlines an 'ideal' service provision process, accounting for the *seamless interaction of both online and offline means of PES provision*, again OC in nature. Steps outlined in the policy consider the following process:

1. Use of MyWelfare for application and notification.
2. Shared informational videos via online means.
3. Nudges and prompts across channels to promote onboarding to employment services.
4. Scheduling of first one-to-one meeting.
5. Support via digital means and offline, via training/employment interventions.
6. Closure of claim via MyWelfare when employment is secured.

Within such strategising, citizens benefit from the multitude of platform offerings, particularly the digitally fronted MyWelfare. Here, caseworker interventions are supported by a homogenised digital platform that provides an array of beneficial information. Additionally, utilisation of a digital tool as part of such provision increases citizen autonomy, providing 'always-on' information provision and the potential for 24/7 service, where and when suits the user. For Irish PES, this tool *should* provide advanced automation and resource-savings not possible in current caseworker-led approaches. However, the importance here lies in providing both online and offline offerings, befitting users with all digital skill levels.

Because of the varying needs of citizens where PES interactions are concerned, *personalisation* of services is a key requirement of modern provision (Fuertes and Lindsay, 2016). This includes consideration for the jobseekers' individual case and circumstances, but also their skills, digital and otherwise.

Such thought is emphasised in the Pathways to Work policy model in Ireland, which promotes personalisation as part of an OC approach. This is delivered primarily via caseworker discretion, supplemented by statistical profiling interventions such as the Irish Probability of Exit model used in initial assessment and supported by MyWelfare as a digital tool for personalised experience tracking and engagement.

Those classed as 'at risk' are particularly noted in planned service delivery, with the outlined aspirations of 'delivering a personalised service and showing flexibility/adaptability and given the need for the service to deal effectively with clients from a range of backgrounds and with a range of capabilities' (Gov.ie, 2022a: 36). Here, a considerable challenge lies in engaging those currently outside of the workforce, perhaps for some time and those who may not have the digital skills expected by modern workplaces. Much has been written globally about such challenges, with the current Irish approach recognising the needs for 'more intensive and personalised support in developing relevant workplace skills and confidence' (Gov.ie, 2022a: 22). This implies a patchwork of digital and in–person approaches are used to deliver services, innately OC in nature.

Recognising the transformative potential of digital technologies in service provision, Irish government policies prioritise the integration of digital tools and platforms in PES. These policies align with global trends and emerging international policies, reflecting a willingness to staying abreast of technological advancements and enhance the efficiency of employment services. Current government expectations are underscored by a comprehensive vision that seeks to harness the benefits of digital means, offering citizens a seamless and user-centric experience across various channels. By embracing digitalisation, Ireland's government aims to not only optimise the delivery of employment services but also to cater to the evolving expectations of citizens in an increasingly digital landscape. However, care must be given to ensure all citizens are included within this. In this, the role of person-led interactions need to be carefully strategised alongside digital tools in reaching all those requiring assistance.

Realities of the unemployed experience in Ireland

In exploring service expectation, policy uncovers what government dictates PES strategising *should* be. In accounting for the reality of such experiences in Ireland, this chapter next explores insights gained from a longitudinal, ethnographic study with the very citizens with whom the government expects to interact, as outlined in these policies. Here, knowledge of actual service provision and day-to-day experiences of PES service in Ireland is gained through 100+ direct interactions with service users across the Irish PES system, with formal interactions supplemented with long-term informal elements of the social welfare landscape, such as social media support groups.

In this, the comparison between expectation of service and the reality within PES is explored.

'If it's not broke, don't fix it'

As digitalisation increases the array of channels and touchpoints engaged across government services in Ireland and beyond, it is not yet, nor may ever be, just to completely eradicate in-person means. For many citizens, fond memories and the community aspect of the 'dole experience' have cemented such spaces as almost a 'third place' of socialisation and connection, between home and work, and as such, their strategising within modern PES efforts must be maintained: 'The people you run into is very interesting. You're as likely to meet a solicitor or a doctor in the queue now as you are anyone else. There's almost an undercurrent of camaraderie in the queue, sometimes. Because it's like "we're down but we're not out"' (Gen, 49).

It is clear from engaging with citizens that an array of both offline and online channels are utilised in engaging with Irish PES today, highlighting potential cause for OC. Online channels arise primarily during service registration, application and information search. Aligning with policy expectations, MyWelfare plays an increasingly necessary role in service configuration and is a requirement for all service registrations and applications within the Irish PES landscape. This tool presents a key turning point in PES digitalisation in Ireland and, to date, it is the primary, front-facing interface in digital service provision.

Offline means, however, as postulated (Wirtz and Langer, 2016; Schenk et al, 2021), are a preferred initial contact method, primarily due to familiarity of approach and wider accessibility. PES offices and the outwardly facing sites of the Department of Social Protection still feature as heavily important for jobseekers engaged in welfare-based activities. Here, personal interaction via caseworkers should be the prime means of both knowledge and service interaction and service individualisation should be a key PES feature (Leibetseder, 2023). However, strains within the Irish system are noted by citizens regularly engaging with PES. In particular, the heavy case load and lack of permanent caseworkers assigned to jobseekers is of concern. While most 'would appreciate the support' of caseworkers, over-complicated and, indeed, reliant on for-profit operational elements, concern jobseekers: '[T]hey just asked me again and again what I wanted to do. I was very vulnerable in that moment, I needed guidance, but there was nothing' (Luna, 52).

Consistency of experiences

It is of interest to citizens that experiences are consistent regardless of channel, partner or means for matters of trust, service quality and efficiency

(Reddick and Turner, 2012; Rey-Moreno and Medina-Molina, 2016). However, the varying service experiences across the Irish PES landscape further cause significant tension. While all services are notionally delivered at a single point of contact – branded as Intreo – a one-stop-shop, this belies a thicket of public and private services and schemes that deliver welfare, and it is now a strong policy expectation and preference that online channels are a substantial part of the service norm. Indeed, for many citizens, it is now common to be passed through a number of contracted service providers. Here, a reoccurring issue for most service users is the lack of consistency across such encounters. This reduces the potential benefits of delivering an OC system for both citizen and PES operator. Despite the policy commitment to a 'one-stop-shop' approach perpetrated by Intreo and the use of MyWelfare as a single-system approach, service provision is actually fragmented with individuals interacting with a range of different PES providers without little integration. Within this, service offerings are often duplicated, providers regularly repeat conditionality demands and there is a general understanding that systems are neither integrated nor aligned: '[K]eep a paper trail. Keep a copy of emails, reports, letters or they'll send you in circles' (Maria, 55).

Clearly, there is no 'one size fits all' approach to service provision, contrary to government policy and considerations for a consolidated approach. Indeed, the 'ideal' process outlined within the Pathways to Work policy is rarely fully enacted. For those already challenged by the experience of unemployment, a supportive and continued PES offering is paramount in both building trust and engagement (Pérez-Morote et al, 2020). Indeed, confounded experiences across private service providers seeks to increase channel complexity (Margetts, 2009). Wherein service differs from provider to provider, the PES experience becomes disjointed, which has considerable ramifications for the empowerment and motivation of the job-seeking individual. Though 'building towards 24–7 services providing consistence, integrated and end-to-end digital solutions' is worthy in enhancing the PES experience (Gov.ie, 2022a: 9), the current citizen reality is far from this ideal. To achieve the ambitious goals for digitalization of PES by 2030, rethinking the current state of PES services should be a priority.

Personalisation of services

In confounding the final OC element that has been touted in leading Irish policy, *personalisation of service* should ideally be a key priority of current service. However, again, service users are unimpressed with the level of actual consideration for their individualised needs. Instead of offering individualised programmes with the aim to assist in the employment process, many citizens engaged felt their PES experience was like a 'bounty process'; pushing activities that will remove the individual from the live register as quickly as possible without factoring in their actual circumstances or, indeed, job suitability. The caseworker is primarily responsible for delivering personalised services within the current model, notwithstanding that service users often fail to recognise their efforts, and interpret the service as impersonal and bureaucratic.

Indeed, for many engaged with local employment services for an extended period of time, a dehumanisation of approach is evident. Rather than assist with positive job search activities and welfare assistance, some citizens engaged report a feeling of suspicion, which regularly manifests itself via confusing and often labyrinthine bureaucracy.

> I haven't had a positive experience of getting onto social support. It would nearly make you feel like you are doing something illegal or wrong. It's like going into your headmaster that's how you feel, some of the people I dealt with can be quite condescending. They make you feel like you are there with your cap in hand begging. (Luna, 52)

This experience is not in isolation and represents an array of quite frank and worrisome indications of depersonalisation within active PES operations. This includes fears that letters received were 'very intimidating' and worries that the service providers themselves were 'trying to catch you out'. Such a reality is not at all fitting policy expectation and compounds concern for current service enactment.

Challenges of omni-channel welfare provision in Ireland

While policy dictates an ideal service approach, a number of challenges emerge in bringing such expectations into reality. Using insight gained from interactions with citizens engaged in Irish PES, the following obstacles of OC service realities emerge.

Risk of exclusion

While service users are increasingly seeking more dynamic mediums for PES service provision, it is also clear that offline channels are still vital for many users. As the digital landscape continues to evolve, not everyone has equal access to the online tools, resources and capabilities necessary to engage with digital PES. Here, digital exclusion remains a key issue to be considered in all future efforts to digitalise. Indeed, in accounting for current policy expectations that 'nobody will be left behind', exploring service realities reveal that PES offerings do not currently reach all citizens on a level playing field.

Access to the necessary digital tools and equipment to engage with PES is a considerable citizen-fronted issue. This is particularly recognised in older adults, who find themselves especially excluded from current Irish social welfare engagement processes. Several complex barriers to labour market integration are identified within this cohort, including lower literacy and general education attainment, self-esteem issues and lower-then-average digital skills: 'There are jobs but they are all looking for skills, I worked in a factory for 18 years those are the skills I have. I don't fit' (Luna, 52). While initiatives to upskill individuals further play key roles in policy, both in the European Union and locally to Ireland, technical laggards and those with lesser digital skills still need to be accounted for in advanced digitalisation of PES so as to ensure reduction in societal, economical and service-based exclusions (Olsson and Viscovi, 2023).

Rural service users

Structurally, rurality is of further concern here. In rural areas, limited internet connectivity and infrastructure often hinder access to essential online services, including PES, creating a significant disadvantage for residents. This not only affects individuals but also impacts the overall economic development of rural communities. In contrast, urban areas generally enjoy better digital infrastructure and connectivity, resulting in increased access to information, PES offerings and remote work possibilities.

Where, access to community spaces assisted in overcoming access issues, the closure of libraries, community centres and, indeed, the move to require digital-PES tools like MyWelfare as the primary contact channels are particularly problematic. To ensure all citizens can access necessary government services, including PES offerings, the rural–urban divide must also be accounted for in digital policy. In this sense, emerging strategy, omni or otherwise, will only work where the needs of all are taken into account.

Disarray with current services

In equating the service experienced by those currently engaged within the PES system, much can be said for policy versus reality. Within the time parameters of the current Irish activation policy, Pathways to Work 2021–2025, there are still shortcomings in meeting citizen expectations. Indeed, current systems routinely fail to deliver the promises of service provision outlined in policies, increasing both distrust of government systems and disarray with current services. Digital channels and online tools, as primary mode of PES digitalisation, are not always accessible or indeed understood by all service users, in particular those with lower than expected digital skills.

This has led to the increased use of non-official channels as primary sources of information by service users. This has manifested in an array of online and social media sources, many with the sole aim of providing welfare information. Intriguingly, most of these groups are citizen-led and citizen-supported, wherein members of the general public share resources, knowledge and tips for navigating the Irish welfare system. Such information appeals to citizens in that it is: non-governmental and, as such, 'more trustworthy'; approachable, written in plain language and vernacular; and expeditious, with 24/7 access and communication potential. The most active of these groups within the Irish system hold communities on Facebook groups wherein pages see between 10,000 and 70,000 users and active questions and answers across the day: '[T]hank you [group admins] for providing such clear insights. It is most appreciated as sometimes the [government] information found is difficult to understand!' (Facebook group user). The challenge of meeting citizens at their level and via mediums fitting their needs is highly apparent here.

Personalisation of service is also problematic when practical realities do not take account of individualised need. Many service users value personalisation, accessing useful services, particular to their needs and flexibly around their timetable Such flexibility is not currently available within Irish PES as rigid controls of interactions are the norm, usually gatekept by service providers. Caseworkers have heavy workloads and, as such, cannot always provide the standard of personalisation expected. While policy dictates the potential for tools like MyWelfare to assist with such personalisation of PES experiences, this reality has not yet emerged. Such tools are not yet used to full capacity or, indeed, are a source of exclusion for those with lower than average digital skills. If Irish PES hope to adopt digital means of personalisation, the challenge lies in reconsidering what personalisation may mean for service users of all types, taking into consideration the digital skills and interaction preferences of all citizens.

Conclusion

Despite expanding efforts to integrate digital PES across Europe, there is a growing gap between policy outlines and the actual experiences of citizens where such tools, platforms and service experiences are concerned. As 2030 looms, the European Digital Decade targets seem more and more out of reach, especially considering the array of variables that need to be considered where the optimisation of PES approaches are concerned. These include consideration for digital skills attainment, current digital infrastructure and the potentialities of integrating traditional, caseworker-led approaches with progressive digital avenues. While ambition seeks to offer significant benefit for citizens, a hastening of efforts to ensure the realities of experience meet assumptions needs to transpire. As seen in the Irish example presented in this chapter, eager policies are often more aspirational than operational, and a significant range of obstacles emerge in providing additional digitalisation of PES approaches.

Significantly, the perimeters of a clear digital divide emerge wherein there is a need to explore how digital tools will affect all citizens, regardless of digital skills and access. In some cases, the removal of in-person services has left a void, and citizens find themselves a gap between the claimed benefits of digitalisation and actual service provision. The transition to digital approaches should not come at the expense of excluding those who may not have use of online platforms, display lower digital skill attainment or prefer traditional in-person interactions. The challenge lies in striking a balance between embracing digital innovation and ensuring inclusivity. Simply removing in-person services without a comprehensive consideration of citizens' diverse needs can lead to dissatisfaction and hinder the overall success of digital initiatives. To address this, an OC strategy, which seamlessly integrates online and offline services, holds great potential. Key perimeters to the application of such strategising need to be acknowledged:

- The utilisation of a range of channels and touchpoints simultaneously.
- The consideration for seamless interaction across such mediums.
- The capacity to personalise individual interactions and engagements.

Such an approach recognises that citizens have varying preferences and needs, providing flexibility and accessibility across different channels. Here, PES should be exploring paths of integration between the traditional and the transpiring.

The journey towards digitalisation in public services requires a careful examination of citizen expectations and a commitment to inclusivity, considering both citizen needs and ability to access and engage with services. As Ireland and other regions embark on this digital transformation, policy makers must ensure that the benefits of a digital-first approach are felt by all citizens, regardless of their preferred channels of interaction or digital skills. The success of digitalisation hinges on the ability to navigate this delicate balance, acknowledging the evolving landscape of citizen expectations and needs and adapting services accordingly. The potential of OC strategies in PES will not be felt until all citizens are considered within strategising and policy and where such expectations become service reality for all.

References

Baum, C. and Di Maio, A.D. (2000) *Gartner's Four Phases of E-Government*. Stamford: Gartner Inc.

Davern, E. (2023) New forms of PES service delivery. European Network of Public Employment Services – European Commission. https://short url.at/DQR58

European Commission (2018) Do you speak 'omni-channeling'. European Commission Policies and Activities. https://ec.europa.eu/social/main.jsp?catId=101&furtherNews=yes&langId=en&newsId=9066

European Commission (2023) *Europe's Digital Decade, Shaping Europe's Digital Future.* https://digital-strategy.ec.europa.eu/en/policies/europes-digital-decade

Fuertes, V. and Lindsay, C. (2016) Personalisation and street-level practice in activation: The case of the UK's work programme. *Public Administration*, 94(2).

Government of Ireland (2021) *Pathways to Work 2021–2025.* Dublin: Government of Ireland. https://www.gov.ie/en/publication/1feaf-pathways-to-work-2021/

Gov.ie (2022a) *Pathways to Work Strategy 2021–2025.* Department of Social Protection Publications. https://www.gov.ie/en/publication/1feaf-pathways-to-work-2021/

Gov.ie (2023) *My Welfare.ie.* Department of Social Protection Publications. https://www.gov.ie/en/service/c87b58-access-mywelfareie/

Gov.ie (2024) *Harnessing Digital: The Digital Ireland Framework.* Government of Ireland Publications. https://www.gov.ie/en/publication/adf42-harnessing-digital-the-digital-ireland-framework/

ILO (2022) *Public Employment Services Diagnostic Tool and Guide.* International Labour Organization Publications. https://shorturl.at/eixB9

Kannan, P.K. and Kulkarni, G. (2021) The impact of COVID-19 on customer journeys: Implications for interactive marketing. *Journal of Research in Interactive Marketing*, 16(1).

Margetts, H.Z. (2009) The internet and public policy. *Public & Internet*, 1(1).

OECD (2020) *Digital Government in Chile: Improving Public Service Design and Delivery.* OECD Digital Government Studies. DOI: /10.1787/b94582e8-en.

OECD (2021) *Government at a Glance 2021.* OECD. DOI: 10.1787/1c258f55-en

OECD (2022) *Harnessing Digitalisation in Public Employment Services to Connect People With Jobs, Policy Brief on Active Labour Market Policies.* https://www.oecd.org/els/emp/Harnessing_digitalisation_in_Public_Employment_Services_to_connect_people _with_jobs.pdf

Olsson, T. and Viscovi, D. (2023) Digitalised welfare: Access, usage and outcomes among older adults. *Media and Communications*, 11(3).

O'Reilly, J., Verdin, R. and McDonald, A. (2023) Introduction. In *Digital Welfare Ecosystems in Europe: Social Protection Systems Preventing Social Exclusion and Enhancing Opportunities to Participate in the Digital Economy.* EUROSHIP Working Paper. DOI: 10.6084/m9.figshare.22060376

Pérez-Morote, R., Pontones-Rosa, C. and Núñes-Chicharro, M. (2020) The effects of e-government evaluation, trust and the digital divide in the levels of e-government use in European countries. *Technological Forecasting and Social Change*, 154.

PESNetwork (2022) *Europe's Public Employment Services Seek a New Post COVID-19 Equilibrium*. European Commission Policies and Activities. https://ec.europa.eu/social/main.jsp?langId=en&catId=1163&furtherNews=yes&newsId=10232

Pieterson, W.J. (2017) *Multi-Channel Management in PES: From Blending to Omnichannelling*. European Commission Analytical Paper. https://ec.europa.eu/social/BlobServlet?docId=18865&langId=en

Pieterson, W.J. and Ebbers, W.E. (2020) Channel choice evaluation: An empirical analysis of shifting channel behaviour across demographics and tasks. *Government Information Quarterly*, 37(3).

Pieterson, W.J., Østergaard Madsen, C. and Ebbers, W.E. (2022) Omni-channel overtunes defining the concept and it's applicability in public sector channel management. In M. Janssen et al (eds) *Electronic Government* (pp 60–72). Cham: Springer.

Reddick, C.G. and Turner, M. (2012) Channel choice and public service delivery in Canada: Comparing e-government to traditional service delivery. *Government Information Quarterly*, 29(1).

Rey-Morero, M. and Medina-Molina, C. (2016) Omnichannel strategy and the distribution of public services in Spain. *Journal of Innovation & Knowledge*, 1(1).

Schenk, B., Dolata, M., Schwabe, C. and Schwabe, G. (2021) What citizens experience and how omni-channel could help: Insights from building permit case. *Information, Technology & People*, 37(2).

Schoyen, M.A. (2023) *'Norway' in Digital Welfare Ecosystems in Europe: Social Protection Systems Preventing Social Exclusion and Enhancing Opportunities to Participate in the Digital Economy*. EUROSHIP Working Paper. DOI: 10.6084/m9.figshare.22060376

Verhoef, P.C., Kannan, P.K. and Inman, J. (2015) From multi-channel retailing to omni-channel retailing. *Journal of Retailing*, 9(2).

Wirtz, B.W. and Langer, P.F. (2016) Public multichannel management: An integrated framework of off and online multichannel government services. *Public Organisation Review*, 17(4).

Zhuang, M, Fang, E. and Cai, F. (2020) How does omnichannel marketing enable businesses to cope with Covid: Evidence from a large-scale filed experiment. *Europe PMC*. DOI: 10.2139/ssrn.3640730

14

Profiling and subjectification of unemployed people: exploring the case of Slovenian public employment services

Sabina Pultz

Introduction

Currently, public employment services (PES) across European countries are under pressure (Fugini et al, 2014; Larsson, 2022). As an example, the Organisation for Economic Co-operation and Development (OECO) recommends a ratio of 1:150 between caseworkers and unemployed people, but the reality in many welfare states is often far from it. In the face of various challenges in PES, digitalisation has been identified as one of the answers to save resources and enhance efficiency in administration (Marston, 2006; Schou and Pors, 2019; Yalçın, 2021). Digitalisation is happening in several different areas from automated simple decision-making to more advanced formats, and the use of big data and algorithms and machine learning has shown great promise in some areas, a proved troublesome in others (Eubanks, 2018; Larsson, 2022; Ratner and Jørgensen, 2024). Increasingly digital services replace face-to-face encounters across the welfare system (Brioscú et al, 2024; Schou and Pors, 2019). As mass citizen data collection intensifies and we enter a 'datafied state', profiling algorithms, such as those employed by PES, play a bigger role in social service provision globally (Dencik, 2022; Hayes and Griffin, 2023). The incorporation of profiling can be viewed as part of this datafied state.

Algorithmic profiling (based on big data, sometimes artificial intelligence [AI]) is one of the most long-term adoptions of AI within PES, enacted in countries such as Australia, Canada, the United States and the United Kingdom since the late 1990s (Griffin et al, 2020; McGuiness et al, 2022). Currently profiling is in use in Ireland, Belgium and Estonia and profiling systems have failed or been cancelled in Poland, Sweden and Austria (Hayes and Griffin, 2023). These profiling tools are part of active labour market policies (ALMPs), with the goal of assisting unemployed people in finding work (McGann, 2023; OECD, 2022). The ideology embedded in profiling systems aligns well with the goal of ALMPs. ALMPs are work-first policy actions aiming to increase 'labour market participation' – either by providing jobseekers with employability orientated training or education, 'human capital building', or by putting pressure on unemployed people to find and accept work, measures referred to as 'welfare conditionality' (Aurich, 2011; McGann, 2023).

Profiling tools are based on categorisations and statistical models predicting who is the most likely to become long-term unemployed. The exact categories and cut-off scores differ between countries, however there are some patterns transgressing the different tools (Desiere et al, 2019). Jobseekers are typically classified into either 'high-risk' or 'low-risk' categories, based on their probability of entering long-term unemployment. Such tools are often additionally used to predict the likelihood of exiting the PES system over a given period, usually based on data given within entry to the PES system (Desiere and Struyen, 2021). Here, decision-making, based on machine discernment, is replacing the judgement of PES employees and replacing both rule-based and caseworker-led profiling activities. The aim of these tools has been to enable PES and counsellors to better be able to identify those in need of more help and spend a minimum of resources on the ones who can find a job on their own; making the system more effective and directing resources to the place they are most needed. Hayes and Griffin (2023) note that there is an expanding need to examine the ramifications of such technologies in front-facing public services.

We know some of the promises that profiling includes (such as efficiency) as well as some of the problems with the tools (lack of accuracy, resistance from case managers, discrimination and legal challenges) (Desiere et al, 2019). Across the European Union there has been limited success with profiling tools, sometimes due to legal grounds. Profiling tools have been criticised for discriminatory effects accentuating existing differences between unemployed people based on variables such as gender and ethnicity (Allhutter et al, 2020; Plümecke et al, 2023). Similarly, Hayes and Griffin note (2023: 7) that 'data is often aggregated from multiple unsuited sources, and these incremental approaches allow for a "people like you" classification instigating increased stigmatisation and stereotyping while labelling citizens based on incomplete views of their social context (Big Brother Watch, 2018)'. Stigma and shame is a challenge to most unemployed people and these technologies potentially exacerbates these dynamics (Pultz, 2018, 2024; Sharone, 2024). However, significant work on labour market discrimination and studies focusing on AI and machine learning technology within employment systems recognise an 'inherent tension between model accuracy and discrimination' (Desiere et al, 2019: 7; Kern et al, 2021). Much current reporting of accuracy figures does not capture the extent to which models fail to identify those at high risk (Griffin et al, 2021). At other times these have proven less effective, also due to meeting some resistance among counsellors.

What we know least about is how citizens experience these tools. As an exception, Pultz (2016) has investigated how the management and unemployed citizens experience a profiling tool in a Danish context. Here, management emphasised the benefits of relying on profiling tools as making decisions more 'objective' and 'scientific', rather than dependent on caseworkers' subjective discretionary judgement calls. The unemployed people were not explicitly informed about the profiling tool. As they became unemployed, members filled in a short survey and, based on survey information and register data within the unemployment fund, a statistical model was developed making predictions about their likelihood of becoming long-term unemployed. Even though the unemployed citizens were not informed about the profiling and categorisation into different risk groups, they expressed feeling as if they were treated in different ways. The ones who were left alone interpreted that as the system believing in their own abilities to secure a job, while the ones who felt as if they had to 'do more', such as participate more often in courses or activities, did not necessarily feel more helped or supported. While these profiling systems are dispersed, we need to better understand: *What are the subjectification processes involved in a profiling system?*

Based on an interdisciplinary research project, HECAT, fieldwork was conducted in Slovenian PES. Based on ethnographic work and in collaboration with counsellors and unemployed people a digital platform called MyLabourMarket (MLM) was developed. Part of MLM is a profiling system. This chapter zooms in and explores how managers, counsellors and unemployed people experience engaging directly with a profiling tool and thus fills an important gap in the literature. The chapter focuses specifically on the subjectification of the unemployed people, more so than the counsellors and managers. Exploring how such tools impact and change the working lives of employees in PES is thus outside the scope of this chapter.

To understand mechanisms of subjectification, it is central to understand the technologies of power involved. Here, profiling is conceptualized as a tool that is part of a wider palette of policies that come under the umbrella of ALMPs. Understanding technology as something that is not only instrumental, but that creates people and that people create through their use and interpretation/meaning-making processes, involves exploring both intended and unintended effects of technologies (Shraube, 2024; Pultz and Dupret, 2023).

Theoretical approach: governing unemployed people through digital technologies

The theoretical framework is based on a Foucauldian approach and in particular the concept of subjectification (Foucault, 1988; 2008). According to his work on governmentality studies, subjects become and emerge in the intersection between what Foucault (1988) terms technologies of power and those of the self (see also Pultz, 2024). While the two are not ontologically separate they each point to different social phenomena. Translated to a PES context, technologies of power largely consist of the various laws, rules and practices that exist to govern unemployed people. Technologies of the self, on the other hand, refer to the various ways that subjects engage with, experience and transform the demands and rules and conditions under which they live. Again, in a PES context, this involves exploring how unemployed people experience the laws, rules and demands they have to live up to as well as it involves exploring how the unemployed people conduct themselves as jobseekers and in general in their everyday life as unemployed (Pultz, 2024). Especially scholars from street-level bureaucracy approaches have successfully argued that there is leap between politics-as-policy and politics-as-made (Lipsky, 2010; Brodkin, 2012; Zacka, 2017) and hence exploring technologies of power involves not only analysing policy documents but also exploring how these are put into practice and given meaning along the way. Here, ethnographic work is particularly helpful. Based on the theoretical approach, profiling is viewed as a technology of power that governs the unemployed in particular ways and for the current purpose I will forefront this technology and relatedly neglect exploring the impact of other technologies as well as the interaction between the many technologies put into use in the PES.

During the last couple of decades, researchers focusing on subjectification processes have increasingly sought to uncover the non-linguistic and material aspects of subjectification processes (Bjerg and Staunæs, 2011; Staunæs and Juelskjær, 2016). These affective dimensions are key to understanding the various and intricate ways that unemployed people are governed today, in what Pultz (2017), with inspiration from Ahmed (2004), calls affective economies. The emotional and affective sides of subjectification processes are also deemed relevant in this context, as profiling systems seek to incentivise action (behaviour) but by ways of motivating unemployed people to act in new ways. Paraphrasing Bjerg and Staunæs (2011), affects are core matters to be managed by and through. Understanding how technologies of power and those of the self work involves looking into the affective sides of subjectification processes. Concretely, it involves investigating whether unemployed people experience fear, insecurity or feel empowered by gaining insights into the statistical probabilities of them exiting PES based on specific ways of measuring this outcome in the context of the Slovenian PES and labour market.

Methods

The research question will be explored based on ethnographic fieldwork conducted in Slovenian PES over the course of three years (2020–2023).

The fieldwork consists of field observations, ad hoc interviews as well as semi-structured interviews. Some interviews were conducted with the help of an on-site translator. Therefore, in this chapter, I will focus on the semi-structured interviews. These lasted on average one hour. All interviews were transcribed and for those conducted in Slovenian they were translated. Data used for this chapter include interviews with management (n=3), counsellors (n=15) and unemployed people (n=45). These were gathered throughout the lifespan of the project in 2020, 2021 and 2023.

During the interviews in 2023 the participants were trying the MLM platform, including the profiling tool. This chapter focuses exclusively on data concerning the profiling part of the platform.

The profiling section has a graph that shows the unemployed person's likelihood of exiting PES expressed in number of days based on the information put into the system (profession, gender, age, ethnicity to mention a few) (see Figure 14.1).

Before showing the participants the actual site we asked them about their expectations about what they thought they would encounter, what the purpose was and how they experienced it. While the participants scrolled around and became acquainted with the profiling tool, the interviewer asked questions, such as 'What are you looking at?', 'What do you make of that?', 'How does it affect you to see this information and in this way?'.

In order to answer the research question at hand – how are unemployed people subjectified by profiling tools? – I investigate the various ways that the three different groups think about profiling and how they experience it while using it. I am in particular attentive to emotional and affective dimensions and less attentive to technical aspects of the platform. I explore both the positive and negative effects of this tool as well exploring the intended as well as the unintended effects of profiling systems (Pultz, 2024).

Findings

The findings section is structured in a way that systematically explores the built-in understandings of the profiling tool, beginning with management level, then consulting counsellors' perspectives, and last exploring the unemployed people's experience with the tool. In all sections, the aim is to shed light on the subjectification processes involved in deploying the profiling tool in PES.

Management level

The built-in promises of profiling: what can profiling do?

As described in the introduction, one of the issues of European PES is the challenge of living up to the recommended ratio between counsellors and number of cases/unemployed citizens. This is also the case in Slovenia. As

Figure 14.1: Average time unemployed

Note: Based on the filled data and historical trends from the last 12 months the mean time to employment is 118 days, with a 90% probability of employment between 63 and 77 days.

one head of office says: 'Profiling is needed in Slovenia. We have to have it. This is also one of the possibilities, so we lower the casework for the counsellors. Our counsellors really have huge discretion.' While discretion is held in high regard as a professional virtue among the caseworkers, it is also clear that it is very time-consuming. Another head of office expresses a similar imagery: 'If the tool will be what we expect, then it will definitely help us within the process of counselling. So we could locate our resource to the population that really needs us.'

Inherent in the quotes is the 'promise' of profiling that it makes the work of PES more effective and hence relieves the counsellor of an otherwise time-consuming task. The profiling system in 2020 consisted of a two-part profiling system: 'Profiling is done in two parts; First from the registration, and then another profiling is done with the counsellor.' A head of office explains that the Slovenian PES has moved away from a more complicated system with seven categories towards a simpler version with only three categories. While this was helpful, the process of profiling based on rules through registration (made by the counsellor at a meeting) and a counsellor-based judgement was time-consuming.

Another head of office also imagines that the profiling system will provide a more objective and 'strong base' for decision-making processes in terms of helping unemployed people steer their career in a good direction and as such important in career guidance. The goal is 'to have a powerful tool to have in the decision-making process, not one that makes 100% decisions, but to have a strong base for the decision making. About career guidance, where to build and which direction to build your career'. The head of office elaborates: 'Profiling is a part of career guidance also, so the counsellor has the knowledge about how to profile the client, but it could help them with some recommendations and some additional information.' In terms of subjectifying the unemployed people, according to the management level the profiling tool relieves resources from overburdened caseworkers by removing a time-consuming task. Additionally, the tool plays an important role in qualifying decision-making processes in terms of career counselling. Overall, the tool is not described in affective language but rather as a support tool for counsellors and thus it only indirectly impacts the subjectification of unemployed people as it enables more help for those who are in need.

The built-in limitations: what profiling cannot do

While the promise of profiling involves targeting resources at the people who need it and thus making more effective use of resources, it is also clear that profiling cannot replace counsellors. Profiling and technology lack the personal touch, as expressed in the following quote, and hence the limitations of the technology are made visible:

Our job is not such a kind. It [the digital profiling] will be only additional to it. They don't believe IT or this new tool could replace counsellors and their work. It's not that kind of work that can be replaced. The personal touch is still the most important thing, so it can't be replaced. Especially with the long termed unemployed, who are staying unemployed at this moment. In the future we expect to have two kinds of populations, one is that young people who will gain from this technology and will turn quickly into the labour market, and on the other hand second population will be long termed unemployed, and those who have some kind of disability, and they will need us more than ever. The personal touch. Corona showed that even young people will have some mental problems, and they will really need this personal touch, because not only older people are at this moment long termed unemployed, but also young people coming from the school, is missing this personal touch.

Especially, the COVID-19 pandemic made it clear that the absence of the personal touch was problematic for several groups that were vulnerable in more than one way. While the hope is that profiling will spare resources and also provide additional information, the current experience with profiling has sparked some resistance, and according to one head of office, the resistance mainly comes from the more experienced counsellors, who describe the tool as time-consuming. The current critique is that no new information derives from using such a tool:

They have some counsellors who can be a bit resistant, but yeah of course. … It's not a problem, but we have some counsellors that everything new is not good; 'we did this for 10 years, why something new?' But the tool should be in that level, where it should be tested by counsellors who don't want it … but at this moment it's not relevant. The current situation is that you really have to put in a lot of information, duplicate the information, I guess this kind of counsellors who are reluctant would say, no this isn't helpful, I have to put in more energy, than I get from the result.

According to the head of office, the resistance is caused by the current problematic procedures that involve writing down the same information several times. It is unclear to what extent the resistance has been explored in-depth by management. However, it is important to note that resistance is identified and needs to be handled.

The managers emphasise the need to balance the statistical tools with counsellors' discretion to avoid problems with counsellors objecting to the introduction of the profiling tool:

P1:   There was also objection in our employment service, because the counsellors could take it too seriously. And yeah there is need for a balance between statistical tools, which is only or less than 95 per cent, 80 per cent or even 60 per cent correct. So it needs to be an additional tool, that helps with the decision. The acceptance within the counsellor could be mixed.

P2:   Yeah it would be great if the counsellor could give his or her assessment.

It is a built-in challenge, that the accuracy of profiling tools is not always very convincing (Desiere et al, 2019). The managers emphasise that the implication is that there should be an element of counsellors' own assessment. While digital technologies of profiling can be decided at management level and implemented in front level service, these technologies of power can be counteracted by counsellors who in fact use their agency to translate politics-as-policy to policy-as-reality. Understanding the subjectification processes thus involves exploring not only the lived experiences of unemployed people as they face digital technologies, but also how they are administered by counsellors as the counsellors' ways of appropriating the technology carry tremendous impact on how the unemployed people come to experience the tool.

Counsellor level

Saving resources

While the management level gives insight into some overall imagined promises and limitations of the profiling tool, the counsellor level offers other perspectives more closely related to the lived experience of providing support to citizens and at the same time being under an immense time pressure dealing with a larger caseload than recommended by the Organisation for Economic Co-operation and Development. These perspectives also allow us to get closer to the meeting between the counsellor and the unemployed citizen.

Counsellors think of profiling tools as a way to distribute resources more efficiently: 'so I think profiling those people that really need help, and those who don't need as much help, that they can be on their own, if I say so. I think this would be the main change'. Directing resources towards the people who need it and leaving the others alone is perhaps the most dominant promise of profiling tools expressed in the interviews, also across management and counsellor level.

At the moment the profiling is done together with the citizen, and as the counsellor says here, a lot of time is spent getting plain information. If that information had been obtained beforehand, or digitally by the citizen, they would not be 'losing time', as one counsellor expresses it:

The other situation is when we try and invite someone to PES for a counselling, you have to send the invitation at least five days ahead. So if I don't do that, I'm also losing our and his time. That's why the profiling is done with the client, so it takes around 20–30 minutes, and the person just sits there and gives information.

In addition to questioning whether time is well spent on this task, it is noteworthy that the counsellor thinks of the interaction as the unemployed citizen 'just sits there and gives information'. There doesn't seem to be any critical reflection in terms of what information is asked for, but it is clear that the citizen is not left with much room for agency but rather is subjectified rather passively as the giver of particular pieces of information. The interaction does not cover customised or personalised interaction, which are key to creating and maintaining relations.

Making citizens anxious or motivated?

Another counsellor addresses the built-in dilemma of profiling tools; what is the actual effect of receiving information about your likelihood of becoming long-term unemployed? He speculates that some people would become anxious rather than better equipped as a jobseeker on the Slovenian labour market: 'I don't know if it even motivates you to know that you are in high risk of getting long-term unemployed. I guess you would just become anxious.' Key to the question of subjectification is what the profiling gives rise to – are the unemployed people left feeling more anxious or motivated to change their predicted outcome?

Another counsellor identifies an important aspect to incentivise citizens: 'a tool that is supposed to work with different scenarios and also possibly actions; so if I do this, how does that change my possibilities and what kind of possible scenarios would there be on various paths into the labour market'. Receiving information about your labour market opportunities should be linked to certain possible actions; it should steer the unemployed in a more promising direction. In that sense, profiling should be seen in a wider perspective, exploring how is it used as well as who, in practice, is made responsible for improving the predicted outcomes. These ethical dimensions are highlighted by the counsellors.

Moulding labour market expectations and reality checks

The counsellors – like the managers – value the flexibility of the categories. A counsellor explains: 'He looked employable, but it's not like that, so we move him. So, it's not finished like that and vice versa. I don't think it is an obstacle.' Beneath this way of thinking is the idea that the unemployed citizen might in fact 'be wrong about himself'. In such cases, the counsellors believe the tool can play a helpful role in terms of offering some kind of reality check:

> So it's kind of a reality check, this tool will need repairs, but if it works, this person could say, okay, with this education and if I search as an administrator, it means it will take me like 350 days in Ptuj. So, he can get some sense of reality, what it means with different education and competences, job experience, if I'm looking in one place, it means it will take me this time.

In this view, the profiling tool works 'at a distance' (Burchell et al, 1991), echoing Foucault's notions of how governmentality works and the change in perspective supposedly happens through the unemployed person's self-reflective capacities. Learning about discouraging outcomes should work by increasing the unemployed people's mobility and willingness to be flexible.

The profiling tool can act as a way to encourage a stepping-stone strategy, accepting a job that is not the dream job, but in the right direction:

> You have to know what you want, because the labour market is like other markets, so you have demand and supply, so if you just settled with one thing, it will stay like that forever. So maybe just step by step, maybe I can't get the dream job right now, but I know what I want long-term, and I think the employers like persons who know what they want. I think that's not a bad idea. Maybe it's not doable, if you have to change your education, you have to know it means you have to put some effort and time. Yes. That's important. If the person sees it could be possible in one year, then they would be more motivated for the not-so-wanted job for a period.

Counsellors have the embodied experience of putting into use different active labour market measures in dealing with their citizens and they emphasise the heterogeneity among the citizens. Numbers speak to some people more than others, so seeing the graph might be motivating to some, while for others it would not have any value:

> Especially clients who says 'I'm looking for a job, but can't because of this and this' and they stick to it. So they don't say I don't get a job because of this, and say I have to solve this problem or search in other places, or have to search for career in other direction. They just stick to it. If you have this automatically, scientific tool, that says okay, this means the probability is that you can get a job in 350 days. You try to persuade people to say, okay that's not good, let's try something

else. I'm trying to tell them that in many different ways, but people are different. Some will find the statistical important, others it doesn't have a value. So I have to choose whether to use it or not. Because different people, different motivation. So it's not for everyone, but some it would be useful.

Looking at the seemingly objective data encourage unemployed people to be more flexible in their job search. Rather than only imagining one job or one scenario, job search and imagined job routes should be broadened through so-called 'persuasion'. The counsellor emphasises heterogeneity among their citizens and hence the technology for some work in a motivating fashion, affectively charging them to change their behaviour and perspective. For others, looking at statistics will not have the same effect and thus it remains a task for counsellors to know who will be 'persuaded' by the technology and who will not. Clearly, a focus on persuasion involves an affective dimension, taking into account the embodied experience meeting the tool in the particular way that it is presented and dealt with by the counsellor and in the meeting between the unemployed person and the counsellor. The meaning of the tool and its impact on subjectification processes go through and are molded by how profiling and its results are handled in the social practices at PES.

Unemployed people

Getting all kinds of information: the good, the bad, the ugly

In the interviews with the unemployed people, it was often discussed whether it makes sense to get all kinds of information, and in particular receiving bad information was discussed at length. In other words, do you want to know the bad news, or would you rather live in ignorant bliss? And what is the effect of being confronted with bad news? An interviewer asks an unemployed man: 'So do you think everybody wants to know this type of [bad] information or some people just wouldn't like it?' The unemployed person answers: 'Yes, I would say pretty much people don't want to stress themselves with … but this is wrong, because if you don't inform yourself, then you cannot expect that you would progress.' In this participant's perspective it would be wrong not to get the information and inherent in his perspective is an underlying belief in the data and the predictions made. He does not challenge the truth or accuracy of profiling but rather interprets it as a 'reality check', also mentioned by the counsellors, and as a necessary input to make 'progress'. Another unemployed person similarly expresses the effect of viewing a discouraging result: 'I mean, because if it's a really long time, maybe I should look in another field.' The tool is perceived as a realistic prediction and the unemployed are conceived of as rational actors who should conduct themselves according to this information.

As the information is, however, sensitive, the unemployed person would prefer getting the information first at home and then openly discuss the results with his counsellor rather than receiving the information at a meeting with the counsellor: 'I wouldn't have any problem discussing this with my counsellor, not at all. But I would first examine, analyse it at home.'

The participant plays around with the tool and changes some of the input going into the algorithm. Changing some parameters results in a change from a predicted unemployment period of 250 days to a little less than 100: 'That gives me more motivation. Because 250, that means two years.'

While many profiling systems are based on a 'one off' calculation, the MLM profiling system developed within HECAT leaves room for unemployed people themselves to change parameters and immediately see the trade-off between the changed choices and the predicted results. According to our participants, that element is motivating as it makes people aware that they have agency and active choices can be made. From the unemployment literature, it is clear, that excactly the feeling of agency and self-determination is squeezed in a situation of uncertainty and often fear about the future (Pultz, 2024).

A one-off prediction thus subjectifies unemployed people more as objects while the possibility of changing parameters involves a more agentic subjectification which has a motivating effect according to the participant.

Relying on labour market information

Another feature of the MLM profiling platform is the possibility of comparing between different jobs:

> I can see what job there's less people unemployed or the least amount of time that you're unemployed. But I don't think this would really affect my choice for what I want to do. … Maybe just for fun to check with your friends and me. But for me, not really.

To this participant it would not really impact her choices to compare between different occupations; it would be amusing to compare, but it would not affect her job search and aspirations on the labour market.

Being presented with a particular graph visualising the average amount of unemployed days for a person with that profile, many unemployed people struggle interpreting the results. There is a line stating what the graph is showing and to many people this communication is pivotal in order to get any information out. A participant says:

> I mean, I usually, I'm not looking at statistics. … I suppose the idea behind it is that mainly either a counsellor or a person can see that

when, if they're unemployed, what's the average time that people go back to work, so they can get an idea of how long it might take them to search for a job.

For this participant, who is not used to looking at statistics, he quickly analyses that the graph must be relevant for others than himself. He mentions counsellors in the quote but also refer to statistics as relevant to look at for researchers. His reaction demonstrates the heterogeneity among the unemployed people and it highlights the dilemma of deploying digital advanced tools. To some people it might be useful, but to others, they feel incapable of understanding the results and are, as such, excluded from obtaining the same information.

While the difference in digital literacy has been explored in the literature (Barna and Epure, 2020), there is also a relevant difference in terms of educational background that affect how different users experience a profiling like this one. Another participant notes that the purpose of viewing these averages is to normalise and destress: 'It's to give that information so maybe they don't get stressed out if they're not finding a job very quickly or something like that. So, it helps.'

Another participant (Lucia) is presented with her result. While she expresses trust in the data presented, she also reflects on the limitations of making such predictions as the last couple of years have been filled with unexpected major events such as the COVID-19 pandemic and wars that impact labour market dynamics extensively:

> It can be true, especially in the time like now. I mean, it's very hard to get that job now. Yeah, I believe that this is true. That's useful to know, but we can know because numbers can change day by day. So there's still something we don't know about, what will happen tomorrow and so on. Especially with the current situation and Europe with the war between Russia and Ukraine and so on.

Another participant, Martej, also voices some scepticism in terms of trusting the data and the underlying assumptions that are built into the profiling tool:

> If I don't do anything, I will get 150 days. Or 500 days. 50 days can be indicated, but if I don't work hard on getting it, it can take me 150 days or more. This can really make me desperate. Because a lot depends on the effort I invest, on the energy I invest into getting a job.

She problematises the fact that it is possible to generate different outcomes and, in her perspective, what it comes down to is whether she puts in the hard work necessary to land a job. Being presented with one number, to her, involves being subjectified in a simplified manner – as if the process of job search was not as complicated as is the case and, importantly, as if the individual's own actions do not matter to the extent that she thinks they do. She also sensed some way of being made passive and treated more as an object than as a person holding power.

From the unemployed people's perspective, it is clear that the profiling tool contain elements that involves subjectifying them in ambiguous ways, sometimes pacifying, and at other times governing them as more active subjects who can make choices that impact predictions and hence also motivational levels.

Concluding discussion

Based on ethnographic field work conducted in Slovenian PES offices, the chapter has explored the subjectification processes involved in using a profiling system. While a digital technology such as a profiling system can be viewed as a neutral instrument that 'just' supports (or replaces) decision-making processes in PES, the chapter shows the intricate ways that such a tool affects the people who use it as well as the people who are governed by it. Incorporating new technologies such as profiling transforms PES into digital services and that leaves open the question of 'what are the extensions and amputations, and what do we break apart and put back weaker?' (see the Introduction to this volume).

The chapter has demonstrated the usefulness of applying a rich qualitative method to explore these matters and open the rich empirical field, digging deeper to understand both the intended and unintended effects of using such a tool. This chapter highlights the need to address the role of technology directly based on an understanding that people do not just use technology in an instrumental manner (Schraube, 2024). Similarly, Pultz and Dupret (2023) who note: 'The exact design, the inherent possibilities and limitations and the actual material make-up influence the users and co-create them. When it comes to understanding technology as part of a socio-material complex – it is shaped by how it is used, but it also shapes the users (Oudshoorn and Pinch, 2003).'

This chapter has made visible some of the tensions present when deploying a profiling technology at the Slovenian PES.

I sum up some of the tensions here:

- trust in data;
- making citizens passive (just feeding information); and
- discouraging or motivating.

The consequences of profiling are directly linked to how the various groups perceive the trustworthiness of data – whether they believe that graph or not. If citizens believe in the graph being scientifically developed and based on undisputable, valid data, they are more likely to be convinced that the graph will have beneficial effects – such as enabling more informed and rational choices and thus increase effectivity.

As street-level bureaucratic researchers scholars emphasise again and again, the ways policies and policy instruments are deployed at the front end matters greatly in terms of what politics really is (Lipsky, 2010; Brodkin, 2012). Some counsellors emphasise the need to combine statistics and the personal touch and allowing for the counsellor's assessment to be considered in order to avoid any resistance against the tool. A potential pitfall is subjectifying unemployed people as passive containers of neutral information that they should feed into the profiling technology. In fact, making visible how profiling is malleable and adaptable to human decision-making was deemed key in terms of motivation and agency for unemployed people. Counsellors repeated some of the same promises narrated by the managers; the tool should help direct resources to where they are most needed and thus take off some of the workload for the counsellors. They also identified the tool as a possible way of offering citizens a reality check and serve as an encouragement towards a stepping-stone strategy in job search rather than only focusing on the dream job. There is a lack of solid results on the consequences on the work of professionals, that is, on the uses they make of digital tools, on how these tools interfere with their expertise, on their consequences on working relations, particularly with hierarchies, and so on. This chapter has touched upon some of these matters, however future research should addresss these questions.

In closing, to really understand the impact of profiling and other digital technologies applied in PES around Europe, this chapter has documented the importance of exploring subjectification processes, more broadly taking into consideration the many (different) perspectives on profiling and its effects; behavioural and affective. Technologies are not neutral instruments that convey objective data; it is human-made constructs that have very real social and ethical implications shaping what kind of unemployed people are made in PES offices all over Europe. We need to understand the emotional effect and the entanglement between data, human beings and the technology as we develop better ways to support unemployed people.

References

Ahmed, S. (2004) Affective economies. *Social Text*, 22(79): 117–139.

Allhutter, D., Cech, F., Fischer, F., Grill, G. and Mager, A. (2020) Algorithmic profiling of job seekers in Austria: How austerity politics are made effective. Frontiers in Big Data, 3: 5.

Aurich P. (2011) Activating the unemployed: Directions and divisions in Europe. *European Journal of Social Security*, 13(3): 294–316.

Barna, C. and Epure, M. (2020) Analyzing youth unemployment and digital literacy skills in Romania in the context of the current digital transformation. *Review of Applied Socio-Economic Research*, 20(2): 17–25.

Bjerg, H. and Staunæs, D. (2011) Self-management through shame: Uniting governmentality studies and the 'affective turn'. *Ephemera: Theory & Politics in Organization*, 11(2). 138–156.

Brioscú, A. et al (2024) A new dawn for public employment services: Service delivery in the age of artificial intelligence. OECD Artificial Intelligence Papers, No. 19. https://doi.org/10.1787/5dc3eb8e-en

Brodkin, E.Z. (2012) Reflections on street-level bureaucracy: Past, present, and future. *Public Administration Review*, 72(6): 940–949.

Burchell, G., Gordon, C. and Miller, P. (1991) *The Foucault effect: Studies in governmentality*. Chicago: University of Chicago Press.

Dencik, L. (2022) The datafied welfare state: A perspective from the UK. In A. Hepp, J. Jarke and L. Kramp (eds) *New perspectives in critical data studies: The ambivalences of data power* (pp 145–165). Cham: Springer International Publishing.

Desiere, S., Langenbucher, K. and Struyven, L. (2019) Statistical profiling in public employment services: An international comparison. OECD – Social, Employment and Migration Working Papers, No. 224.

Eubanks, V. (2018) *Automating inequality: How high-tech tools profile, police, and punish the poor*. New York: Picador.

Febiri, F. and Hub, M. (2021) Digitalization of global economy: A qualitative study exploring key indicators use to measure digital progress in the public sector. SHS Web of Conferences, 92.

Foucault, M. (2008) *The birth of biopolitics, lectures at the College de France, 1978–1979*. Basingstoke: Palgrave Macmillan.

Foucault, M. (2010) *The government of self and others, lectures at the Collège de France 1982–1983*. Basingstoke: Palgrave Macmillan.

Foucault, M., Martin, L.H., Gutman, H. and Hutton, P.H. (1988) *Technologies of the self, a seminar with Michel Foucault*. London: Tavistock.

Fugini, M.G., Maggiolini, P. and Valles, R.S. (2014) *E-government and employment services: A case study in effectiveness*. Cham: Springer.

Griffin, R. et al (2021) Report: Ethical, social, theological, technical review of 1st generation PES algorithms and data use. HECAT, Project Deliverable, Number D1.3.

Hayes, O. and Griffin, R. (2023) Algorithm profiling in public employment services (PES): Reporting standards policy brief. [HECAT] D7.2 Policy briefing report. https://doi.org/10.5281/zenodo.7921614

Haug, K.B. (2023) Structuring the scattered literature on algorithmic profiling in the case of unemployment through a systematic literature review. *International Journal of Sociology and Social Policy*, 43(5/6): 454–472.

Kern, C., Bach, R., Mautner, H. and Kreute, F. (2021) *Fairness in algorithmic profiling: A German case study*. New York: Cornell University Press.

Lipsky, M. (2010) *Street-level bureaucracy: Dilemmas of the individual in public service*. Russell Sage Foundation.

Marston G. (2006) Employment services in an age of e-government. *Information, Community and Society*, 9(1): 83–103.

McGann, M. (2023) *The marketisation of welfare-to-work in Ireland: Governing activation at the street-level*. Bristol: Policy Press.

McGuinness, S., Redmond, P., Kelly, E. and Maragkou, K. (2022) *Predicting the probability of long-term unemployment and recalibrating Ireland's statistical profiling model* (No. 149). Research Series.

Niklas, J., Sztandar-Sztanderska, K., Szymielewicz, K., Baczko-Dombi, A. and Walkowiak, A. (2015) *Profiling the unemployed in Poland: Social and political implications of algorithmic decision making*. Warsaw: Fundacja Panoptykon.

OECD (2022) Harnessing digitalisation in public employment services to connect people with jobs. Policy Brief on Active Labour Market Policies. https://www.oecd.org/els/emp/Harnessing_digitalisation_in_Public_Employment_Services_to_connect_people_with_jobs.pdf

Oudshoorn, N.E. and Pinch, T. (2003) Introduction: How users and non-users matter. In N. Oudshoorn and T. Pinch (eds) *How users matter. The co-construction of users and technology* (pp 1–25). Cambridge, MA: MIT Press.

Plümecke, T., Wilopo, C.S. and Naguib, T. (2023) Effects of racial profiling: The subjectivation of discriminatory police practices. *Ethnic and Racial Studies*, 46(5): 811–831.

Pultz, S. (2024) Emotionally indebted: Governing the *unemployed people* in an *affective economy*. Palgrave Macmillan.

Pultz, S. (2018) Shame and passion: The affective governing of young unemployed people. *Theory & Psychology*, 28(3): 358–381.

Pultz, S. (2017) It's not you, it's me: Governing the unemployed self in the Danish welfare state: Phd dissertation, Københavns Universitet, Det Samfundsvidenskabelige Fakultet.

Pultz, S. (2016) Governing homo economicus: Risk management among young unemployed people in the Danish welfare state. *Health, Risk & Society*, 18(3–4): 168–187.

Pultz, S. and Dupret, K. (2023) Emotions online: Exploring knowledge workers' emotional labour in a digital context in an agile IT company. *Human Arenas: An Interdisciplinary Journal of Psychology, Culture, and Meaning.* https://doi.org/10

Ratner, H.F. and Jørgensen, R.F. (2024) *Essay til Magtudredningen: Kunstig intelligens i* velfærdssamfundet. https://ps.au.dk/fileadmin/Statskundskab/Billeder/Forskning/Forskningsprojekter/Magtudredning/Essays/Tema11/Ratner___Joergensen__Tema_11_.pdf

Schou, J. and Pors, A.S. (2019) Digital by default? A qualitative study of exclusion in digitalised welfare. Social Policy & Administration, 53(3): 464–477.

Schraube, E. (2024) *Digitalization and learning as a worlding practice: Why dialogue matters*. New York: Taylor & Francis.

Staunæs, D. and Juelskjær, M. (2016) Orchestrating intensities and rhythms. *Theory & Psychology*, 26(2): 182–201.

Yalçın, E.C. (2021) Efficiency measurement of digitalization on EU countries: A study based on data envelopment analysis. International Journal of Management, Knowledge and Learning, 10(1): 323–333.

Zacka, B. (2017) *When the State Meets the Street: Public Service and Moral Agency*. Cambridge, MA: Harvard University Press.

15

Conclusion

Didier Demazière, Ray Griffin,
Magnus Paulsen Hansen and Janine Leschke

A neat conclusion to this volume on the digitalisation of public employment services (PES) is not possible. Across 14 chapters more issues are opened than resolved, and we find ourselves at a critical juncture. Some PES are now contemplating and envisaging entirely digital services and it is hard to predict how this utopian vision will unfold in practice. Contemporary excitement about generative artificial intelligence is adding to the zeitgeist. Strangely, we are at least 40 years into digitalising PES, and development is still a contested jumble of software and systems, administration, policy and politics – with nothing cohering as a definitive way forward. In this, we have some digitally mature services such as profiling, job search and matching services; a patchwork of technology enabled services from online registration, self-assessment, skills training, case management, counselling and labour market information – and yet, often these are piecemeal, ad-hoc efforts or responses to crises. This fragmentation and contestation around services such as profiling highlights the broader challenges of adopting and integrating new technologies within established administrative and policy frameworks.

So, while PES represent some of the largest social investments by contemporary governments, typically having large, capable in-house ICT departments, their efforts to harness the potential of digital technology in an ethical and just manner are often poor. These chapters surface how complex and challenging the digitalisation of PES is proving, parsing between top-down policy directives and bottom-up service user imperatives, legal and operational consideration, the legal considerations of algorithms, and the unpredictable impact of digital tools on both jobseekers and counsellors. It is obvious that we are only starting to think more broadly about a coherent and inclusive approach to digital welfare, addressing issues of digital exclusion, digital literacy, communication confusion, tensions between professional discretion and automation, and the governance of unemployed people through digital services. As we navigate these complexities, it is crucial to start thinking beyond traditional approaches to consider how digital tools can create more inclusive, personalised and responsive services that truly meet the needs of all jobseekers.

Indeed, across this volume, the most obvious theme is the dispiriting absence of a shared vision of development, a unified field of action or even a convergence of practice. Promoters and advocates of the digitalisation of the PES nevertheless stress the advantages – both sought and supposed – of this technological innovation: facilitating access to welfare state services by lowering access costs for users; fostering anticipatory public action thanks to predictive indicators of users' difficulties; improving equality of treatment by routinising the decision-making procedures of front-line agents; optimising the efficiency of services rendered by assisting social workers in prescribing adapted, tailor-made interventions, and so on. But the PES digitalisation varies considerably from one country to another, in terms of pace of development, in terms of the ways in which tools are introduced – imposed or negotiated – with public employees, and how their jobs are transformed, in terms of degrees of decision-making automation, in terms of reaction and appropriation of advisors, in terms of the level of trust that both they and the unemployed place in algorithmic instruments and artificial intelligence tools. A recurring tension emerges, between the expected benefits, efficiency and financial costs against the potential risks that surround opacity and the hidden ethical costs of public services – discrimination, reinforcement of inequalities, various biases. The outcome of these tensions is, at present, uncertain. However, it can be argued that it depends directly on the quality of the data used, and above all, on the opportunities offered to front-line actors – advisers and unemployed people – to be actively involved in the process and influence decision-making.

In the contemporary practice we explored across the 14 chapters, there is little that models excellence – how best to approach developing digital PES. Nor are there substantial efforts to broaden out development practices beyond a narrow elite of policy makers and technicians that currently produce, steward and disseminate knowledge on digital PES. As a number of chapters touch upon, the voice of caseworkers and the unemployed are largely absent from the digitalisation agenda. Also the narrative on what is animating this policy movement is surprisingly vague (as Jordan and Griffin suggest in Chapter 2) beyond top-down visions for cutting-edge, state-of-the-art public services. These logics are extensions of more than 30 years of New Public Management and entrepreneurial government, at least in some settings animated by the ambitions to do more for less, prioritising efficiency and cost. Also receiving glib attention is data protection and digital inclusion and literacy; two issues that profoundly limit the scope of digital PES.

At the moment, the goal of development of digital PES risks heading off further into the wrong direction. One of the most significant digital techniques used in PES today is statistical profiling, which in theory rations access to expensive casework supports, including activation, parsing between those likely to be long-term unemployed from those likely to be frictionally unemployed. However, using big data and novel algorithms for statistical profiling may jeopardise core values of transparency, accountability, ethics and professionalism. Strangely, social policy and more broadly the socio-economically orientated social sciences are only starting to contemplate the social consequences of digital PES.

Digitalisation more broadly has a utopian and hopeful history, nucleated in the cybernetic countercultures of the 1970s where technology was understood to open things up, expand possibilities, democratise, equalise and collapse boundaries and divisions. In general, these hopes have dwindled and been dashed in the face of the corporate internet, data surveillance and subjectification, the age of anxiety and social media. Much of the scholarship on digital PES thus starts from a critical and hopeless standpoint. Absent is an understanding of how the move from analogue to digital recomposes welfare, reimagines the order and the hierarchies of current welfare states – qualitatively, interpretively, experientially, emotionally and creatively, in ways we do not yet fully understand. Current understandings of digital PES at best crudely grasp the sheer complexity of welfare, the deep historical context, analytical depth, critique and interpretation. It is difficult to imagine how the order and the hierarchies of the welfare state can be kept alive in a digital service, as we do not even have a good handle on the byzantine complexity of the existing welfare state. And because of this, rather than thinking of digital PES as an opportunity, it is largely perceived as a threat.

PES is one of the most expensive social services provided by governments. In most countries PES has been stitched together as a bricolage of activities and services over decades, so much so that it is almost impossible to consider whole scale redevelopment. There is now a large hidden opportunity to put the development of digital PES on a more considered footing. Rightfully, much of the scholarship on digital PES, including many chapters in this volume, starts from a critical and rather pessimistic standpoint. Instead of ending the volume with yet again pointing to the broken promises of digitalisation, we suggest an alternative pathway for digital PES.

So, what is to be done? A manifesto for digital PES

Digital public services are coming, along with raised expectations for accessibility, lower administrative burdens, costs and effort. Digital PES holds out the possibility of being available 24/7, with clear digital interactions that, for citizens, should take less time and effort as well as reducing the administrative burden for PES. Equally, automating case handling supports improved productivity, with less repetitive tasks, and frees up PES capacity for higher value human-to-human interactions. It is clear that citizens and front-line workers want a seamless experience, akin to the best that can be found in the sector. So, while the potential of digitalisation is manifest, as of now, it seems to be largely unrealised.

Starting by unpacking the citizen's experience

Becoming unemployed is an anxiety-inducing life event, and approaching PES for the first time or any time is bewildering. Information on how to access welfare and services is often presented inconsistently in hard-to-comprehend bureaucratic language. Applications routinely require hard copies of supporting documents, with service users needing to maintain scrupulous records, formulate and repeat their story consistently, in a way that is positively understood by PES. Individuals routinely must navigate between different parts of government for housing, health, unemployment, tax and a range of other services, often with multiple accounts and digital IDs. Service journeys are often more to do with legislation and rules, and principles of fairness and equality than the care that service users need. Digital PES holds out the potential to substantially improve the service for users through reimagining the user's digital journey – with clear, simple instructions, less duplication, using a single, seamless, transparent, coherent and accessible service.

Here the voice of the unemployed person, and the practical wisdom of caseworkers, is vital to development and implementation. Capturing that voice goes beyond inclusion to paying significant and deep attention using various collaborative and observation-based research methods. In other words, it requires an ethnographic inquiry to the entanglement of (digital) PES with the lives of unemployed persons.

Back to first principles with a deep understanding of the welfare state and its institutional context

Digitalisation alters the welfare state, and without an understanding of how the institutional context of PES is deeply intertwined with its historical foundations, reform is undertaken in a void. As a result, developing digital PES should be rooted in the broader historical and institutional context of the welfare state. In particular, the welfare state was formed out of post-war logics that explicitly understood the safety net and support structures for the unemployed as essential to preserve and promote peace, prosperity and to protect against war and social agitation. Over the 70 years since the great European wars, the welfare state and PES have proved remarkably durable and adaptable – navigating the COVID-19 pandemic, global financial crisis, oil shocks and wars, working as an automatic stabiliser to preserve the political and economic system in times of stress. The shift towards digitalisation within PES has to be understood as part of this ongoing adaptation and calibration, rather than more immanent issues of cost, efficiency, control and responsiveness, or short-term political marketing needs. Again, digital transformation developments using only a narrow seam of policy makers and technicians increases the likelihood that such historically attuned understanding of welfare, the labour process and how and why we offer welfare in particular ways, is not integral to service renewal.

In general, PES needs to focus more acutely on access, particularly against the rising issue of non-claiming and non-participation in PES services among economically inactive people, including due to perceptions of stigmatisation. Many unemployed people struggle to use digital services – through low digital literacy, lack of digital access or resources, or even because of barriers they face in their lives that cannot be addressed through digital and self-service portals. In these situations, exclusion from the labour market is compounded by a double exclusion from accessing welfare.

For some, digital alternatives only compound the barriers to employment. An important lesson from recent digitalisation efforts is that governments need nuanced strategies that accommodate those who prefer or require person-to-person support in order to minimise the risk of these clients getting lost or left behind.

Beyond automating existing services

In contemplating the future of PES, it is vital to move beyond merely automating existing processes. While the digitalisation of PES has introduced efficiencies in profiling, job search and matching services, the true potential of digital transformation lies in envisioning novel services that leverage data in innovative and user-friendly ways to enhance the core functions of PES. This requires a fundamental rethinking of service delivery that goes beyond streamlining operations to reimagining how data can be used to proactively support jobseekers and employers and support their quality labour market integration. The integration of advanced data analytics and artificial intelligence into PES can unlock new opportunities for personalised service delivery and ultimately better experiences of jobseekers. For instance, predictive analytics can anticipate labour market trends and individual career trajectories, offering tailored advice to jobseekers based on real-time data. Machine learning algorithms can identify skills gaps and recommend targeted training programmes, ensuring that jobseekers are not only matched with existing opportunities but are also prepared for future demands. By harnessing the power of big data, PES can shift from a reactive to a proactive approach, offering support that is not just responsive to immediate needs but also anticipatory of future challenges. However, the pursuit of such innovative services must be carefully balanced with ethical considerations and the need for inclusivity. The deployment of data-driven solutions requires robust safeguards to ensure data privacy and prevent algorithmic bias as much as possible. Transparent and accountable use of data must be prioritised to build trust among users. Furthermore, digital services must be designed with inclusivity at their core, ensuring that all jobseekers, regardless of their digital literacy or access to technology, can benefit from these advancements. Addressing digital exclusion is crucial to prevent the exacerbation of existing inequalities. Despite significant investments and the presence of capable in-house ICT departments within PES, the development of digital services remains a contested and fragmented endeavour. The current landscape is characterised by a mix of digitally mature services and a patchwork of ad-hoc, piecemeal efforts. This lack of coherence reflects the broader challenges of successfully integrating new technologies within established administrative and policy frameworks. To overcome these hurdles, a more coordinated approach is needed, one that aligns technological innovations with the strategic goals of PES and the broader welfare state.

From target groups to inclusive personalisation

In envisioning new services, it is crucial to transcend the traditional focus on target groups that label 'problem people' – such as older low-skilled workers, single mothers, individuals with disabilities, and NEETs (Not in Education, Employment, or Training). This commonly used approach risks stigmatising these groups and perpetuates a fragmented service delivery model. Instead, to fully embrace digital possibilities and imaginaries, we can think of the potential for inclusive personalised services that genuinely address the diverse individual needs of all service users. Such a shift requires a fundamental rethinking of how digital tools and data are utilised to create more holistic, responsive and empowering services. The power of digital technology lies in its ability to offer personalised services at scale. By leveraging advanced data analytics, machine learning and artificial intelligence, PES can develop tailored interventions that are responsive to the unique circumstances of each individual and their specific needs and preferences. For instance, personalised job matching algorithms can consider a massive and complex range of factors – such as skills, experience and personal preferences – beyond the simplistic categorisations of target groups. Similarly, personalised training and development programmes can be designed to address specific skills gaps and career aspirations, thus empowering jobseekers to achieve their full potential. Furthermore, digital PES can foster a more inclusive environment by ensuring that services are accessible to all users, regardless of their digital literacy or access to technology. This involves designing user-friendly interfaces, providing digital literacy training and offering multiple channels of support – including in-person assistance for those who need or prefer it. By focusing on inclusivity, PES can avoid the pitfalls of digital exclusion and ensure that all jobseekers, including those from traditionally marginalised groups, can benefit from digital advancements.

Embracing interdisciplinary and inclusive research for digital public employment services

Finally, to overcome the fragmented development of digital PES and unlock their full potential, we must adopt interdisciplinary and inclusive research and development methods. This approach involves embracing open innovation and integrating diverse research approaches and traditions such as ethnographic and contextual fieldwork, in-depth interviews, and participatory input from caseworkers, street-level organisations, and actual service users. The key is to work with people, rather than on people, ensuring that the voices and experiences of those directly impacted by PES are central to the design and implementation of digital tools and solutions.

Ethnographic and contextual fieldwork can provide deep insights into the lived experiences of jobseekers and the challenges they face when interacting with PES. By immersing researchers in the environments of service users, this method allows for a more nuanced understanding of the barriers and opportunities within the existing system – particularly what is possible and what is feasible. In-depth interviews with both service users and front-line workers can further enrich this understanding, capturing the practical wisdom and tacit knowledge that are often overlooked in top-down policy approaches. These qualitative methods can reveal the complexities and subtleties of user needs, informing the development of more intuitive and effective digital services that will likely have greater acceptance by users, caseworkers and jobseekers alike.

Open innovation, which encourages collaboration across disciplines and sectors, is essential for creating imaginative and powerful digital solutions. By engaging a wide range of stakeholders – including technology developers, social scientists, policy makers and the service users themselves – PES can benefit from a diverse array of perspectives and expertise. This collaborative approach fosters creativity and ensures that digital tools are not only technologically advanced but also socially relevant and user-friendly. For instance, co-design workshops and hackathons can bring together different stakeholders to brainstorm and prototype innovative solutions, ensuring that the end products are grounded in the real-world experiences and needs of users.

Involving caseworkers and street-level organisations in the development process is particularly important. These professionals possess invaluable insights into the practicalities of service delivery and the day-to-day realities of supporting jobseekers. Their input can help ensure that digital tools are designed to enhance, rather than replace, the human elements of PES.

By prioritising the input of those who interact with the system daily, we can develop digital services that support and empower both service users and providers.

Ultimately, the future of digital PES lies in a collaborative, interdisciplinary approach that prioritises inclusivity and user engagement. By working with people, leveraging diverse research methods and fostering open innovation, we can create digital tools and solutions that are not only efficient and effective but also equitable and empowering. This approach will help transform the fragmented and ad-hoc landscape of digital PES into a coherent and integrated system that truly meets the needs of all jobseekers.

Index

Page numbers in *italic* type refer to figures; those in **bold** type refer to tables.